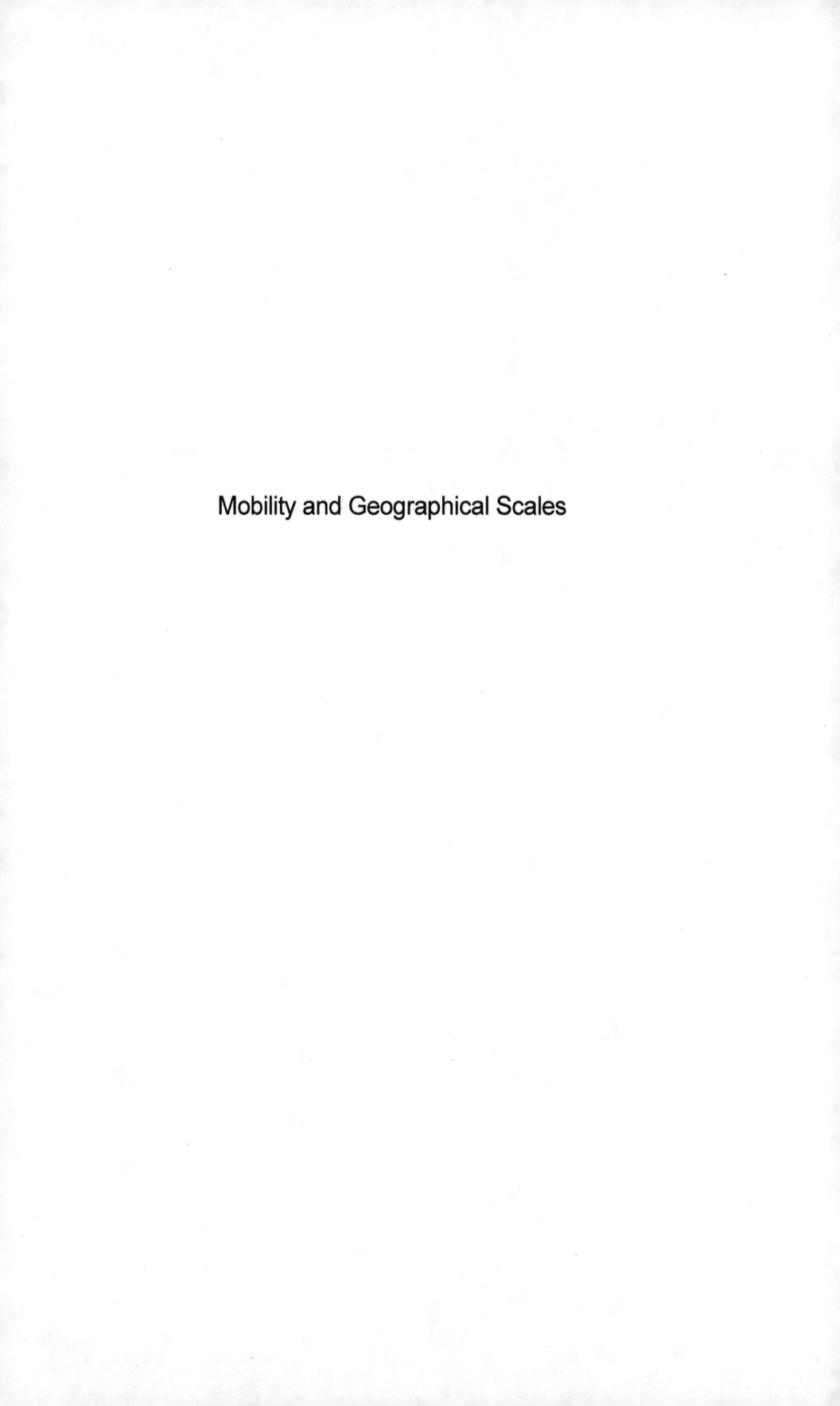

Mobility and Geographical Scales

SCIENCES

Geography and Demography, Field Director – Denise Pumain

Infrastructure and Mobility Networks Geography, Subject Heads – Hadrien Commenges and Florent Le Néchet

Mobility and Geographical Scales

Coordinated by
Guillaume Drevon
Vincent Kaufmann

WILEY

First published 2023 in Great Britain and the United States by ISTE Ltd and John Wiley & Sons, Inc.

Apart from any fair dealing for the purposes of research or private study, or criticism or review, as permitted under the Copyright, Designs and Patents Act 1988, this publication may only be reproduced, stored or transmitted, in any form or by any means, with the prior permission in writing of the publishers, or in the case of reprographic reproduction in accordance with the terms and licenses issued by the CLA. Enquiries concerning reproduction outside these terms should be sent to the publishers at the undermentioned address:

ISTE Ltd
27-37 St George's Road
London SW19 4EU
UK

www.iste.co.uk

John Wiley & Sons, Inc.
111 River Street
Hoboken, NJ 07030
USA

www.wiley.com

© ISTE Ltd 2023

The rights of Guillaume Drevon and Vincent Kaufmann to be identified as the authors of this work have been asserted by them in accordance with the Copyright, Designs and Patents Act 1988.

Any opinions, findings, and conclusions or recommendations expressed in this material are those of the author(s), contributor(s) or editor(s) and do not necessarily reflect the views of ISTE Group.

Library of Congress Control Number: 2022945772

British Library Cataloguing-in-Publication Data
A CIP record for this book is available from the British Library
ISBN 978-1-78945-064-4

ERC code:
SH2 Institutions, Values, Environment and Space
    SH2_8 Energy, transportation and mobility
SH3 The Social World, Diversity, Population
    SH3_1 Social structure, social mobility

Contents

Chapter 1. Collective Thinking About Mobility Scales 1
Vincent KAUFMANN and Guillaume DREVON

   1.1. Introduction 1
   1.2. The notion of mobility in social sciences 3
   1.3. The need for an integrative approach 5
   1.4. A new research arena 8
   1.5. Articulating spatial and temporal mobility scales 9
   1.6. References 11

Chapter 2. A Society with No Respite: Mobility as an Interdisciplinary Concept 15
Christophe MINCKE

   2.1. Introduction 15
   2.2. Mobility as a scale of magnitudes in a reticent capitalism
   (Boltanski and Chiapello) 17
      2.2.1. Justifying inequalities 17
      2.2.2. Inequalities in a reticular context: the project-based city 18
      2.2.3. Project-based cities and mobility 19
   2.3. Movement: the central element of liquid modernity (Bauman) 20
      2.3.1. Dissolution and anchoring of solid modernity 20
      2.3.2. The fading of ends and limits 21
      2.3.3. The individual, the model, shopping 22
   2.4. The alienating acceleration (Hartmut Rosa) 24
      2.4.1. Acceleration 24
      2.4.2. Three critiques of acceleration 25
   2.5. The turning point of mobility (Urry and Sheller) 27
      2.5.1. Mobilities as an analyzer of social matters 27
      2.5.2. Mobilities in weak link societies 28
      2.5.3. The social aspect of mobility 29
   2.6. Mobility as an injunction (Mincke and Montulet) 29

2.6.1. Two spatiotemporal morphologies 30
2.6.2. Mobility shifts. 31
2.6.3. The mobilitarian ideal 32
2.7. Contextualizing research on mobilities 34
2.8. References 36

Chapter 3. Mobility Justice as a Political Object 37
Caroline GALLEZ

3.1. Introduction 37
3.2. Inequality and mobility justice in contemporary Western societies . . . 38
3.3. Social justice and mobility, theoretical approaches 40
3.4. Inequalities and equity in transport and urban planning 42
3.4.1. Integrating equity in the evaluation of transport policies 43
3.4.2. Moving from inequalities in mobility to inequalities in access
to facilities. 44
3.4.3. Evaluating equity of access to facilities 45
3.5. Mobility justice: contributions from the social sciences 47
3.5.1. Ambiguities of mobility 48
3.5.2. Mobility regimes and differentiation of mobility rights 49
3.5.3. Mobility justice in the face of the ecological emergency and
social inequalities 51
3.6. Beyond inequalities, mobility justice 53
3.7. References 54

Chapter 4. Appropriations and Uses of Travel Time: How to
Inhabit Mobility 63
Juliana GONZÁLEZ

4.1. Introduction 63
4.2. The emergence of a research field in search of a position 64
4.3. The basis for exploring the uses of travel time 65
4.3.1. What are the uses of travel time for each mode of transport? 67
4.3.2. What theoretical frameworks should be used to address the
qualitative dimension of travel time? 72
4.4. Inhabiting travel time: at what cost to the environment? 74
4.5. The relevance of mixed methods for building a common survey base . 75
4.6. Major research studies 77
4.7. Discussions and research perspectives 78
4.8. References 79

Chapter 5. Designing Space for Walking as the Primary Mode of Travel 87
Sébastien LORD and Mathilde LOISELLE

5.1. Introduction 87
5.2. A diversity of approaches to the objective conditions of walking, first of all a question of scale?. 90
   5.2.1. Walkability of the city and the neighborhood 90
   5.2.2. The urban quality and the walking environment 91
   5.2.3. Applications for the development of walking environments 93
5.3. The conditions of operation, what is the place for the walker's experience? 95
   5.3.1. The subjectivity of walking in its social and sensory dimensions . 95
   5.3.2. The atmosphere and its components 97
   5.3.3. On the hermeneutic significance of atmospheres in the practice of walking. 100
5.4. What are the challenges of the scales of analysis for intervention in living environments? 101
5.5. References 103

Chapter 6. Residential Trajectories and Ways of Living: An Overview of France and Europe. 107
Samuel CARPENTIER-POSTEL

6.1. Introduction 107
6.2. Residential choice as social positioning 108
   6.2.1. Classical models... 109
   6.2.2. ... to mobility turn. 110
6.3. Elements of analysis of residential mobility in France and Europe .. 112
   6.3.1. General spatial dynamics of residential mobility 112
   6.3.2. Differentiation by life course 114
   6.3.3. Differentiation by social position. 117
6.4. Discussion and perspectives: toward new ways of living 121
   6.4.1. Multifaceted emerging practices 121
   6.4.2. Toward comprehensive and biographical approaches 124
6.5. Conclusion 126
6.6. References 127

Chapter 7. City, State, Transnational Space: Scales and Multidisciplinary Approaches of Migrations 133
Garance CLÉMENT and Camille GARDESSE

7.1. Introduction 133
7.2. Myths and realities of contemporary migration 134
   7.2.1. A majority of interregional migration 134

7.2.2. More diversified and feminized international migration? 135
7.2.3. Deconstructing the European "migration crisis" 137
7.3. "Transnationalism", "privilege" and "bordering": taking into account
other scales of migration. 139
 7.3.1. From "immigrants" to "migrants" 140
 7.3.2. The notion of migratory privilege 141
 7.3.3. The contributions of border studies 143
7.4. Cities in migration studies 144
 7.4.1. Spatial dispersion policies and practices 145
 7.4.2. A local turn in migration governance?. 146
 7.4.3. Thinking about reception and hospitality 147
7.5. Investigating migration 148
7.6. Conclusion 151
7.7. References 152

Chapter 8. Work and High Mobility in Europe 161
Emmanuel RAVALET

8.1. Introduction 161
8.2. High work-related mobility 162
 8.2.1. Intensive daily commuting 163
 8.2.2. Weekly commuting. 165
 8.2.3. Fluctuating commuting patterns 166
 8.2.4. Frequent travel for work 167
8.3. The profile of the highly mobile population 168
8.4. Reasons for the use of large-scale work-related mobility 169
8.5. The experience of high work-related mobility 172
8.6. High mobility linked to work and digital technology, what
prospects? 173
8.7. Conclusion 175
8.8. References 176

Chapter 9. Event-Driven Mobility: From a Theoretical Approach
to Practical Management 185
Pascal VIOT

9.1. Introduction: the challenges of contemporary event-driven mobility. . 185
9.2. Mobility and major events: testing the host territory 187
9.3. A qualitative and quantitative test. 188
9.4. Road policing strategy 189
9.5. Toward a mobility turn of event-driven management practices 191
 9.5.1. The engineer's planning strategy 192
 9.5.2. The user-spectator's experience pathway 194
 9.5.3. The development of event mobility management practices 196

9.6. Conclusion: toward a sociology of event-driven mobility 197
9.7. References 198

**Chapter 10. Inland Navigation: Rethinking Mobility from an
Aquatic Perspective** 201
Laurie DAFFE

10.1. Introduction. 201
10.2. Societal and environmental issues of inland navigation. 202
  10.2.1. Modal share of inland waterways in the European Union 202
  10.2.2. Prospects for the development of river activities and the shift
  from road to waterways 203
  10.2.3. Faster, less far, more anchored: the scales of future navigation. . 206
10.3. Current state of knowledge 207
  10.3.1. Aquatic mobility, an emerging field of research 208
  10.3.2. Small-scale inland navigation and "people of the river,"
  flurban lifestyles 209
  10.3.3. Trajectories of houseboats and river dwellers 210
  10.3.4. Toward "wet ontologies". 211
  10.3.5. The watery turn: grasping mobilities from an aquatic perspective 213
10.4. Conclusion: meeting between water and land 216
10.5. References 217

Chapter 11. Temporary Mobilities and Neo-Nomadism. 221
Arnaud LE MARCHAND

11.1. Introduction. 221
11.2. State of current knowledge and major references 222
  11.2.1. Socioeconomics of temporary labor migration 222
  11.2.2. Neo-nomadism and countercultures 224
11.3. Challenges for contemporary societies 226
11.4. Survey methodologies, analysis with missing data 229
11.5. Place in general sociology 232
11.6. Status of scientific debates and controversies in the field. 234
11.7. References 235

Chapter 12. Towards a Rhythmology of Mobile Societies 241
Guillaume DREVON and Vincent KAUFMANN

12.1. Limitations of the concept of mobility 241
12.2. Thinking about the entanglement of mobilities using forms of rhythm 243
12.3. Responding to the challenges of mobility research with a rhythmology
of mobile societies 244
12.4. References 246

List of Authors 249

Index 251

1

Collective Thinking About Mobility Scales

Vincent KAUFMANN[1] and Guillaume DREVON[1,2]

[1] *Laboratoire de sociologie urbaine (LaSUR), École polytechnique fédérale de Lausanne, Switzerland*
[2] *Urban Development and Mobility Department, Luxembourg Institute of Socio-Economic Research, Esch-sur-Alzette, Luxembourg*

1.1. Introduction

In our globalized world, the coexistence, meeting, and sometimes friction between the different spatial and temporal mobility scales are permanent. Thus, contrasting forms of mobility coexist in a world perpetually in motion (Drevon et al. 2017). These movements, however, unfold according to different temporalities and spatial extents. At the one end of the spectrum are local and everyday mobilities; at the other are migrations characterized by uprooting and then permanent anchoring in a new social and geographic context. Between the two extremes are the more atypical or hybrid forms of mobility, such as large-scale work-related mobility, second homes, and temporary or seasonal mobilities. These different forms of mobility are distinguished by their contrasting temporal and spatial scales. Together, all these forms of mobility set the pace for our societies and punctuate the life journeys of individuals. Intertwining these different forms of mobility requires social science researchers to construct new ways of interpreting our societies, as proposed by Urry (2000) to describe and analyze contemporary societies through the prism of mobility.

Mobility and Geographical Scales,
coordinated by Guillaume DREVON and Vincent KAUFMANN. © ISTE Ltd 2023.

However, approaches to the different forms of mobility that constitute the broad spectrum mentioned above remain fairly disciplinary. Thus, local daily mobility is most often studied by the socioeconomics of transport and urban geography, while migration and residential mobility are largely rooted in the field of demography. Atypical mobility, due to a lack of available data, is most often the domain of anthropology and ethnography. The fact that these different forms of mobility coexist within the same society requires a common approach for the different fields of social sciences in order to think collectively about the different spatiotemporal forms of mobility. This book attempts to meet this interdisciplinary challenge by offering a set of chapters from various disciplinary backgrounds in an attempt to document and describe most forms of contemporary mobility.

Collective thinking about the different spatial and temporal mobility scales is all the more important as the butterfly effects multiply, sometimes carried by long-haul flights from China. In fact, crises directly linked to mobility and referring to different forms of collisions of scales are occurring at an increasingly rapid pace: strong demand for the right to stroll in Istanbul's Taksim Square in 2013, a call to develop public transport rather than finance the Olympic Games in Rio in 2016, the rejection of speed limits and the carbon tax by the Gilets Jaunes in the winter of 2018 in France, a general strike in Chile following the increase in the price of a metro ticket in October 2019, reinforcement of migratory controls at the gates of Europe following the Syrian conflict, and finally, in 2020, forced immobilization of a large part of the planet to fight the spread of Covid-19 and the exit of the United Kingdom from the European Union. All spatial and temporal mobility scales are affected by these crises, as we can see: pedestrians and the ultralocal and the everyday, urban transport, the automobile and the national territory, air traffic, as well as residential and international migration.

In this general context, we are at an exciting moment for dealing with the spatial and temporal dimensions of mobility, especially since the major social science research traditions on mobility are still struggling to think of time and space together in a single, nondeterministic, and dynamic approach.

In this chapter, in order to delve into the topic, we propose discussing the history of the notion of mobility in social sciences, before returning to the understanding of the spatial and temporal scales of this phenomenon. After this conceptual and epistemological exploration, Chapter 1 ends by presenting the different contributions that constitute the key ideas of this book.

1.2. The notion of mobility in social sciences

The term "mobility" appeared in German, English, and French dictionaries in the 18th century to evoke mental agility and therefore the ability to change. It is therefore a question of:

> Ease of change, of modification. Mobility of features, of physiognomy. Mobility of light, of reflections. Mobility of character, of mind, of imagination, ease of passing promptly from one disposition to another, from one object to another. Mobility of feelings, of mood. Mobility of opinions (Dictionnaire de l'Académie française du XVIIIe siècle)

The term mobility entered into the terminology of social sciences in the 1920s, with a double arrival: the work of Sorokin and that of the Chicago School.

In 1927, a Russian researcher who had emigrated to the United States, Pitirim Sorokin, published a book entitled *Social Mobility*, in which he laid the foundations for what was to become one of the most classic fields of investigation in sociology. He defines mobility as a change of occupation and identifies two types of movement:

– vertical mobility, which implies a change of position in the socio-professional ladder, which can be upward or downward (e.g., the worker who becomes his own boss);

– horizontal mobility, which refers to a change in status or category that does not imply any change in relative position in the social scale (for example, changing to a job with identical levels of qualification and remuneration). In Sorokin's conception, mobility may involve space, but movement in geographical space has, in his opinion, meaning only through a change in status in the social space that it reveals or implies.

The work of the Chicago School in the 1920s and 1930s focused on the spatial dimension of mobility. Faithful readers of Georg Simmel, researchers placed the analysis of mobility in a dynamic analysis framework inspired by internationalism. While the interactions between the city, its morphology, and social relations are at the heart of the Chicago School's work, their attention is focused, above all, on the social system, its functioning, its organization, and its transformations. Geographic mobility, whether residential or daily, is considered an integral part of urban life. The originality of this approach lies in the fact that mobility is thought of as a factor of disorganization or disruption of equilibrium, and therefore as a vector of change.

From the outset, this work has been concerned with international migration to the United States. In this respect, it is in line with researchers interested in migration phenomena who have proposed numerous "laws" and models, such as Ravenstein's seven "laws" (1885), Stouffer's (1940) models of attraction and repulsion processes, and Zipf's (1946) model, which introduces the effects of distance into attraction/repulsion models.

At the start of the Second World War, the field of mobility was already divided between sociological research, which defined mobility primarily as a change of position, role, or status, and an ecological approach, which considered it as a flow of movements in space.

Since the 1950s, analyses of social mobility have focused on the career paths and the intergenerational transmission of occupational categories. This last theme crystallized essential questions relating to the construction of social inequalities, such as social reproduction and the possibilities of ascending or descending the occupational ladder. It mobilized sociology to the point of becoming one of the most dynamic fields of research, which was to become totally autonomous in relation to the work in the city and in the urban setting. In this movement, sociology came to adopt the definition of mobility as a change of status, role, or position, which was the only one retained until the present day.

At the same time, geographical approaches to mobility have been developing since the postwar period (Kaufmann 2014) and are based around the four main forms of spatial mobility present in the societies of the time: daily mobility, travel, residential mobility, and migration. These are the main forms that can be differentiated according to the temporality to which they address (long or short term) and the space in which they take place (internal or external to the catchment area) (see Table 1.1). Each of these four forms is the subject of an abundant piece of literature and develops its own concepts, arenas, and journals. In short, it is constructed as a field of research. This conception clearly refers to spatial and temporal scales. Yet, if we delve into the research, we quickly realize that, although the temporal dimension is integrated, it is often not really questioned in the academic reflections that insist more on the spatial dimension of mobility.

However, the conceptualization of mobility remains common to all four domains: it is a movement between an origin and a destination. Implicitly, this approach combines a definition of mobility as the crossing of space and a definition as change. In fact, it postulates a coupling of these two orders of phenomena.

	Short time frame	Long time frame
Inside of a catchment area	Daily mobility	Residential mobility
Outside of a catchment area	Travel	Migration

Table 1.1. *The four main forms of spatial mobility*

Dividing spatial mobility analysis into four domains has produced significant scientific advances, even if it has not made it possible to deal with all their links, because of the autonomy of the research domains that it has produced. Although approaches to mobility have often emphasized geography, temporal approaches are an important dimension of the analysis of mobility, especially daily (Drevon 2019) and temporary mobility. An examination of the temporalities of mobility cannot be free of the theoretical foundations of the geography of time (Hägerstrand 1970). Indeed, the Lund School and its most illustrious representative, Torsten Hägerstrand, laid the foundations for an approach to mobility and activities that take into account both space and time. This spatiotemporal consideration of human activities allows us to understand their ordering and coordination within a constrained space–time framework (the prism). The geography of time has received renewed interest from researchers over the last 20 years. This approach to human activities and behaviors is the result of a critique of economically inspired models that postulate a supposed rationality of individuals, thus reinforcing the need to rethink the analysis of mobilities, particularly by reinterpreting the sociology of social mobility.

1.3. The need for an integrative approach

The movement of people, goods, capital, and ideas is at the heart of global change and affects all areas of economic, political, and social life. These intrinsically structural changes appear to be the consequences of globalization and, in particular, of the fluidity of the circulation of capital, goods, and people on a scale never seen before. For example, the mobility of the main factors of production has increased considerably. On the side of capital, mobility has gone hand in hand with the development of the financial industry and increased returns. Liberalization, the development of information and communication technologies, and the continuous development of new services by the financial industry have led to an extremely rapid circulation on a global scale. The spatial and temporal organization of cities and territories is now penetrated by considerable differences in speed, ranging from walking to the immediacy of telecommunications, thus articulating particularly contrasting spatial and temporal scales.

In this context, a person's ability to move in space and time has become a central resource for social mobility and more generally for social integration. In doing so, it raises the question of the relationship between social mobility and spatial mobility. This question was extensively addressed in the 1970s and 1980s by numerous studies that showed that international or inter-regional migration was a "social elevator." The research of Bassand et al. (1985) went even further by analyzing the links between central and peripheral locations and upward or downward social mobility.

To account for these transformations, a new integrative approach is strongly needed, one that does not postulate the "Russian doll" type inclusions between the spatial and temporal forms of mobility or of a sequential type, like the four-stage models used to generate daily movements. Indeed, understanding mobility behavior is fundamentally a question of "why do we move?"

We move around to go to work and carry out the tasks of daily life. But we also move around to relax for leisure activities, which are becoming more and more prevalent. We also move around to fit in with lifestyles where frequent long-distance travel is valued. We travel to cohabitate with a partner, and we also travel following a divorce. Shifting from one activity to another also makes us change our role, our emotional state, and even our social status. These forms of mobility unfold on different temporal and spatial scales, from movement in the vicinity to international migration, and from a brief move in the neighborhood to a move to the other side of the world. Understanding mobility thus implies establishing a holistic approach to the phenomenon, which integrates the spatial, temporal, and social dimensions of mobility, thus making it possible to fit together the pieces of the puzzle that the history of research has sometimes misplaced and often scattered around.

In this endeavor, the work of Michel Bassand is essential and pioneering. In the book entitled *Mobilité spatiale*, Bassand and Brulhardt (1980) laid the foundations for such an approach. They consider mobility as a total social phenomenon in the sense of Marcel Mauss and define it as all movements involving an actor's change of state or system under consideration. With this definition, mobility has a dual spatial and social quality, which makes it richer than purely spatial or purely social approaches.

Since the beginning of the 2000s, many thoughts on mobility have been developed under the banner of mobility turn. They aim to develop an integrative definition of the phenomenon in order to provide a real concept. These reflections concern the theoretical understanding of the phenomenon (Cresswell 2006; Urry 2007), the way in which mobilities are experienced (Merriman 2012), the role that mobilities play in the constitution of the contemporary individual (Kellerman 2006), the way in which they have evolved over time, etc. These works deconstruct spatiotemporal mobility scales and see this phenomenon as fully integrating migration. They insist that crossing geophysical space is generally a means to an end, not the end itself, and that therefore it is essential to look at the nature of this end in order to understand the motivations of mobility. This is how the mobility paradigm was born, which is a way of analyzing societies by paying attention to the role played by the movement in the organization of social relations. Such an approach allows us to legitimize questions concerning the practical, discursive, technological, and organizational devices implemented by societies to manage distance, as well as the methods necessary to study these devices.

The integrative approach to the notion of mobility, which stems from the work of Michel Bassand and the mobility paradigm, makes it possible to consider mobility in a resolutely interdisciplinary multiscale approach. In particular, it has the advantage of making it possible to approach mobility as (1) a socio-spatial phenomenon, (2) an analytical indicator, and (3) a social value. These three modalities of the notion of mobility are specific and complementary:

– *Mobility as a socio-spatial phenomenon.* The first modality is the observation that being mobile refers to a double faculty: that of moving, of changing place, but also that of transforming ourselves, of adapting to a new situation, of changing status, position, skills, etc., these two dimensions being strongly intertwined.

– *Mobility as an analytical indicator.* The second modality is that mobility can be considered as an analytical indicator of social reality. In this sense, measuring mobility can, for example, help us to understand the dynamics of family relationships. It can also, for example, make it possible to measure the rhythmic pressures to which working women with young children are subjected in terms of reconciling family life, social life, and professional life (Kaufmann 2011).

– *Mobility as a social value.* In preceding developments, mobility was understood as a primary good (Gallez 2015), within the meaning of Article 13 of the Universal Declaration of Human Rights relating to freedom of movement. The mobility value is, however, marked by a fundamental ambivalence: when movements are rapid, distant, and frequent, therefore reversible, they have very positive connotations; when, on the other hand, it is a question of migrations, in other words migrations of poor populations, therefore irreversible, they have a negative connotation. In contemporary Western societies, reversible mobility has thus become a dominant social norm, which is constructed particularly on the basis of a fantasy that associates rapid and distant movements with positive experiences of self-enrichment through travel experiences.

1.4. A new research arena

Mobility conceptualized with the help of the three modalities just described opens up the social sciences to new questions and thus renews the debates on social and economic differences, differentiations, and inequalities in relation to time and space. Over the last 15 years, work on mobility has been largely based on a broad, integrative approach to the phenomenon of mobility, considering it as a total social fact in the sense of Marcel Mauss, which allows for interdisciplinary recompositions around several epistemologies likely to produce a renewal of knowledge. More specifically, concerning the spatiotemporal mobility scales, four complementary approaches based in social science are developed, through the hybridization of urban geography, urban sociology, and the analysis of public policies with a spatial impact.

The first approach considers that the generalization of reversible forms of mobility requires an adaptation of the approach of contemporary societies. In his book *Sociology beyond Societies*, Urry (2000) is very clearly situated in this perspective, as is Manuel Castells (1996) in *The Network Society* or Jeremy Rifkin (2000) in *The Age of Access*. In this approach, social categories become blurred, and the traditional metric distances of geography lose their meaning. By looking through the lens of a network-based apprehension of the world, we make all that is related to fixity disappear and thus to the instituted substance of societies and their stratifications (Offner and Pumain 1996; Montulet 1998).

The second approach consists of considering the transformations of mobility as the practical consequence of an ideology of speed characteristic of modernity, to which people are now subjected. In this perspective, the social injunction to mobility is becoming more and more pressing, particularly in the world of work (Vignal 2005). Moving fast, far and often becomes imperative for those who want to prove that they are dynamic, motivated, or ambitious (Amar 2010). This posture is clearly that of Bauman (2013) in *Liquid Modernity* or of Janelle (1969) and Harvey (2001) when they speak of the compression of space–time. The vision of mobility as an ideology is very strongly focused on the world of work: daily commutes between home and work do indeed constitute a significant part of contemporary movement, but because of their rational motivation, they play only a minor role in the construction of a relationship with space between the traveler and the places they pass through; however, mobility also comes under the heading of other fields, such as leisure and tourism, which contribute to shaping a pace of life.

The third approach involves interpreting changes in mobility as one sign among others of the advent of a society of individuals (Drevon 2019). In this view, society as a whole is then based on the idea of freeing human beings from the clutches of community and traditional attachments to make them more rational and reflexive with regard to their own development (Ascher 1995; Bourdin 2005). The multiple rhythm lifestyles that are developing, as well as the hybrid forms of travel such as long-distance commuting, "digital nomads," or dual residents, are to be considered as reflections of individual aspirations. The central issue of this individualization becomes a social cohesion: how can so many differences be made to cohabit harmoniously (Tasan-Kok et al. 2013)?

The fourth approach to transformations in mobility is inspired by *Time Geography* (Hägerstrand 1970; Pred 1977) and also finds its extension with the concept of accessibility (Lenntorp 1976; Burns 1979) and of activity programs in time and space (Hensher and Stopher 1979). In this approach, the modalities of the simultaneous consideration of space and time are linked to three types of constraints: the capacity to appropriate a potentially available geographical context, the need for co-presence between individuals (knowing where, when, how, and for how long), and the conditions of availability of the activity opportunities offered (opening hours, teleworking, etc.). From this point of view, the transformation of mobilities is interpreted by a spatiotemporal enlargement of the possibilities to carry out activity programs.

Despite their epistemological differences, these four ways of interpreting the relationship between mobility and society converge on the diagnosis of a growing fragmentation and diversification of the temporalities of mobility (David 2007; Drevon et al. 2020), as well as the enlargement of the potential for speed provided by transport systems and connected objects and their accessibility. These observations support the theory developed by Rosa (2010) concerning the acceleration of life rhythms when he states that this results from the conjunction between technical acceleration and the multiple injunctions linked to social acceleration.

1.5. Articulating spatial and temporal mobility scales

In order to take the description and detailed understanding of the transformations of mobility and societies that have just been outlined in this chapter further, the book brings together a dozen contributions from researchers from different disciplinary backgrounds: sociology, geography, demography, anthropology, and political science.

Each of these contributions attempts to describe the different spatial and temporal mobility scales from a specific angle and according to a common sequence. Thus, each chapter in this book opens with a detailed review of scientific knowledge. From the presentation of the major references in the field, it then proposes a synthesis of different research works carried out in Europe on the subject discussed to finally lead to the outline of future research perspectives based on the discussion of the current debates and controversies that animate it. This writing device has the advantage of providing a didactic and comprehensive overview of the different spatial and temporal mobility scales as well as the issues related to each of them.

The book follows a path that tends first to put the conceptual and theoretical issues into perspective. Chapter 1, written by Vincent Kaufmann, a professor at the École polytechnique fédérale de Lausanne (EPFL), and Guillaume Drevon, a researcher at the Luxembourg Institute of Socio-economic Research and associate researcher at the LaSUR of the EPFL, proposes a review of the concept of mobility and its current perspectives. In Chapter 2, Christophe Mincke, a visiting professor at the Université Saint-Louis and researcher at the Institut national de criminalistique et de criminologie de Bruxelles, positions mobility as an interdisciplinary notion based on the main theoretical contributions of the last decades, which have tended to link different mobility scales. Chapter 3, written by Caroline Gallez, the director of research at the Laboratoire Ville Mobilité Transport, puts into perspective the eminently political dimension of mobility, particularly the inequalities it generates. Based on an in-depth review of the state of knowledge, Caroline Gallez outlines the principles of mobility as a vector of social justice at both the individual and the city level.

The second part of the book is dedicated to the main forms of mobility, which are also the most studied in social sciences. In Chapter 4, Juliana González, a researcher at the Laboratoire de sociologie urbaine of the EPFL, addresses the issue of inhabiting mobility by proposing an original approach that focuses on the experience of travel time. In Chapter 5, Sébastien Lord and Mathilde Loiselle from the École d'urbanisme, d'architecture et de paysage and the Faculty of Planning at the University of Montreal highlight the central dimension of walking and outline the principles of planning that promote its development. Chapter 6, by Samuel Carpentier-Postel, from the Université de Bourgogne Franche-Comté, is dedicated to residential mobility in France and Europe. In this chapter, Samuel Carpentier-Postel puts into perspective the dynamics of residential mobility and their determinants. Chapter 7, provided by Garance Clément, a researcher at the Laboratoire de sociologie urbaine of the EPFL, and Camille Gardesse, from the École d'urbanisme de Paris, discusses migration at different spatial scales from a critical perspective.

Finally, the third part of the book is dedicated to atypical forms of mobility. In Chapter 8, Emmanuel Ravalet, a researcher at the Université de Lausanne, describes the complexity of the different forms of large-scale work-related mobility. Chapter 9, by Pascal Viot, an associate researcher at the Laboratoire de sociologie urbaine of the EPFL, looks at the issue of mobility and urban rhythms related to major events. Laurie

Daffe, a researcher at the Laboratoire de sociologie urbaine of the EPFL, highlights in Chapter 10 the theme of river mobility from an anthropological and ethnographic perspective. Chapter 11, by Arnaud Le Marchand of the Université du Havre, focuses on the different forms of temporary and seasonal mobility. Chapter 12, written by Guillaume Drevon and Vincent Kaufmann, suggests putting the limits of the concept of mobility into perspective. In this last chapter, the authors also suggest renewing the approach to mobility through the prism of the concept of rhythm, thus prefiguring a rhythmology of mobility and more broadly of contemporary societies.

1.6. References

Amar, G. (2010). *Homo mobilis : le nouvel âge de la mobilité : éloge de la reliance*. FYP, Paris.

Anderson, J.E. and van Wincoop, E. (2004). Trade costs. *Journal of Economic Literature*, 42(3), 691–751.

Ascher, F. (1995). *Métapolis : ou l'avenir des villes*. Odile Jacob, Paris.

Bassand, M. (1985). *Les Suisses entre la mobilité et la sédentarité*. Presses polytechniques et universitaires romandes, Lausanne.

Bassand, M. and Brulhardt, M.-C. (1980). *Mobilité spatiale : bilan et analyse des recherches en Suisse*. Georgi, Lausanne.

Bauman, Z. (2013). *Liquid Modernity*. John Wiley & Sons, New York.

Bourdin, A. (2005). *La métropole des individus*. Éditions de l'Aube, La Tour-d'Aigues.

Burns, L.D. (1979). Transportation, temporal, and spatial components of accessibility [Online]. Available at: https://trid.trb.org/view.aspx?id=1211105 [Accessed 23 January 2018].

Castells, M. (1998). *La société en réseaux*. Fayard, Paris.

Cresswell, T. (2006). *On the Move: Mobility in the Modern Western World*. Taylor & Francis, New York.

David, O. (2007). Vie familiale, vie professionnelle. Une articulation sous tension. *Espace populations sociétés*, 2–3, 191–202 [Online]. Available at: https://doi.org/10.4000/eps.2080.

Drevon, G. (2019). *Proposition pour une rythmologie de la mobilité et des sociétés contemporaines*. Alphil/Presses universitaires suisses, Neuchâtel.

Drevon, G., Gwiazdzinski, L., Klein, O. (2017). *Chronotopies : lecture et écriture des mondes en mouvement*. Elya, Grenoble [Online]. Available at: https://halshs.archives-ouvertes.fr/halshs-01522381 [Accessed 13 April 2018].

Drevon, G., Gerber, P., Kaufmann, V. (2020). Dealing with long commuting and daily rhythms. *Sustainability*.

Gallez, C. (2015). La mobilité quotidienne en politique. Des manières de voir et d'agir. Doctoral thesis, Université Paris-Est, Paris [Online]. Available at: https://halshs.archives-ouvertes.fr/tel-01261303 [Accessed 10 February 2021].

Hägerstrand, T. (1970). What about people in regional science. *Papers in Regional Science*, 24(1), 7–171.

Harvey, D. (2001). *Spaces of Capital: Towards a Critical Geography*. Taylor & Francis, New York.

Hensher, D.A. and Stopher, P.R. (1979). *Behavioural Travel Modelling*. Croom Helm, London.

Janelle, D.G. (1969). Spatial reorganization: A model and concept. *Annals of the Association of American Geographers*, 59(2), 348–364.

Kaufmann, V. (2011). *Rethinking the City: Urban Dynamics and Motility*. EPFL Press, Lausanne.

Kaufmann, V. (2014). *Retour sur la ville : motilité et transformations urbaines*. Presses polytechniques et universitaires romandes, Lausanne.

Kellerman, A. (2006). *Personal Mobilities*. Routledge, London/New York.

Lenntorp, B. (1976). Paths in space-time environments: A time-geographic study of movement possibilities of individuals. PhD thesis, Royal University of Lund, Lund.

Merriman, P. (2012). *Mobility, Space and Culture*. Routledge, London/New York.

Montulet, B. (1998). *Les enjeux spatio-temporels du social : mobilités*. L'Harmattan, Paris.

Offner, J.-M. and Pumain, D. (1996). *Réseaux et territoires : significations croisées*. Éditions de l'Aube, La Tour-d'Aigues.

Pred, A. (1977). The choreography of existence: Comments on Hägerstrand's time-geography and its usefulness. *Economic Geography*, 53(2), 207–221.

Ravenstein, E. (1885). The laws of migration. *Journal of the Statistical Society*, 48, 167–227.

Rifkin, J. (2000). *L'âge de l'accès : la révolution de la nouvelle économie*. La Découverte, Paris.

Rosa, H. (2010). *Accélération : une critique sociale du temps*. La Découverte, Paris.

Stouffer S. (1940). Intervening opportunities: A theory relating mobility and distance. *American Sociological Review*, 5, 845–867.

Urry, J. (2000). *Sociology Beyond Societies: Mobilities for the Twenty-first Century*. Routledge, London/New York.

Urry, J. (2007). *Mobilities*. Polity Press, Cambridge.

Vignal, C., Miot, Y., Fol, S. (eds) (2016). *Mobilités résidentielles, territoires et politiques publiques*. Presses Universitaires du Septentrion, Villeneuve d'Ascq.

Zipf, G. (1946). The P1 P2/D hypothesis: On the intercity movement of persons. *American Sociological Review*, 11, 677–686.

2

A Society with No Respite: Mobility as an Interdisciplinary Concept

Christophe MINCKE

Institut national de criminalistique et de criminologie, Brussels, Belgium

2.1. Introduction

A book that examines mobility scales must, logically, seek to shed light on how local or international, daily or long-term, and temporary or long-term mobility differs.

This approach, however, should not lead one to think that mobility can only be approached through the prism of scale. This would be tantamount to considering that mobilities cannot be considered in a global manner. If mobility is a concept with any sociological depth, it must be studied in an interdisciplinary manner through the scales at which it manifests itself. Indeed, to limit the concept of mobility to a particular scale would imply that a considerable number of situations, social practices, and representations are totally foreign to it. Thus, if mobility could only be conceived at an individual level, it would be impossible to use it to analyze public policies, social representations, or institutions. In the same way, if mobility only concerned long-distance travel, it would be impossible to use it as a tool for understanding everyday relationships with space, especially local space. Similarly, if we were to talk about mobility at various scales, but at the cost of establishing definitions of this mobility specific to each scale considered, we would have to give up the idea of a global social phenomenon, called mobility, whose ramifications at various scales would be united by a set of common characteristics. In this book, this chapter will explore mobility beyond the distinctions of scale. We shall therefore set about describing some theoretical proposals that have sought to link the different mobility scales and describe a relationship to mobility that is free of them.

In order to carry out this task, we have chosen to examine five theoretical proposals that seek to shed light on the meaning of mobility in our societies, the social representations with which it is associated, the context in which it takes on meaning, and, of course, the normative investments of which it is the object. It is thus the relationship of our contemporary societies with mobility that will be examined here.

The theories selected here are those that we consider to be major and recent contributions to this question. The aim here is not to make history of the thinking on mobility, but to present proposals that may shed light on contemporary phenomena related to mobility. It should be noted that the fifth proposal is ours, conceived with Bertrand Montulet, and is not presented here because it would be on a par with the others, but because we assumed that it was one of the reasons why the editors had asked us for it. Rather than attempting an overview of the productions of each selected author, we preferred to stick to their major work – from the perspective of a multiscale reflection on mobility – and to take these productions as milestones of a global perspective on mobilities.

We will begin our overview with the proposal of Luc Boltanski and Ève Chiapello (see section 2.2), who question what, today, justifies inequalities within our societies. Proposing a normative framework – the project-based city – they offer a first approach to mobility as part of an evolution of contemporary value systems, born in companies, expressed in management literature, and now widely shared in society. We then turn to the contribution of Zygmunt Bauman and his reflection on the emergence of a liquid modernity, based on lability, lightness, and the race for mobility (see section 2.3). Closely linking modernity and capitalism, it makes mobility the instrument of a domination of the mobile over the less mobile. This question of domination will also be present in our third author's work, that of Hartmut Rosa, who is the author of a critical theory of acceleration (see section 2.4). Articulating his thought around the notion of alienation, he characterizes our societies by the fact that they have entered into a process of endless acceleration, feeding and justifying themselves. He makes it a major factor of a headlong rush leading to a subjection of the individual to the imperative of speed. Our fourth milestone will be the work of John Urry (see section 2.5). Based on the idea of a paradigmatic shift in mobility in a society marked by the figure of the network and by weak social ties, his intervention is both a formalization of the centrality of mobility in social relationships and a call for a (re)centering of the social sciences on it, to make it a major analyzer of social matters. We will conclude by presenting the work we are proposing, with Bertrand Montulet, around the question concerning the evolution of social representations of space–time and mobility. In this work, we have endeavored to integrate the contributions of the authors who have preceded us, first and foremost the four of whom we will speak here. Our specific contribution is, undoubtedly, beyond this work of integration to propose a more explicit extension of the reflections on mobility to non-material spaces and to propose a grammar of the injunction to mobility, articulated in four imperatives.

The work discussed here must be seen in a broader context, including Ehrenberg's (1998) contribution to the reflection on the exhaustion of the contemporary individual in pursuit of himself, Cresswell's (2001, 2006) proposals on sedentary and nomadic metaphysics structuring contrasted relations to space and mobility, or Kaufmann's (2004, 2008) contribution via the concept of motility. We should not forget, in this broader context, the significant contributions, albeit of lesser magnitude, that encourage reflection on the social frameworks related to mobility, a living field, such as that of Borja et al. (2014) or Debarbieux (2014).

2.2. Mobility as a scale of magnitudes in a reticent capitalism (Boltanski and Chiapello)

The first theoretical approach that we feel is necessary to report is that presented by Boltanski and Chiapello (1999) in their landmark work entitled *Le nouvel esprit du capitalisme* (English version: *The New Spirit of Capitalism*). This book is an extension of another one: *De la justification: les économies de la grandeur* (English version: *On Justification: Economics of Worth*), by Boltanski and Thévenot (1991). In order to understand the latter, it is necessary to briefly recall the ambitions of the first book.

2.2.1. *Justifying inequalities*

Boltanski and Thévenot, in *On Justification: Economics of Worth*, question the mechanisms of justification of social orders, in other words, of social inequalities between individuals. They ask how, in societies based on the principle of common humanity – human beings are equal because of their humanity – inequalities can exist, be maintained, and be considered perfectly admissible. To answer this question, they formalize various registers of justification by relying on a common grammar, which includes all the necessary elements for a system of legitimating inequalities. They call these universes of meaning "cities." Each one allows for classifying objects and persons hierarchically, after the tests.

It is on the basis of this grammar of justification of orders of magnitude that Boltanski and Thévenot formalize various cities, corresponding to as many ways of classifying people and objects. They identify five of them: inspired, domestic, opinion, civic, and industrial cities. However, they conclude their work by recognizing that none of these seem to describe the current order of magnitude in a valid way, and that they are trying hard to identify the system currently at work.

Eight years later, Luc Boltanski is back on the scene with *The New Spirit of Capitalism* written with Ève Chiapello (Boltanski and Chiapello 1999). Together, they propose the project-based city that they consider to describe the most contemporary system in economy of greatness, one whose domination has been established since the 1960s.

2.2.2. Inequalities in a reticular context: the project-based city

The project-based city is characterized by a particular affiliation to the figure of the network. It is based on a fundamental value, the common higher principle: activity. This requires everyone to be active at all times, whatever the field. Activity takes the form of participation in the projects that bring together a group of participants in a network mode. Every project is temporary; activity therefore consists of moving from one project to another and managing a global integration process in a successive or concomitant set of networks. The distinction between large and small within the social hierarchy is based on respect for this common superior principle.

Since the state of greatness is linked to the ability to integrate projects, its central quality is its employability, i.e., the interest it represents in the eyes of its networks of relations, an interest that motivates its solicitation for many projects. In order to build a broad network, mobility and adaptability are essential qualities. The large subject is flexible, unlike the small subject, who is fixed, rigid, and unable to integrate and change projects. The small subject is the one who cannot commit or be committed.

However, the large one does not achieve this status without difficulty because they have to sacrifice to the formula of investment. This term refers to the price to be paid to rise in terms of social hierarchy. In this case, the large subject has had to give up everything that could hinder their mobility: geographical and material attachments, regular working hours, personal principles, long-term planning of their life path, etc. Any obstacle to total flexibility must be removed, including their own morality and institutional power, as well as all categorization and compartmentalization of their various activities (work/leisure, friendships/professional relationships, etc.).

But the project-based city is also legitimate because it is redistributive through the ratio of size. This term refers to the fact that the large contributes, by its size, to the well-being of the small. In this case, the large of the project-based city redistributes connections and projects to the small in exchange for their enthusiasm. The small ones have access to networks that would otherwise be closed to them. This networking helps them to grow. This is how the large one serves the common good. Without it, of course, none of the projects would see the light of day.

The test that leads to the attribution of great quality, which demonstrates greatness, is the articulation between projects: going from one to another to manage several at the same time, but also being able to find new ones when one of them comes to an end, is a pivotal moment. The large one then shows its agility, demonstrating its greatness.

The whole system is based on a particular conception of the human being and their behaviors, called "natural relationship between beings". In the project-based city, it is the establishment of connections with others. It itself is derived from a specific conception of dignity, based here on the natural capacity of each person to establish connections and on the desire to do so. In this framework, the harmonious figure of the natural order is the network. The human being is a social being, a being that is part of a network, and this is why the project-based city is the right order for human societies.

2.2.3. Project-based cities and mobility

Although their aim is not directly to examine the relationship of our societies with mobility, Boltanski and Chiapello introduce in the project-based city – and thus in their presentation of the reasons for the justification of inequalities – elements that are closely linked to this question.

This is how the large one shows themself as permanently capable of movement. They are thus always active, never immobile, always ready to embark on a new project, and always looking for new links to establish with others. Free of all grounding, freed of all weight, they embody mobile lightness.

Thus, if the purpose of Boltanski, Thévenot, and Chiapello's theoretical advances is above all to better understand the way in which our societies, which recognize the equality of human beings in principle, tolerate inequalities, the formalization of the project-based city puts the question of mobility into perspective and provides elements for thinking about the reasons why we are mobile and value this mobility.

It should be noted that the point here is not to understand mobility in the narrow sense of the term, as a movement in material space, but, more broadly, as a set of social practices concerning both material and social spaces. Let us note that Boltanski and Chiapello, from the title of their work, insert their reflection in the specific framework of capitalism.

2.3. Movement: the central element of liquid modernity (Bauman)

Boltanski and Chiapello are of course not the only ones to question the place of mobility in the current economic and social context, nor to consider that the division of anchorages is a striking phenomenon, central to recent social developments. Bauman (2000), in his seminal work *Liquid Modernity*, questions its emergence and proposes an explanation based on the evocations of capitalism.

Handling concepts of heaviness, lightness, liquidity and solidity to handle the comparative destinies of modernity and capitalism, he proposes both a reflection on socioeconomic structures and on the destiny of individuals.

2.3.1. *Dissolution and anchoring of solid modernity*

Modernity would have, at the time of its emergence, dissolved the entirety of the existing social institutions, in the name of the obstacle that they constituted to freedom, but also to the instrumental reason. Then, it would have created new solids, new forms of political and economic organizations that were stable and resistant to change. For Bauman, this time is over because modernity has changed, becoming a continuous process of dissolution, becoming an end in itself and no longer founding anything that offers resistance to change. A compulsive tendency to modernization has developed, a kind of creative destruction theorized by Schumpeter.

For Bauman, the origin of modernity lies in the dissociation of time and space. When technical means made possible a considerable acceleration of travel, space was no longer measured by the time it took to travel through it. A place, which for a long time had been a 2 days' walk from another, became accessible in different times, depending on the technical means used to reach it: the steamboat, the train, and soon after the automobile or the bicycle thus opened up the prospect of differentiated travel times that were constantly contracting as progress was made. Time then became the dynamic element of space–time, one that we were constantly trying to shorten in order to travel through space, fighting against the resistance of distances.

The most powerful technologically or economically became the fastest, the one who had new means to catch their competitors at speed. This is how the globe was soon covered in all directions and colonized. The empires took each other by storm and conquered immense territories, stopping only when they came up against a similar one and considering as empty any space not under the domination of one of them.

Certainly, mobility and speed were important, but the conquered spaces had to be ruled, controlled, bounded, and closed off. The world of modernity, based on the decoupling of time and space, was solid because it was made of borders, controls, and territorial claims. The conquest of space meant a spatial stabilization within borders.

It is this spatiotemporal arrangement that, for Bauman, has survived. The advent of information technology has now abolished space by moving from speed to instantaneity. Since today we can increasingly free ourselves from space, communicating instantly with the whole world and acting remotely, space has lost its value. What made it expensive was the difficulty of accessing it, the time it took to travel, and the competitive advantages that technology could offer. Now that everyone can be everywhere in the blink of an eye, the devaluation of space is total.

This evolution finds a striking echo in the corresponding evolution of capitalism. In the era of space resistance, heavy capitalism reigned. This was based on important infrastructures that tied capital to the ground. Factories, machines, stocks, and concessions for the exploitation of resources were then indispensable to economic activity. In order to exploit them, an innumerable workforce was recruited and chained to the infrastructure. Neither the capital nor the workers thought of escaping, as the anchoring of the economic activity seemed obvious: the weight and the size were the signs of success and power. Workers and employers lived together and fought against each other. In order to achieve productivity gains, production had to be faster and more efficient, and manufacturing processes had to be increasingly organized. The Fordist organization was the model, a model of order, based on the maximum predictability of each gesture and on the domination of time. The time of the flash of crossing space in order to conquer it corresponded here to the monopolization of land to develop productive activities, the strict delimitation of their perimeter, the extreme control of movements, and the routinization of time. In this world, it was up to rational leaders to define the steps to be taken to achieve clear and predefined objectives.

2.3.2. *The fading of ends and limits*

But, as Bauman teaches, no one is concerned with the ends anymore, so that production systems are deprived of a clear direction. The economic elites themselves no longer wish to anchor their activities. They think only in terms of light, mobile capitalism. Any choice made today must be the seizure of an opportunity, but it must not obviate the future agility of structures. Companies are relocating, subcontracting, refocusing on their core activities, laying off employees, and constantly adapting their strategies. There is no longer any question of long-term objectives, nothing being conceived as predictable. The industrial heaviness may be the power of the moment, but it will inevitably be a barrier to change tomorrow. But only one thing is certain: change.

In this light capitalism, limits have disappeared. Nothing hinders action in a world of instantaneity. From then on, an incessant movement can develop: it is not that we hurry to reach a fixed goal, but that in the absence of a goal, there is no finish line, no final gratification, just a movement cultivated for itself, because it is all that remains.

As Bauman points out, we are not equal in the face of movement. Thus, the dominant ones, today, are no longer those who hold space and are masters of borders. They are those who are able to escape from everyone, to change places without difficulty, while the dominated remain attached to space. Thus, capital enjoys more and more the ability to vanish, to teleport away, while workers remain localized. To force someone to stay in a place is, in liquid modernity, the preferred way to dominate them, while escapism is the faculty that determines power.

In a world largely based on the abolition of space, time becomes an eternal present. If the instantaneity of the movements and communications seems to be within our reach, it appears possible to indefinitely stretch each instant, to accomplish, the time of its duration, an infinity of tasks. The duration is thus without value if it is possible to accomplish everything in an extremely short period of time.

The combination of immediacy and lightness allows us to escape the consequences of our actions, to reap the rewards, and to avoid having to assume our responsibilities, which are left to those left behind.

2.3.3. *The individual, the model, shopping*

These developments of course have far-reaching consequences at the individual level. Thus, solid modernity assigned stable positions to individuals: they were freed from the society of order so that they could be assigned to the social function where they would be most productive. If mobility was possible, it was on the condition that it led to establishment in a status and role that would endure.

There is nothing like this today, in a society that no longer thinks in terms of centralized coordination, fixity, and the collective. Individuals are summoned to show autonomy and to take their destiny in hand. Nothing seems to be written in advance, and the injunction is to become oneself, rather than to conform to pre-existing models.

In this context, the state is experiencing a significant decline, which during solid modernity was both the target of the struggle for liberation and the vehicle for that same liberation. For the direction taken collectively no longer depends on clearly identified authorities, and ordering behaviors. It derives from the influence of innumerable models, which, by their example, invite autonomous individuals to imitate them. The trajectory of each individual is thus the result of innumerable successive and unpredictable choices, which Bauman calls shopping. It is not surprising, therefore, that the individual consumer – satisfying his desires one after the other, before seeing them revived – rather than the individual producer – responsible for a defined task in the production activities – is the focus of interest. Shopping has become a relationship with the world in its own right to the extent that individuals consume not only goods but also, for example, identities, which are always variable and changing, profoundly modifying our perception of ourselves.

The fragility of identity resulting from shopping pushes individuals to avoid contact with otherness, which weighs heavily on the relationship with public space, which has been designed to avoid contact. Drawing on Claude Lévi-Strauss, Bauman proposes that public places can be emic – designed to reject the foreign and the undesirable – or phagic – designed to avoid contact with the other so that everyone feels accepted, but at the cost of erasing their particularities. These two techniques make it possible to increase indifference to difference and to avoid any problematic relationships with otherness. He adds, on the one hand, the non-places of Georges Benko and Marcel Augé, in which the presence is only physical data, without social meaning, and which cannot be spaces of interaction, as well as, on the other hand, the empty spaces of Kociatkiewicz and Kostera, which remain unthought of and cannot be invested in by those who ignore them.

A pathology of public spaces emerges and leads to a political pathology: the loss of the ability to – and even the awareness of the usefulness of – living with difference, as well as the development of flight techniques.

We thus see the development, in Bauman's work, of a thought centered on the question of movement: from solid modernity as the conquest of space and establishment, to liquid modernity as the constant rearrangement of positions in a definitively defeated space, mobility is central. It is so central that, in both models of modernity, and in the capitalisms that correspond to them, it is a central factor of domination. The speed of conquest and the ability to escape are forms of mobility that underpin power.

The relationship with mobility remains, in this context, rather univocal: the power belongs to those who move and the constraints to mobility are little considered. Similarly, the importance of instantaneity and the disappearance of space can lead to the question of the reappearance of spatial resistance in the era of global warming and the limitation of greenhouse gas emissions.

2.4. The alienating acceleration (Hartmut Rosa)

While, as we have seen, Zygmunt Bauman makes the acceleration of change a central characteristic of liquid modernity, he is not the only one to do so. For example, Rosa (2012) offers a vision of the modern condition centered on this concept.

His project is to question the modern temporal regime in terms of alienation, that is, the dispossession of individuals of their capacity to define autonomously the criteria of the good life. These criteria derive from individual aspirations that push each person to seek to give his life a particular turn. To be deprived of our capacity to define our criteria of the good life autonomously – to be alienated, therefore – leads to the pursuit of exogenous goals, which, for Rosa, inevitably leads to suffering.

2.4.1. *Acceleration*

Rosa's starting point is the acceleration, which is consubstantial with modernity. This was, from the beginning, a process of intensification of change, aiming to free the individuals from the shackles of the past. However, today, this mechanism would have escaped any control.

Rosa distinguishes three types of acceleration. The first, technical, concerns processes oriented toward defined goals, notably productive activity. Like Bauman, he diagnoses a loss of importance of space due to the acceleration of transport and the development of non-localized activities and non-places. This acceleration is intentional. The second acceleration, that of social change, is based on a compression of the present and an accelerated downgrading of our understanding of the world. Thus, the social institutions organizing the processes of production and reproduction – the world of work and the family, for the most part – have seen their rates of change accelerate, moving from intergenerational to intragenerational cycles. Indeed, the changes that were once perceptible from one generation to the next are now being felt within the same generation. Finally, the third area of acceleration is pace of life, perceived through the experience of the frequency of demands. Beyond the subjective complaint about acceleration, Rosa points to the objective of compression of time devoted to ordinary activities – such as eating or sleeping – the multiplication of activities carried out in parallel, as well as the reduction of downtime.

For Rosa, there are three driving forces of acceleration, and they do not stem from technological advances. The first is competition, central to our thinking about the allocation of social positions, which has become an end in itself, with a strong focus on speed as a means to gain competitive advantage. The second driving force is what Rosa calls "the promise of eternity", that is, the invitation to fulfill ourselves in this world, through the realization of an ever-increasing number of actions. The contemporary individual is then caught in a headlong rush, which leads them to desire to accomplish more and more, and to experience increasing frustration due to their inability, despite frenetic activity, to achieve a significant number of their ambitions. The third driving force is the cycle of acceleration, a runaway process itself, leading to a succession of technical acceleration, acceleration of social change, and acceleration of the pace of life in successive rounds, each step leading to a strengthening of the next.

For Rosa, constant acceleration leads to totalitarianism. Our being in the world is profoundly modified by it, notably because of the contraction of space, which loses its primacy as a result. Social relations develop without the need for any physical proximity, which has, as a consequence, an increase of meetings, until saturation. Our human relationships are weakened by this because they are easily made and broken. Not even our own identity is affected by evanescence. Deprived of a life plan, letting ourselves be carried along by the current of opportunities encountered in the course of our lives, we adopt temporary and fluctuating positions. Even our material environment is dizzy, so much so we quickly replace the objects that surround us, not because they are out of use but because they are exceeded by the race in which we are taken. In this context, the notions of progress or history lose their consistency.

2.4.2. *Three critiques of acceleration*

Rosa develops three critiques of acceleration. The first, a functionalist one, questions the sustainability of the current acceleration regime. The main problem here is the danger of desynchronization due to acceleration differentials. For example, the movement has been much bigger in the social, economic, and technological spheres than in the political sphere. Yet, in a democracy, decision-making processes take time – the more complex the society – and cannot be radically accelerated. Democratic processes therefore threaten to be outpaced by the changes in the socioeconomic phenomena they claim to govern. The specter of deregulation arises, carried by conservative liberals, who call for the removal of the political from collective management, on the grounds that it would be a factor of slowing down. Rosa points out, similarly, the dangers linked to the desynchronization of speculation and the activities of production and consumption, or that of the generations, unable to work on the symbolic reproduction of society because they would live in realities too different to understand each other.

The second criticism is normative and questions the respect of justice in the current context of acceleration. Modernity is characterized by two contradictory features: on the one hand, individuals are increasingly interdependent, which increases the need for social regulation, while on the other hand, liberal societies tend to recognize a large degree of freedom for individuals. Modern societies are thus inhabited by a tension between the need for coordination and the recognition of freedom. Coordination is nowadays pursued through the imposition of a regime of urgency and immediacy. In such a context, individuals fall prey to guilt without remission: that of never being able to catch up. The situation is all the more problematic because the temporal regime of our societies is presented as a natural fact, which makes it difficult to criticize.

The third criticism, ethical, concerns the betrayal of the promise of modernity. Indeed, the latter was largely based on the project of an emancipation of the individual and on the idea that, after a phase of acceleration and production, an era of abundance would allow us to free ourselves from economic struggles and achieve self-determination. Acceleration and competition were to be a transitional phase. Today, all goals, values, paradigms, and practices serve acceleration as a goal in itself. In an unstable environment, pursuing a goal no longer makes sense. It is therefore necessary to ride out the wave, to take advantage of opportunities as they arise. Acceleration is no longer at the service of an objective that would exceed it.

Acceleration would define the outlines of an alienation of the individual, understood as the distortion of relationships between the self and the world. The alienation is fivefold, affecting our relationships with space (loss of familiarity with space due to the intensity of mobility), with things (due to their replacement rate, making them foreign to us), with our actions (due to the hyperactivity constraint that weighs on us), with time (because the time of hyperactivity, not only does not satisfy us but also leaves few traces in our memories), and with ourselves as well as with others (because we live in a state of social saturation, unable to integrate ourselves in a stable experience).

As we can see, while Rosa does not focus specifically on mobility in the material sense of the term, by positing the concept of acceleration as central to our world, he gives social rhythms a preponderant importance, including those that govern our movements. Moreover, it is acceleration as such that attracts his attention, and not the variability of social rhythms. The question of immobility is therefore not addressed, although we may ask to what extent it can also be a mechanism of alienation.

2.5. The turning point of mobility (Urry and Sheller)

John Urry is the first of the authors we will examine here to be concerned with mobility as such, and not as an adjunct to broader changes.

We will focus here on his book *Mobilities* (2007), which has strongly influenced mobility studies by developing the idea of the emergence of a *new mobility paradigm*. At the heart of his concerns is the desire that space should no longer be considered by scientists as a framework in which the game of social actors takes place, but as an integral part of the social game.

2.5.1. *Mobilities as an analyzer of social matters*

Urry's vision is based on the idea that social relations are made of connections, which imply regular connections and separations. Therefore, anyone who looks at social matters must be interested in mobilities. Urry therefore invites us to take an approach to mobility that respects its richness, by considering the way it is experienced by social actors, but also the social and political technologies that allow it to be regulated.

The movements that underlie social relations may be necessitated by legal, economic, or family obligations, the desire to maintain rich social relations with others, the elaboration of material or social productions, the desire to frequent certain places and meet other users, or the desire to experience the materiality of certain places. Urry thus proposes a global reading of social matters from the perspective of mobility.

Of course, the movements thus envisaged must be considered in the light of the specific characteristics of the beings and objects that move, which have a considerable influence on the possibilities and modalities of movement. If mobilities structure social matters, the reverse is also true.

These mobilities are also challenges to governmentality in that they force societies to manage the space and social devices that facilitate or impede movement. Thus, he reminds us that all movements are socially constructed and depend on public policies, from walking to train travel, from car travel to air travel. Mobility is not naturally given, but a social construction.

As such, Urry calls for mobility to be analyzed in terms of movement potentialities and reticular capital (a concept close to that of motility of Kaufmann (2004)). For him, mobilities are indeed the result of the interweaving of behaviors and potentialities (both material and normative or personal). In the context of a mobile and mobilizing capitalism, everyone is summoned to become autonomous and mobile.

The essential thing is not so much about actual mobility as network capital, which allows one to maintain relations with distant people by relying on a set of resources linked to the planning and management of travel, to remote communications, and to temporal control.

2.5.2. Mobilities in weak link societies

The context in which mobilities should be thought of is that of a reticularized society, which has seen the dependence of social relations on co-presence diminish – individuals need to meet less and less to create a bond – and the weak links become denser and more intense – superficial and easily separable relationships that unite people who do not have face-to-face relationships. The movement affects social relationships in a very broad way, at all levels, from the family to long-distance social relationships.

Thus, rather than belonging to a fixed place or group, what becomes crucial is to be able to access the people, places, and services necessary to maintain one's social network. Therefore, the notion of access corresponds to the figure of the network. However, this access is extremely variable over time and requires, among other things, a big effort of coordination with other actors. It is no longer a question, for example, of rubbing shoulders with people close to us in places to which they belong in a stable manner – the company, the family home, traditional places of socialization – but rather of accessing places – real or virtual – in a coordinated manner in order to maintain social relations, and therefore of taking into account the constant variation in the conditions of access and coordinating with the people with whom we maintain relations.

Of course, these new models of relations with space are promoted in particular by new technologies and computerized social networks that become essential social mediations. Urry points out, however, that these technical systems do not promote egalitarian networks. In fact, they support the development of aristocratic networks, which favor the nodes of networks that already occupy an important position, to the detriment of the weakest. Weak link networks and the technologies that support them are therefore tools of social stratification that reinforce inequalities.

In this context, physical mobility remains necessary in that it allows face-to-face encounters with others and the maintenance of relationships that are much richer than those mediated by remote communication technologies. Once again, this mobility will depend on the unevenly distributed network capital.

2.5.3. *The social aspect of mobility*

As we can see, Urry makes mobility a crucial social analyzer, indeed the essential point of entry for thinking about and understanding contemporary social relations. It is through social networks, reticular capital, inequalities of access to people, and resources that he proposes to think about social structures and the struggles that inhabit them.

In this respect, he thinks jointly of the evolution of society and – that which he calls upon – the social sciences. A new program, a mobility turn, is necessary to apprehend new realities, which must affect not only the objects studied but also the methods.

For him, however, recent social developments remain tinged with a negative connotation: weak social relations, the characterization of long-distance relationships as virtual or imaginary, and the maintenance of physical co-presence as necessary for social relations in the full sense of the term all point to the prospect of a loss, an impoverishment of the collective experience.

It is also worth noting that, while he re-examines the centrality of mobility in our societies, he does not reconsider its definition as such, as if being mobile today were essentially what being mobile had always been.

2.6. Mobility as an injunction (Mincke and Montulet)

We will end this brief overview of global – and multiscale – theories of mobility with a proposal that we authored, together with Bertrand Montulet (Mincke and Montulet 2019). The aforementioned authors literally founded this approach, since our first task was indeed to rely on their work to try to combine them into a coherent theoretical approach, which we were then able to complete when the need arose.

The ambition of this work is to understand the evolution of social representations of space–time – and therefore of mobility – and the concomitant evolution of norms relating to mobility. The structuring hypotheses of our work are, on the one hand, that what is identified as mobility today would not have been so identified a few decades ago and, on the other hand, that the particularities of current representations of space–time explain the contemporary normative regime.

2.6.1. *Two spatiotemporal morphologies*

Building on a previous work by Montulet (1998), we suggest that we are living in a moment of articulation of two spatiotemporal morphologies, i.e., two ways of representing space and time in an interdependent way.

The first, the limit-form, characteristic of the modernity of the 19th century and the first two-thirds of the 20th century, is based on the figure of the border, a device par excellence for structuring space, otherwise reduced to an unorganized expanse. The border is a device defining a circumscription and distinguishing an interior from an exterior. Its fundamental principle is to gather within it a set of entities sharing common characteristics and to exclude those that lack them. Of course, the border lends itself to the game of internal subdivisions, just as the national territory can be subdivided into regions, departments, provinces, communes, etc., in a game of Russian dolls. The drawing of a border is accompanied by the definition – whether explicit or not – of the conditions for its crossing. Thus, national borders are devices for delimiting the territory of a state and for controlling movements.

The very idea of a border is inseparable from that of a long time frame. Without stability, it is an illusion, as one could not conceive that it changes constantly, according to social and political evolutions. The space–time morphology of the limit-form, founded on the border for the spatial pole, thus associates the latter with a time made of an alternation of stases and divisions, of stability and sudden changes. Thus, the time of the national border is made of stability, interrupted by sudden changes: conquests or treaties reconfigure its course and open a new era of stability.

It is necessary here to bring about a precision on the outline of the concept of space. For us, the concept of space includes any result of a process of spatialization, that is to say of the structuring of a reality by means of systems of proximity, distance, and positions, relative or absolute. Now, the processes of spatialization, undoubtedly because they belong to the fundamental frameworks of the human thought, are at work in the structuring of an infinity of realities as much material as social, religious, philosophical, political, etc.

Thus, the border that circumscribes the national territory is matched by borders that do the same for the national language, the national community, the national culture, the legal competence of the State, etc. Even the game of internal subdivisions is replicated in the competences of local political institutions or in those of the deconcentrations by services. A wide range of phenomena can therefore be considered from the point of view of spatiotemporality and understood through identical concepts, such as that of the border.

The limit-form is opposed to the flow-form, which is a more recent spatiotemporal morphology based on the network figure. In societies representing time, not as an alternation of stases and sudden divisions, but as a constant flow eroding everything permanently, the spatial structuring by the border cannot be maintained. If reality is constantly rearranging itself, it is no longer possible to draw a stable border, and thus a border in the true sense. To this constant temporal flow corresponds a space structured across the network. The question is no longer that of external outlines traced on a stable and pre-existing space but rather that of the identification of relations uniting points – the nodes of a network.

Thus, a city is no longer defined by its territorial and administrative outlines, a border that one would search for in vain in the incessant flows of reality, but as a set of relationships. Through the circulations and communications of which it is the epicenter, variable "hinterlands" are defined, beating according to the moments of the day, the evolution of demands, consumption, and social practices.

2.6.2. Mobility shifts

While the social representations of space–time evolve, we can expect the same to happen to those of mobility. Is mobility not, after all, a displacement in space over time?

To the limit-form corresponds a representation of mobility based on the transgression of borders. What is mobile is what crosses borders, for example, in a company, the individual who, through examinations or "seniority", climbs the ladder of hierarchy. This mobility crossing is replicated at all scales, whether it involves crossing the limits of the city, the province, the country, or the continent. This mobility implies leaving a defined territory to gain a new one, temporarily or not. It is thus teleological and directional, since it implies the fixing of a goal preliminary to the movement. It is therefore a second and even intermediate state. An inclusion in a constituency always precedes it and a new inclusion follows it. From one anchor point to another, mobility franchising corresponds to specific practices that have nothing to do with wandering, loitering, or drifting. In this respect, it should be remembered that the crossing of borders is most of the time conditional and therefore implies planning and control.

On the other hand, to the flow-form corresponds a drifting mobility consisting of a constant movement, of which it is important to take advantage or which it is advisable to amplify, of a kinetic mobility, motivated by itself. In a space whose structure is based on the network, the positional games do not depend on a prior positioning within a space conceived as a playground, on a ground marked by boundaries. The positions are relative and depend on the games of relations between nodes of the network. Now, the position of each of these nodes is itself relative to other nodes, and so on. Therefore, if the relative positions of some of these nodes change, the position of other nodes will change as well, and so on. In the hinterland city, it is not a question of how far one is from the city center, but how easy it is to get there. At peak times, the center can therefore move away from an observer who is *a priori* immobile (at least in the sense of mobility franchising) and, at weekends and in off-peak hours, move closer. As we can see, in a network, immobility is hardly conceivable since the reticular pulsations lead to constant relative movements.

Mobility is here first. No fixity precedes it nor will it succeed it. Immobility can only be relative and proceed from an effort not to be left behind by certain points – among a multitude – of a network.

2.6.3. *The mobilitarian ideal*

It is against a background of a flow-form and drifting mobility that, in our opinion, a valorization of mobility for its own sake is developing. Since any attempt at immobility is futile, the only defensible attitude is to ride out the wave, to take advantage of the currents that discuss the network, to get closer to the coveted nodes, and to exploit the accesses that we temporarily enjoy. In this universe of meaning, material and non-material (relative) immobilities become dysfunctional, and mobility is not only desirable but also mandatory. This injunction to mobility takes the form of a mobilitarian ideal that is embodied in four imperatives.

The activity imperative is based on the obligation of constant activity. In the private or professional sphere, young or old, for free or for a fee, we must be constantly active. Rest has become illegitimate, and overload is no longer a dysfunction but a necessary and legitimate attitude. From the activity report of a company to the measurement of workload in administrations, through the litany of people "who do not stop", while declaring themselves passionate about their multiple activities, everyone tries to legitimize themselves through the staging of their overload.

The imperative of activation clarifies the former: the activity to be developed must not be the conformation to an order, the servile execution of actions determined by third parties. It must be the fruit of an activation of the actors considered, who must therefore find in themselves the sources of their activity. Proactivity, initiative, and autonomy are some of the mantras that structure our relationship with activation. It is not only social welfare recipients who should be activated, not by ordering them to go to such and such a place to take up a job that awaits them, but by training themselves, by conceiving of a personal project, by relentlessly seeking a job, or even by creating one.

The imperative of participation specifies the modalities of the expected activity: it must be reticular and collective. It is exercised through concomitant and successive[1] projects, relying on the coordination of multiple and always temporary actors. It is not a matter of settling into a status or a role, but of jumping with agility from one position to another, according to the circumstances and the project that one is experiencing at a given moment. Family, professional, sports, or leisure projects follow one another in a participative logic. Thus, the social welfare recipient is not taken charge of by an expert in charge of finding an assignment on the job market. They are surrounded by advisors, coaches, and facilitators who participate, along with many other partners, in the project to reintegrate them into a professional trajectory that corresponds to their personal project.

The last imperative is adaptation. Individuals and organizations in constant motion, binding and accumulating multiple projects, need to demonstrate unfailing flexibility. Any rigidity, barrier, or constancy is problematic in that it diminishes the ability to engage in new participations, to take advantage of network movements, or to ensure consistency of activity.

It is clear that these four imperatives, if they weigh on each individual or organization, do not have the same weight for all. The capacities of some and others to produce the appearance of mobility and to mask their immobility are not equal. Thus, the unemployed are often stigmatized for their supposed immobility, and are called upon to become active, to engage in reintegration projects, and to adapt to the labor market, whatever the cost. Those of independent means, who could be similarly reproached for contravening mobility imperatives, are only very rarely questioned. Like any normative corpus, the mobile ideal is thus susceptible to very variable uses, far from the rigorous and egalitarian application of norms.

In this theoretical framework, the dominant are not only those who are capable of mobility but also those who can escape, as Bauman would say, while the dominated would have their mobilities impeded. The dominated may be those who are forced into painful, disadvantageous, or unwanted mobilities, while the dominators have their immobilities ignored or forgiven.

Moreover, the mobilitarian ideal is not only a vector of alienation, like acceleration in Rosa's thinking, it is a normative framework that lends itself to a wide variety of uses, including emancipatory mobilities. Thus, the imperative activation can be as much an instrument for shifting the burden of solving the organizational problems encountered by the company onto the worker as for taking into account the worker's voice in the organization of work in a valorizing and useful way. In the same way, can

---

[1] This of course refers to the project-based city described above (see section 2.2.2).

participation be a pretext for denying and invisibilizing the opposing interests of workers and employers, but also a way for the former to refuse to be pure instruments in the hands of the latter?

2.7. Contextualizing research on mobilities

If the study of mobility must focus on its diversity and its particularities, and if it must therefore take into account the question of scales and avoid confusing everything with a facade of uniformity, it is nonetheless useful to try to integrate these analyses into a broader framework. This is what the five theoretical works presented above propose. Each in its own way, they integrate the issue of mobility into a broader framework.

Of course, it is not a question of finding a definitive truth about mobility but of trying to understand what interdisciplinarities can be identified. Whether it is a question of the emergence of a new register of justification of inequalities based on the project, disengagement, and activity, or of the liquefaction and lightening of capitalism and modernity allowing for constant reconfigurations and mobilities, or the alienation of individuals by their submission to a self-sustained acceleration without any other object than itself, or to make mobility the pivot of our social systems and thus the focal point of any social science, or finally to make mobility an injunction linked to an evolution of social representations of material space–time or not, it is each time a question of the search for a global perspective. It is not a question of finding an ultimate principle, or an absolute origin, but of ascending in generality.

It is through this work that trends observed in independent fields a priori can be brought together: the evolution of the organization of companies and that of individual travel in the private sphere, the valuing of mobility for its own sake, but the ignorance of certain of its forms, the lability of territorial, but also emotional, professional, philosophical or political attachments, etc.

While the ambition of this chapter is to draw a partial overview of the field and not to propose a theory of the whole field, a metatheory integrating the five presented here – it must be noted that they maintain close links – which undoubtedly owe as much to comparative readings as to common observations of reality.

At the center, certainly, is the valorization of mobility for its own sake, rather than as a means of connecting two predefined points. Each in their own way, the authors studied here note the abandonment of a system in which anchoring, heaviness, attachment, constancy, and stability were essential, and in which mobility was a temporary uprooting, a way of joining two places. Whether they formalize it explicitly or not, they chronicle a change in the meaning and use of mobility and a tendency to make it an end in itself.

Rather than a practice, mobility is becoming an almost natural state of being, unequally accessible, but less and less requiring the support of specific legitimacies.

Of course, all the authors included here diagnose a radical, if not sudden, change. None of them, however, intend to take up the naturalization of mobility, its depoliticization into pure movement. On the contrary, it is a question of defining what is changing and what that change implies in turn. In the line of sight, in a broad way, the question of the domination and that of the disruption or the prolongation, under other forms, under other norms, of social hierarchies. In what way is mobility, today, an instrument of social stratification? How does it allow values to be attributed, behaviors to be imposed, or situations to be justified?

In addition, each of these theories proposes to reconsider social phenomena that have long been studied by the social sciences: the work and the organization of the company, social rhythms, the economy, travel, or social representations of space–time. As such, they are likely to constitute the conceptual substratum of innumerable empirical research studies.

Finally, and this is perhaps the justification for the present chapter, all these authors remind us that the question of mobility, in the social sciences, cannot do without the question of meaning. The meaning that actors give to their practices, but also to the world, to the reality in which they are immersed and in which, precisely, they develop their action. This question can only be answered through a dialogue between empirical research and theory. What our text could invite us to do is to explore a simple and infinite question: that of the link between empirical research, often precise, local, and extremely close to the field, and theoretical, globalizing, and generalizing research. Any generalization is necessarily, in some way, an error, but only a generalization allows us to avoid the empirical research becoming the chronicle of an isolated field. Any empirical research presupposes, inevitably, a spurious abstraction from a larger context, but only empirical research allows us to avoid the pitfall of the discourse, taking itself for an object. It is thus in the dialogue between these two extremes that lies, without any doubt, the possibility of a progression of science on the question of mobility and its meaning.

It is through this dialogue that questions such as meaning, but also synchronization and desynchronization, speed differentials, borders (protective or oppressive), quality of life, the political dimension of the relationship with space, the conditions of possibility of a critique of social norms relating to space and mobility, and the differentiated uses of these norms, can be clarified. Each of these questions requires the use of not only fieldwork but also generalizations. Each offers the prospect of research that goes beyond the pure description of social practices.

2.8. References

Bauman, Z. (2000). *Liquid Modernity*. Polity Press/Blackwell, Cambridge/Malden.

Boltanski, L. and Chiapello, E. (1999). *Le nouvel esprit du capitalisme*. Gallimard, Paris.

Boltanski, L. and Thévenot, L. (1991). *De la justification : les économies de la grandeur*. Gallimard, Paris.

Borja, S., Courty, G., Ramadier, T. (2014). Trois mobilités en une seule ? *EspacesTemps* [Online]. Available at: http://www.espacestemps.net/articles/trois-mobilites-en-une-seule/ [Accessed 3 June 2015].

Cresswell, T. (2001). The production of mobilities. *Mobilities*, 43, 11–25.

Cresswell, T. (2006). *On the Move: Mobility in the Modern Western World*. Routledge, New York.

Debarbieux, B. (2014). Enracinement – ancrage – amarrage : raviver les métaphores. *L'espace géographique*, 43(1), 68–80.

Ehrenberg, A. (1998). *La fatigue d'être soi : dépression et société*. Odile Jacob, Paris.

Kaufmann, V. (2004). La mobilité comme capital ? In *Mobilités, fluidités... libertés ?* Montulet, B. (ed.). Presses de l'Université Saint-Louis, Brussels.

Kaufmann, V. (2008). *Les paradoxes de la mobilité : bouger, s'enraciner*. Presses polytechniques et universitaires romandes, Lausanne.

Mincke, C. and Montulet, B. (2019). *La société sans répit. La mobilité comme injonction*. Éditions de la Sorbonne, Paris.

Montulet, B. (1998). *Les enjeux spatio-temporels du social : mobilités*. L'Harmattan, Paris.

Rosa, H. (2012). *Aliénation et accélération. Vers une théorie critique de la modernité tardive*. La Découverte, Paris.

Urry, J. (2007). *Mobilities*. Polity Press, Cambridge/Malden.

3

Mobility Justice as a Political Object

Caroline GALLEZ

Laboratoire Ville Mobilité Transport (LVMT),
Université Gustave Eiffel, Champs-sur-Marne, France

3.1. Introduction

In the spring of 2013, hundreds of thousands of people demonstrated in several Brazilian cities to denounce the increase in public transport fares. It was against a backdrop of increased public spending, following the organization of the soccer World Cup. In October 2018, in France, the so-called *Gilets jaunes* movement emerged in reaction to the increase in fuel prices linked to the application of a carbon tax and the reduction of the speed limit on interurban road networks. In mid-October 2019, in Chile, a social movement, on an unprecedented scale since the end of the dictatorship, unfolded following an increase of more than 3% in subway tickets in the capital. In all three cases, the increase in the cost of travel was the trigger for social anger. The protests denounced, among other things, measures that infringed on the freedom of movement and aggravated the daily difficulties in accessing essential resources.

In a globalized world where the movement of people, goods, capital, and information is one of the foundations of capitalist economies, a plurality of associations, collectives, organizations and individuals are calling for the respect or extension of mobility rights. While spatial mobility has become an indispensable condition for participation in social life, inequalities in mobility remain very marked, undermining the idea of a universal right to movement, despite the fact that national and international declarations and constitutions affirm it. These inequalities are expressed on different geographical scales, in the form of infringements of freedom of movement, forced displacement, highly constrained mobility practices, or differentiated access to public space or modes of transport. In this context, mobility justice is the subject of growing demands, placing public and political debates on the problems of inequality and respect for the right to mobility from a moral perspective.

In this chapter, we propose to approach mobility justice in its political dimension, i.e., with regard to the power issues that it reveals, both in the analysis of observed inequalities and in the policies or protest movements that defend mobility justice objectives. To do so, we begin by discussing the main issues of mobility justice in contemporary Western societies (section 3.2). We then outline the most commonly applied social justice theories on mobility (section 3.3). Thirdly, we present the major research works applied to mobility justice and its policy implications: firstly in the field of transport and urban planning (section 3.4), then in the broader field of social science (section 3.5). In conclusion, we return to the scientific and political controversies surrounding the issues of mobility justice (section 3.6).

3.2. Inequality and mobility justice in contemporary Western societies

Presented as having a rising value in contemporary urban societies (Bacqué and Fol 2007), associated with the "new spirit of capitalism" (Boltanski and Chiapello 1999), equated with flexibility, a cardinal virtue in the world of work, mobility has not always been positively valued. From the Middle Ages to the modern period, rootedness and community attachment have been the dominant social condition. The term "mobile" refers to inconstancy; mobile people arouse distrust, and vagrancy is punished as a crime (Castel 1999; Roche 2003; Cresswell 2005). It was not until the rise of modern capitalism that the relationship between liberty, mobility, and citizenship changed significantly (Blomley 1992). The right of individuals to move freely was asserted during the revolutionary period, in connection with citizenship, and then strengthened during the Enlightenment, with the advent of liberal political philosophy. In 1948, the Declaration of Human Rights established that the right to move is a universal right, an integral part of citizenship.

However, the emergence of a right of free movement, which benefits specific groups of individuals (citizens) and which applies to certain goods, goes hand in hand with the establishment of control mechanisms that restrict or prevent the movement of other people or goods. These measurement and control devices, such as the passport or customs, contribute to the construction of national communities (Noiriel 1998; Denis 2006). The development of rapid means of transport and the technological changes that accompanied the Industrial Revolution accelerated the development of mobility and contributed to its commoditization. The growth of flows of people, goods, information and capital supports fundamental economic and spatial transformations, generalized urbanization, metropolization, peri-urbanization and globalization of economic exchanges. Nevertheless, it masks significant differences between individuals and social groups at different spatial scales.

Within national areas, inequalities in mobility became a major public policy issue as problems of access to employment and urban amenities became more pronounced in the late 1960s. The rise of individual mobility, which came later in Europe than in the United States, accompanied extensive urban growth and disjointed movements of residential and employment suburbanization. Some populations without access to a car suffer from a lack of accessibility, often poorly compensated for by the availability of public transport services. In urban areas marked by strong social and racial inequalities, as in the United States, this problem is identified as one of the major causes of poverty and unemployment (Sanchez 2008). The social issue of improving urban public transport was also affirmed in Europe in the 1960s and 1970s (Gallez and Motte 2018). The development of public transport services was part of the provision of a "social" transport offer for people who did not have access to a car – the "captive users". In France, this is reflected in the inclusion of a "right to transport" in the 1982 law on the orientation of domestic transport.

The social issues of access to mobility were reinforced from the 1990s onward, with the rise of the fight against exclusion, which reflected a transformation of the social question (Fol and Gallez 2017). In Europe, back-to-work policies, aiming at empowering and giving responsibility to people in precarious situations, gradually replaced the redistributive approach to aid for the unemployed created after World War II (Elbaum 1995). In this context, access to mobility was presented as an essential factor of people's employability (Fol 2009). While individual mobility is becoming a social norm imposed on the whole population (Massot and Orfeuil 2005), public policies target individuals or social groups deemed to be lacking in access to mobility, thus resulting in a targeted and conditional right to mobility (Jamar and Lannoy 2011; Féré 2013).

At the international level, due to the increase in migration flows linked to the globalization of trade, conflicts and ecological disasters, public authorities are faced with the contradictory injunctions of the neoliberal economy. While the role of modern states is weakening to the benefit of economic actors, national governments are faced with growing demands to maintain security, economic protectionism and national priority in access to employment, which are opposed to the generalization of the right to mobility, as well as to the application of principles of reception and aid to refugee populations. The pressure exerted against NGOs rescuing shipwrecked people in the Mediterranean Sea, the multiplication of barriers, walls and border controls, development of detention centers and evacuation of camps in urban areas are all examples of coercive measures taken by public authorities against migrants or their supporters. They underline the limits of the right to mobility, which is reserved for nationals of some 30 Western countries, i.e., less than a quarter of the world population (Gay et al. 2011).

In this context, many collectives, associations, and NGOs have placed the right to mobility or the right to access resources at the heart of their demands (Sheller 2018). The forms of these demands, which apply equally to the expansion of access to mobility or freedom of movement, as well as the fight against forced displacement or evacuation, reveal the ambivalent character of mobility claimed as a right or denounced as oppression.

Finally, the ecological crisis is profoundly changing the spatial and temporal scales at which the issues of mobility justice and injustice are defined. The energy and environmental impacts of transport and the movement of people and goods are major. Today, it is estimated that transportation accounts for about a quarter of global greenhouse gas emissions (AEE 2018). However, this environmental contribution is very unevenly distributed, with the weight of the most advantaged social groups, who use air travel more often, for business or leisure purposes, clearly in the majority (Nicolas et al. 2012; Büchs and Schnepf 2013). Moreover, the least economically endowed populations are also the most exposed to the environmental impacts of transport (air pollution, noise) because of their residential location being near major infrastructures or their professional activity. Precarious workers, who are sometimes highly mobile (Jouffe 2007), are also the most vulnerable to increases in mobility costs, as shown by a number of recent social movements.

All of these issues have received increasing attention from social scientists, particularly in the last 10 years. These works refer, in a more or less explicit way, to different theoretical conceptions of social justice.

3.3. Social justice and mobility, theoretical approaches

Social justice refers to a normative approach that aims to establish the fairness or unfairness of social inequalities, based on principles such as equality or equity. There are different conceptions of justice in the field of political philosophy (Kymlicka 1999; Savidan et al. 2018). The principle of justice, i.e., the way in which the fairness or unfairness of observed inequalities is defined, constitutes a first differentiating element. An aggregative theory aims to maximize the total or average amount of a resource in society, whereas a distributive theory advocates for a fair distribution of that resource. Between the two, several distributive principles have been defined, which move away from strict equality; these principles refer to the notion of equity, i.e., a distribution of resources that, although not equal, is considered fair. A second differentiating element is that of the object or objects targeted by social justice, in other words, the resource or resources that we wish to maximize, equalize, or distribute. As for the temporal, spatial, and social scales at which social justice is defined, they are becoming increasingly important in theoretical and political debates, as evidenced by the notions of intergenerational justice, global justice and animal ethics.

Several theories of justice serve as recurring references for thinking applied to mobility (Pereira et al. 2017).

Associated with the work of economist John Stuart Mill, inspired by Bentham's moral philosophy, *utilitarianism* is based on the principle of maximizing collective well-being, defined as the sum of the utilities of the individuals making up society. Because the distribution of utility among the individuals that make up society is unknown, utilitarian theory believes that any policy that aims to improve the well-being of some individuals without worsening the situation of others is legitimate.

The *Theory of Justice* by Rawls (1971) is a distributive approach to justice that is opposed to utilitarian theory. It is based on the notion of "primary social goods" that allow people to accomplish their projects (fundamental rights and freedoms, freedom of movement and free choice of profession, access to positions of authority, income and other resources, social bases of self-respect). This approach advocates a double principle: an egalitarian distribution of fundamental rights and freedoms, in the largest possible proportion, an access to positions of authority distributed according to a principle of equality of opportunity (individuals can decide whether or not to occupy these positions) and a distribution of other primary goods favorable to the most disadvantaged.

With the *capability approach*, the economist Sen (2009) and the philosopher Nussbaum (2011) suggest looking at power inequalities rather than the inequalities of individuals' resources. This theory starts from a critique of the Rawlsian approach, which does not allow us to grasp the differences in people's ability to convert primary goods to serve their goals. Sen proposes to evaluate the quality of life on the basis of what individuals are really able to achieve, in terms of *beings* and *doings*, which he describes as functionings. *Capability*, which represents the individual's freedom to function, is defined as the set of potential functionings that the individual can achieve.

The application of justice to mobility issues raises several specific problems, including that of taking into account the spatial dimension, which is absent from most theories of justice. Following the publication of the *Theory of Justice* (Rawls 1971), which was part of the social mobilizations of the late 1960s and marked a major break away from the utilitarian foundations of political economy models, several geographers took up the issue of justice (Brennetot 2011). In *Social Justice and the City*, the geographer Harvey (1973) proposed to understand the problems of resource allocation in urban spaces from the perspective of social justice. Contesting the effectiveness of reformist distributive approaches, he gives a Marxist reading of urban inequalities, which he describes as territorial, by associating them with the power structures that underlie them.

This work was taken up, discussed and criticized by other geographers, claiming to be part of the radical geography movement (Smith 1987) or social geography (Bailly et al. 1978; Reynaud 1981; Séchet 1989). Later, Soja (2010) developed an approach to spatial justice that questions the equity in the distribution of urban resources, including in terms of access to transport. This approach, which does not focus specifically on mobility issues, is an extension of Lefebvre's (1968) work on the production of space and the right to the city. Soja (2010) is interested in the way in which inequalities in access to space or in the spatial distribution of resources reflect and emerge from power relations between social classes. Advocating a distributive conception of justice, in which all forms of inequality could be understood in an interdisciplinary manner based on their spatial inscription, he suggests that a more equitable distribution of access to urban resources constitutes the basis of social justice.

The state of the art of the international literature shows that reflections on the issues of ethics and justice in the face of mobility are both rapidly growing and relatively recent. It is not that issues of inequality of access to mobility or mobility practices have not been the subject of longstanding work and debate, particularly in the field of transport (Fol 2009; Ohnmacht et al. 2009). However, this work has long been confined to specialized fields and disciplines that have focused on the actual movement of people, particularly urban travel and migration at different spatial scales. From the 1980s to the 1990s, the questioning of the fight against social inequalities and the sharp increase in unemployment were accompanied by a renewal of theoretical approaches to equity and the factors of social exclusion. It is in this context that scientific productions on the issues of equity or justice in transport and mobility are reactivated.

We will distinguish between the work that circumscribes thinking in the field of transportation (Litman 2002; Martens 2016; Pereira et al. 2017) and the work that places the debate at the heart of broader social science approaches to mobility (Cook and Butz 2018; Sheller 2018), which fall under different conceptions of mobility itself.

3.4. Inequalities and equity in transport and urban planning

In terms of urbanized areas, inequalities in mobility, access to modes of transport, or urban amenities have been the subject of a large body of literature since the late 1960s, particularly in relation to the spatial mismatch hypothesis developed by Kain

(1968; Wachs and Kumagai 1973). The consideration of equity issues in the evaluation of transportation projects and policies or in access to urban amenities has steadily increased over the past decade (Martens and Golub 2012; Martens 2016; Di Ciommo et al. 2017).

3.4.1. *Integrating equity in the evaluation of transport policies*

A substantial body of work on the redistributive effects of transport policies has focused on socioeconomic appraisal methods (Grant-Muller et al. 2001; Thomopoulos et al. 2009). In terms of evaluation of transport infrastructure *ex ante*, the "cost–benefit balance" method is still the most widely used in Western countries. This approach is based on a utilitarian conception of justice that aims to maximize the "global surplus" of users, thus limiting the consideration of social and territorial equity. Firstly, the method assumes an optimal distribution of income, which reveals the indifference of the public decision to the way in which individuals benefit from the advantages or bear the costs of the future infrastructure (Bonnafous and Masson 2003).

This first limitation is amplified by the assumption of increasing rates of return, according to which profitability depends on an infrastructure and its use: the more the infrastructure is used, the higher[1] the sum of expected time savings, and the greater the estimated profitability. The profitability objective directs choices toward satisfying the most important "demands": priority infrastructure is that which carries the most traffic, and priority individuals in the use of infrastructure are those with the highest "value of time". This approach, as Bonnafous and Masson (2003) argue, is at odds with the principle of territorial equity that guides the traditional vision of land-use policy.

Questions about the redistributive effects of transport policies have also been addressed from the perspective of pricing infrastructure usage, particularly in relation to the implementation of congestion charges (Banister 1993; Di Ciommo and Lucas 2014). As Vanoutrive and Zijlstra (2018) point out, there is considerable variability in the pricing principles proposed by economists, each of which has been extensively debated from the perspective of social impacts, including through the notion of social acceptability (Viegas 2001) and the progressive or regressive effects of pricing (Levinson 2010). Some authors suggest that the acceptability of pricing could be improved, and the negative effects corrected, by earmarking toll revenues, for example, for public transport funding (Eliasson 2014). Although subject to debate, this use of funding for alternatives to the private car is part of a trend that seeks to reconcile environmental objectives while safeguarding the principles of economic growth and efficiency.

---

1 The benefits of an infrastructure are usually estimated from the time saved, converted into a monetary value by applying a "value of time".

3.4.2. *Moving from inequalities in mobility to inequalities in access to facilities*

Inequalities in individual travel have also been the subject of numerous empirical studies, highlighting in particular the weight of income: poorer households travel less and lesser distances (Pucher and Renne 2003; Orfeuil 2004; Renne and Bennett 2014). These disparities can be explained in part by differences in motorization rates and access to a driver's license (Orfeuil 2010). They also refer to differences in the availability of public transport: certain neighborhoods or certain types of territories (suburban, rural) are less well served by public transport (Kaufmann et al. 2007). These disparities have been blamed, in particular, for the difficulties in accessing employment. However, inequalities in mobility practices remain difficult to interpret in the sense that they do not systematically reproduce a social hierarchy (Le Breton 2005, 2006). Precarious people can be highly mobile, while at the same time forced to make daily trips for which they choose neither the mode of transport nor the time of day, which weighs heavily on their budget (Jouffe 2007). In everyday life, high mobility is not necessarily a sign of a well-to-do social situation (Wenglenski 2013). As a result, the reduction of mobility inequalities is difficult to formulate in terms of social justice.

The use of the notion of accessibility allows us to partially circumvent these limitations and ambiguities. The starting point is that transport is not an end in itself, but a means of satisfying a need to access places where different social activities can be performed (Levine et al. 2019). In the transportation domain, accessibility is most often reduced to the "ease of access to places", neglecting the dimension that is very much present in planners' understanding of the density of amenity distribution (Hansen 1959).

The problem with this approach, which equates improved transport performance with improved accessibility, is that it does not take into account the retroactive impacts of improved travel conditions on the spatial organization of urbanized areas, particularly in terms of diffuse urbanization (Handy 2002), nor does it take into account the inequalities between individuals in terms of the appropriation of the speed potential thus created (Fol and Gallez 2014).

There has been no shortage of criticism of an approach that focuses on network performance, including from some transport specialists, who question the relevance of time saved as a major benefit of infrastructure (Ben-Akiva and Lerman 1985; Metz 2008). It is from these reflections that alternative approaches have emerged that aim to evaluate the benefits of an infrastructure on the basis of the gains in accessibility that it provides (Koenig 1974, 1980). These "utility-based" measures of accessibility make it possible to distance ourselves from the assumption of increasing rates of return. It is indeed possible to choose utility functions that simulate a benefit that is all the higher the lower the initial accessibility, and thus guide decision-makers toward projects that give priority to less well-served territories or to populations suffering from low accessibility (Martens 2006; Nahmias-Biran et al. 2017).

A very large body of empirical work, including some outside the field of transport, has applied the concept and indicators of accessibility to the analysis of inequalities in access to urban amenities. They have highlighted significant differences in access to employment, services, facilities, or shops for people living in the poorest neighborhoods or those with limited income (Fol 2009; Fol and Gallez 2014). Differential access to modes of transport, particularly the car, is seen both as an indicator of inequalities between social groups and as an index of inequalities in the performance of these modes in providing access to opportunities. Inequalities are due both to the spatial organization of amenities to the level of vehicle equipment or transport service provision, which vary according to the environment of the places of residence, work, or activities, and to individual characteristics, which differentiate, in a given urban and material environment, people's effective access to transport. Golub and Martens (2014), for example, define an indicator of "access poverty" by comparing accessibility by car with accessibility by public transport and testing the impacts for different population groups (by income) of several investment scenarios aimed at reducing this gap.

Most authors agree that transport accessibility is a necessary but not sufficient condition for guaranteeing people's freedom of choice and promoting equal opportunities in terms of access to employment, health care and services (Church et al. 2000; Welch 2013). Wenglenski (2004) shows, in particular, that inequalities in access to employment between managers and employees in the Paris region stem both from differences in access to the car and from differences in the spatial distribution of jobs corresponding to these social categories. Due to a greater concentration in the dense areas best served by transport networks, managers' jobs are more accessible. The actual weight of structural factors such as distance or access to transport modes remains a matter of debate (Fol 2009; Korsu and Wenglenski 2009). Regarding the spatial mismatch thesis (Kain 1992; Gobillon et al. 2007), several authors insist on the decisive weight of individual characteristics, especially when people are racialized, in effective access to jobs (Ellwood 1986; Preston and Rajé 2007).

3.4.3. *Evaluating equity of access to facilities*

Beyond the measurement of inequality, the question of equity of access has been tackled both from transport policy evaluation and individual access to opportunities (van Wee and Geurs 2011; Martens et al. 2012). A great deal of methodological thought has been devoted to the scale of measuring inequalities (referring to notions of social or territorial equity), the theoretical principles of equity, and their translation into indicators or operational criteria.

Various types of indicators or variables are used, which refer to different notions of equity (Litman 2002). Authors agree on the need to cross-reference spatial and individual approaches at a minimum by disaggregating accessibility indicators by social category (Neutens et al. 2010; Di Ciommo and Shiftan 2017). This raises the question of the variable chosen to differentiate social groups (income or individual needs), which in turn refers to the underlying principle of justice. Several indicators have been proposed to measure the fairness or unfairness of the distribution of accessibility and to estimate the impact of transport policies in reducing inequality: the gap between the most and the less well endowed (Martens 2012), Gini indices (Lucas et al. 2016), or correlation coefficients (Adli and Donovan 2018).

Two distributional principles of accessibility are commonly used to assess the equity of public policies: strict equality or meeting a threshold of accessibility deemed "sufficient" to certain essential goods or services, such as employment, education, health and basic shopping (Pereira et al. 2017). The nature of essential goods and services, as well as the level of accessibility to be guaranteed, are, however, the subject of debate that engages normative judgments on the relative importance given to one good over another (Martens et al. 2012). While some authors agree that, like Rawls, a transport policy is equitable when it distributes transport services and investments in a way that reduces inequality of opportunity and prioritizes the most disadvantaged social groups (Pereira et al. 2017), others insist on the need to develop a more appropriate theoretical foundation (Nahmias-Biran et al. 2017). From the perspective of Walzer's (1983) circles of justice theory[2], some authors advance the idea that accessibility is a specific social good whose distribution must be distinguished from that of other goods and resources, particularly income (Martens 2012; Martens et al. 2012).

This approach is nevertheless subject to criticism: apart from the fact that it does not provide a clear principle concerning the distribution of accessibility, the risk is that this meaning is linked to the interests of dominant groups. Other authors point to the risk of paternalism associated with the definition of a sufficient threshold of access to

---

2 According to Walzer (1983), the fairness of the distribution of goods produced in a society depends on the value systems associated with these goods. The distribution of a good that has a particular social meaning, different from everyday consumer goods (e.g. education), must be determined according to a principle that is specific to it (e.g. ensuring equal access to education to guarantee equal opportunity). The second criterion of justice advanced by Walzer is that of the autonomy of the spheres of justice in relation to one another, making it possible to avoid the accumulation of inequalities or dominant positions of certain individuals or social groups.

transport for disadvantaged groups: for Vanoutrive and Cooper (2019), it is an assignment of these groups to accept a minimal service, of lower quality than the access of better-off people. The challenge to this method of defining a minimum threshold of access rather than a universal approach underlies, in particular, the demands made by groups defending the rights of disabled people for the generalized accessibility of transport networks and, more generally, of public services and facilities.

Sen's (1985) and Nussbaum's (2011) capability theory has been used to define levels of accessibility differentiated according to individuals or social groups. Accessibility is seen as a resource necessary for the realization of a series of functions specific to each individual. According to the capability approach, which emphasizes the difference between the distribution of resources and the ability to mobilize resources to carry out projects, equity in access to resources must take into account the possibilities of different individuals or social groups to translate resources (objective accessibility) into capabilities (real accessibility).

Therefore, equity should be defined in terms of minimum thresholds of accessibility (which guarantee minimum capacities), integrating the characteristics of social groups and the features of the transport system and land use. In this context, several authors insist on the need to take account of the people affected in the definition of these needs and thresholds, raising the question of "procedural justice" and the concrete participation of individuals in decision-making processes (Levinson 2009; Beyazit 2011).

When applied to the problems of transport and access to urban amenities, equity is the subject of methodological proposals and empirical work that refer to different philosophical and political conceptions of justice. Taking for granted the role of mobility as a condition of access to resources, these works focus on the conditions for extending the right to mobility or reducing inequalities in the face of mobility. On the contrary, the works carried out in the field of social sciences broaden the perspective by questioning the role of mobility in social dynamics, as well as the factors of production or reproduction of inequalities, at different scales.

3.5. Mobility justice: contributions from the social sciences

The new attention paid to spatial mobility, starting in the 1990s, was not immediately accompanied by a major interest in social justice issues (Cresswell 2006). Criticizing the assimilation of mobility and social change, several authors point out the paradoxes and the strong inequalities between individuals and social groups that are hidden by the misleading vision of a "world in motion" (Massey 1991; Bauman 2000; Cresswell 2001; Kaufmann 2005). The questions of inequality and justice, in their perspective, concern mobility as much as immobility, and touch upon the representations, values and regulations associated with the social production of mobility.

3.5.1. Ambiguities of mobility

Often confused with flows, mobility is an ambivalent object with regard to questions of equality or social justice. For many sociologists, mobility refers first and foremost to *social mobility* (Sorokin 2009), referring to changes in status, particularly professional status, within the social sphere (Gallez and Kaufmann 2009). The new interest in spatial mobility carries the risk of equating the trivialization and *reversibilization* of mobility[3] with a process of social fluidity, with a democratization that would be a sign of egalitarianism (Kaufmann 2005). To avoid confusion between movement and mobility, Kaufmann (2002) defines the concept of *motility* as "the way in which an individual or a group appropriate the scope of possibilities and make use of it", i.e., the capacity to appropriate a potential for mobility.

Many notions such as "appropriable virtuality" (Rémy 2000), "spatial capital" (Lévy 2000), or "networked capital" aim to analyze the potential offered by mobility beyond the actual practices (Urry 2007). In these approaches, mobility is considered a form of "resource" or "capital", concepts classically used in works of various inspirations on social mobility (Boudon 1973; Bourdieu 1979; Coleman 1988). For Urry (2007), while social inequalities are partly due to the unequal distribution of network capital, this capital is not directly proportional to economic capital: thus, poor migrants are among the individuals who maintain the greatest number of long-distance relationships. He recognizes the ambivalence of a capital that cannot be viewed solely in terms of the resources it provides: while network capital increases as the scale and scope of circulation in a society increases, the role of mobility in lifestyles becomes unavoidable, and the likelihood that this mobility is constrained or forced becomes more significant.

The use of the term capital for mobility has given rise to various criticisms. Some authors question the positive valorization associated with mobility potential and underline the limits of an understanding limited to urban mobilities or to the organization of lifestyles, to the detriment of a more global approach, integrating international migrations or questioning the impact of political or economic structures on the ability of individuals to appropriate these potentials (Glick Schiller and Salazar 2013; Leivestad 2016). For example, while arguing that poor migrants may be endowed with significant network

---

3 The term reversibilization refers to the process whereby the most reversible spatial mobilities, those that refer to social experiences with the least definitive impact, tend to be substituted for mobilities that reflect more salient or lasting social experiences (see Kaufmann (2005)).

capital, Urry does not question the impact of their heavy reliance on mobility (Larsen and Jacobsen 2009).

Other authors call into question the very notion of a "need" for mobility. The focus on mobility as an essential need for individuals, which underlies the proclamation of a right to mobility, calls for the multiple forms of mobilization of people throughout their life course to be questioned (Jamar and Lannick, 2007). According to these authors:

> The polymorphous yet massive character of these programmed[4] mobilizations makes us understand that mobility as a "need" is above all defined by the dominant economic and political logics, which are declined at different scales (global, continental, regional, metropolitan) (Jamar and Lannoy 2011).

Bacqué and Fol (2007) emphasize the risk of drift in the dominant academic, political, and media discourse, which operates "a shift from the right to mobility to the inability to be mobile", prohibiting questions about both the resources of immobility and the costs of mobility. Several authors show that the normalization of mobility leads to the encouragement and valorization of certain movements considered "normal", while excluding other movements considered "deviant", unacceptable, or unable to adapt (Langan 2001; Jamar and Lannoy 2011; Kotef 2015; Sheller 2018). All of these works encourage us to consider mobility from the perspective of the modalities of its production.

3.5.2. Mobility regimes and differentiation of mobility rights

These rights are some of the major "sites" for the production of mobility, demonstrating the gap between the discourse on the right to mobility and the conditions of its concrete implementation (Cresswell 2006). When it is asserted as every human being's fundamental freedom, the right to free movement is freed from any social and spatial context. However, the implementation of a social right to mobility implies the definition and application of technical devices, regulatory and legal tools, tariffs, categories and borders, which authorize or facilitate the movement of certain individuals or social groups and prevent, limit or control the movement of others. For

---

4 "Some examples of which are: policies of professional activation, 'lifelong' training, student mobility, flexibilization of statuses and jobs, organized displacement of labor, calls for the consumption of space by automobile and tourist advertising, development of new poles of attractiveness, etc" (Jamar and Lannoy 2011).

Cresswell (2006), the principle of universality of the right to mobility comes up against the spatial dimension of mobility practices.

Although frequently associated with the idea of freedom, mobility is never a universal attribute: each human being is born unable to move independently, and then grows up and evolves in a social and material environment that shapes mobility (Langan 2001). Research on disabilities shows that the ability to move, although a partially embodied characteristic (in the sense that it is relative to the body), cannot be reduced or essentialized to this physical dimension. The ability to move and the actual movement of people are in fact strongly dependent on sociocultural attitudes and practices, as well as the design of the built environment (Imrie 2000). For Chouinard (2001), people with disabilities are often relegated to spaces of "phantom citizenship", where the "law as discursively represented and law as lived are fundamentally at odds" (Chouinard 2001).

This differentiated production of the right to mobility according to the status or condition of the persons has been studied from the point of view of its links with citizenship. Based on the decisions of the US Supreme Court, Cresswell (2006) shows that the freedom of movement is affirmed as an intangible principle of citizenship, even though this right is not enshrined in the constitution. The production of a mobile, autonomous North American citizen, whose movements contributed to the founding of the nation, implicitly goes hand in hand with the production of noncitizens, whose mobility is strictly controlled, or even prevented, as was the case with the Chinese immigrants (noncitizens) who contributed, in the 19th century, to the construction of the transcontinental[5] railroads. In other words, it is the logic of otherness that prevails in the foundation of the right to mobility rather than that of exclusion, underlining the segmentation principle of the application of a supposedly universal right to mobility. The same process forms the liberal subject and citizen through the right to mobility and produces, according to logic of differentiation, the one who suffers from exclusion, confinement, imprisonment, and violence (Kotef 2015).

Several authors use the notion of the "mobility regime" to analyze the power relations, normalization, and regulation that characterize the government of movements and the production of mobility. Referring to the notion of a political regime, Kesselring and Vogl (2013) state that "mobilities regimes hence represent specific sets of principles, norms and rules that regulate, in a fundamental way, the movement of individuals, artifacts, capital, data, etc. in a given context of action". These regimes involve different spatial and organizational scales, and their functioning is based on the maintenance of inequalities that enable some people to benefit from rights and favorable concrete

---

5 The Chinese Exclusion Act of 1882 prohibited the travel of non-citizen Chinese immigrants to the United States.

conditions, while others are prevented, controlled and limited in their ability to move. For Kesselring (2014), mobility regimes are political in the sense that they are instruments for structuring contexts of social interaction.

The impact of mobility regimes in terms of reducing social inequalities can be positive, when they increase access to mobility for a growing number of people, or negative, for those excluded from access to mobility (Kesselring 2014). They can contribute to strengthening equality of opportunity, but they can also be a factor in aggravating social exclusion. Thus, globalization is often discussed in terms of the generalization of transnational flows, whereas it also corresponds, simultaneously, to a strong increase in controls and restrictions on movements. According to Shamir (2005), the mobility regime characteristic of globalization is based on the paradigm of suspicion toward certain groups associated with threats or risks (terrorism, immigration, crime). In opposition to the movement of extension of human rights and its impacts on individual rights, this mobility regime limits and prevents access to certain rights by regulating social space.

3.5.3. *Mobility justice in the face of the ecological emergency and social inequalities*

The context of ecological emergency, increasing migration flows and increasing social inequalities accentuates the paradoxes and ambivalences of the discourse on the right to mobility.

Within national spaces, the norm of mobility, which Orfeuil defines as "the level of mobility practices that society considers 'normal' and likely to be demanded of individuals", has increased sharply (Orfeuil and Ripoll 2015). By incorporating the population's increasing mobility capacities into their strategy, public and private actors have in effect promoted an increasing dispersion of amenities in geographic space. The resulting reorganization of social positions within urbanized spaces is marked by strong inequalities in access to housing, employment, and resources (Lévy 2009). For the less economically endowed, mobility is an adjustment variable to constraints in the labor and housing markets. By forcing some people into long, financially or time-consuming mobility, this spatialization process of urban societies raises issues of sustainability, both socially and spatially.

We have hypothesized that public policies on transportation, land-use planning, and housing that are part of these social and spatial transformations contribute to generating, maintaining or aggravating forms of dependence on mobility (Gallez 2015, 2018). This dependence can be measured by the harm suffered by people with limited mobility suffering from a lack of access to resources or essential local services, or by the people whose daily mobility practices are severely constrained.

However, these issues of dependence are only partially integrated into the discourse of "inclusive mobility", which only takes into consideration the lack of mobility of certain social groups, without integrating the risk of reducing access to resources that an increase in the costs of daily mobility imposes on a large number of people with modest incomes (Gallez and Motte 2017). Moreover, mobility regulation measures, which focus on sustainability at the scale of urbanized spaces, leave aside the challenges of reducing the mobility of the most financially endowed social groups, who also contribute most strongly to the carbon footprint.

For Gössling and Cohen (2014), the failure of transport policies to address climate issues is explained by the persistence of taboo subjects around the reduction of travel demand, particularly on international passenger travel, which mostly concerns the most affluent categories of the population.

Following Sheller (2018), mobility justice is different from both transport justice and spatial justice. The former, by confining itself to urbanized spaces, tends to isolate the production of inequalities from a broader political, social, historical context, both in terms of spatial and temporal scales. As for the spatial justice approach theorized by Soja (2010), it highlights spatial disparities in access to resources and occupation of territories, but does not provide a clear understanding of the mobility inequalities that generate them.

Thus, the question of inequalities in mobility and mobility justice cannot be reduced to a problem of inequalities in terms of access to the transport system, to technical or material aspects, or to an approach to accessibility limited to ease of movement. They encompass, in a much more general way, the way in which mobility is socially produced and the way in which the institutional regulation of mobility generates forms of inequality and injustice that are not very visible when the point of view is limited to a functional approach to the organization of travel or access to urban amenities (Sheller 2018). Sheller points out that mobility practices and the institutional regulations that affect them stem from gendered and sexualized relationships to space, linked to colonial histories, capitalist exploitation and land appropriation. She states, "I argue that debates over sustainable urbanism, transport justice and urban accessibility should be placed in the context of wider transnational mobility regimes, including questions of colonialism, borders, tourism and migration" (Sheller 2018). Implicit in this perspective is the recognition that mobility may not always be a form of freedom, but may also be a form of coercion (Sager 2006).

These criticisms refer to different conceptions of the theory of justice and how to take the spatial dimension into account in these reflections. Drawing on Young's (1990) recognition theory and Massey's (1991, 2005) relational approach to space, Sheller (2018) suggests moving beyond the notion of distributive justice, which she sees as necessary but insufficient. She calls for a deliberative approach to justice, which allows for the recognition of the legitimacy of minorities or discriminated social groups to participate in defining rights. In this proposition, it includes both issues of environmental justice or injustice, the right of migrants, and the consequences of ecological disaster on migration. Also, restorative justice may be necessary, in view of the damage caused to the environment. For Ehrhardt-Martinez and Schor (2015), the most advantaged social groups, who contribute the most to greenhouse gas emissions, should admit their responsibilities for the harm suffered by those who have contributed little to global warming.

3.6. Beyond inequalities, mobility justice

Mobility justice appears as a complex and ambiguous notion, referring to the paradoxes and ambivalences of mobility, as an ability to move in space or to change status. Far from being reduced to a neutral social practice, mobility is socially produced through sets of representations, norms and rules that authorize, value and favor certain mobilities and prohibit, discredit and limit others.

Mobility justice as a political issue is characterized by different difficulties and tensions.

Proponents of a distributive approach to justice call for a correction of inequalities through a more equitable distribution of potential mobility. The necessary diagnosis of inequalities can benefit from an approach based on mobility potentials, which makes it possible to assess the social impacts of mobility regulation policies and question the fairness of the distribution of these potentials. It is less relevant when it comes to estimating the inequalities in the appropriation of these potentials and taking into account the coercive aspects exerted by mobility regimes on people's active movements, which can take various forms: hypermobility of the working poor, discrimination in access to public space or during travel, evacuations and forced travel. These findings call for a more systematic dual analysis of mobility potential and that of actual practices and experiences, which must complement each other in order to assess mobility-related inequalities and implement measures to reduce them.

In addition, notwithstanding the obviousness of discourses, the right to mobility is based, in practice, on a differentiation of people with regard to their nationality, physical condition and racial, gender and social identities they are assigned. Beyond the redistributive approach, taking these inequalities into account requires the recognition of persons or minorities who suffer from discrimination and the implementation of procedures allowing the legitimization and participation of these discriminated minorities or social groups. Based on Fraser's (2011) theory on social justice, which states that in order to overcome the opposition between distributive justice and justice based on the recognition of minorities, we must implement a parity of participation, Sheller (2018) places several principles at the heart of mobility justice, notably associating equity distribution of mobility potentials, deliberative justice and restorative justice.

Finally, mobility justice invites us to think holistically about the scales at which institutional regulations are defined, which range from the individual to the global scale. For Sheller (2018), the approach to mobility justice has to be holistic, in the sense that it must incorporate the intersectional and transnational nature of inequalities in the face of mobility or immobility. The environmental crisis, by reminding us of the limits of an expansion of mobility as a norm, implies a reflection on the sobriety of lifestyles and places the question of social justice at the heart of the means to act in favor of the ecological and solidarity transition. In this context, the joint consideration of social justice and mobility regulation issues appears more essential than ever, inviting us to pursue theoretical, methodological and empirical research applied to the measurement of inequalities in (im)mobility.

3.7. References

Bacqué, M.-H. and Fol, S. (2007). L'inégalité face à la mobilité : du constat à l'injonction. *Revue Suisse de Sociologie*, 33(1), 89–104.

Bailly, A., Claval, P., Rochefort, R., Kesteloot, C. (1978). Espace et justice sociale. Débat autour d'un article de D. Harvey. *L'Espace géographique*, 7(4), 300–310.

Banister, D. (1993). Equity and acceptability questions in internalising the social costs of transport. OECD/ECMT Seminar, Internalising the Social Costs of Transport, Paris, 153–175.

Bauman, Z. (2000). *Liquid Modernity*. Blackwell, Cambridge/Oxford/Malden.

Beyazit, E. (2011). Evaluating social justice in transport: Lessons to be learned from the capability approach. *Transport Reviews*, 31(1), 117–134.

Blomley, N.K (1992). The business of mobility: Geography, liberalism, and the charter of rights. *The Canadian Geographer*, 36(3), 236–253.

Boltanski, L. and Chiapello, E. (1999). *Le nouvel esprit du capitalisme*. Gallimard, Paris.

Boudon, R. (1973). *L'inégalité des chances. La mobilité sociale dans les sociétés industrielles*. Armand Colin, Paris.

Bourdieu, P. (1979). *La distinction. Critique sociale du jugement*. Éditions de Minuit, Paris.

Brennetot, A. (2011). Les géographes et la justice spatiale : généalogie d'une relation compliquée. *Annales de géographie*, 678(2), 115–134.

Büchs, M. and Schnepf, S. (2013). Who emits most? Associations between socio-economic factors and UK households' home energy, transport, indirect and total CO_2 emissions. *Ecological Economics*, 90, 114–123.

Castel, R. (1999). *Les métamorphoses de la question sociale. Une chronique du salariat*. Gallimard, Paris.

Chouinard, V. (2001). Legal peripheries: Struggles over disabled Canadians' places in law, society and space. *The Canadian Geographer*, 45, 187–192.

Church, A., Frost, M., Sullivan, K. (2000). Transport and social exclusion in London. *Transport Policy*, 7, 195–205.

Coleman, J.S. (1988). Social capital in the creation of human capital. *American Journal of Sociology*, 94, 95–121.

Cook, N. and Butz, D. (eds) (2019). *Mobilities, Mobility Justice and Social Justice*. Routledge, Abingdon/New York.

Cresswell, T. (2001). The production of mobilities. *New Formations: A Journal of Culture, Theory, Politics*, 43, 3–25.

Cresswell, T. (2005). Justice sociale et droit à la mobilité. In *Les sens du mouvement. Modernité et mobilités dans les sociétés contemporaines*, Allemand, S., Ascher, F., Lévy, J. (eds). Belin, Paris.

Cresswell, T. (2006). The right to mobility: The production of mobility in the courtroom. *Antipodes*, 38(4), 735–754.

Denis, V. (2006). The invention of mobility and the history of the state. *French Historical Studies*, 29(3), 359–377.

Di Ciommo, F. and Lucas, K. (2014). Evaluating the equity effects of road-pricing in the European urban context. *Applied Geography*, 54, 74–82.

Di Ciommo, F. and Shiftan, Y. (2017). Transport equity analysis. *Transport Reviews*, 37(2), 139–151.

Ehrhardt-Martinez, K. and Schor, J. (2015). Consumption and climate change. In *Climate Change and Society: Sociological Perspectives*, Dunlap, R. and Brulle, R. (eds). Oxford University Press, New York.

Elbaum, M. (1995). Justice sociale, inégalités, exclusion. *Revue de l'OFCE*, 53, 197–247.

Ellwood, D.T. (1986). The spatial mismatch hypothesis: Are there teenage jobs missing in the ghetto? In *The Black Youth Unemployment Crisis*, Freeman, R.B. and Holzer, H.J. (eds). University of Chicago Press, Chicago.

Féré, C. (2013). Vers un droit au transport ciblé et un droit à la mobilité conditionnel. L'évolution de la prise en compte des inégalités de mobilité dans les politiques urbaines. *Flux*, 91(1), 11–20.

Fol, S. (2009). *La mobilité des pauvres. Pratiques d'habitants et politiques publiques*. Belin, Paris.

Fol, S. and Gallez, C. (2014). Social inequalities in urban access: Better ways of assessing transport improvements. In *Getting There/Being There: Financing Enhanced Urban Access in the 21st Century City*, Sclar, E., Lönnroth, M., Wolmar, C. (eds). Routledge, New York.

Fol, S. and Gallez, C. (2017). Évaluer les inégalités sociales d'accès aux ressources. Intérêt d'une approche fondée sur l'accessibilité. *Riurba*, 4 [Online]. Available at: http://riurba.net/Revue/evaluer-les-inegalites-sociales-dacces-aux-ressources-interet-dune-approche-fondee-sur-laccessibilite [Accessed 6 January 2020].

Fraser, N. (2011). *Qu'est-ce que la justice sociale ? Reconnaissance et redistribution*. La Découverte, Paris.

Gallez, C. (2015). La mobilité quotidienne en politique. Des manières de voir et d'agir. Spatial planning and urban planning HDR thesis, Université Paris-Est, Paris.

Gallez, C. (2018). Dépendance à la mobilité et politiques urbaines. Réflexion sur les enjeux sociaux de la mobilité face à l'urgence climatique. *Swiss Mobility Conference*, Lausanne.

Gallez, C. and Kaufmann, V. (2009). Aux racines de la mobilité en sciences sociales : contribution au cadre d'analyse socio-historique de la mobilité quotidienne. In *De l'histoire des transports à l'histoire de la mobilité*, Guigueno, V. and Flonneau, M. (eds). PUR, Rennes.

Gallez, C. and Motte-Baumvol, B. (2017). Inclusive mobility or inclusive accessibility? A European perspective. *Cuadernos Europeos de Deusto*, 56, 79–104.

Gay, C., Kaufmann, V., Landriève, S., Vincent-Geslin, S. (eds) (2011). Quel droit à la mobilité ? In *Mobile Immobile. Quels choix, quels droits pour 2030/Choices and Rights for 2030*. L'Aube – Forum Vies Mobiles, La Tour d'Aigues.

Glick Schiller, N. and Salazar, N.B. (2013). Regimes of mobility across the globe. *Journal of Ethnic and Migration Studies*, 39(2), 183–200.

Gobillon, L., Selod, H., Zenou, Y. (2007). The mechanisms of spatial mismatch. *Urban Studies*, 44(12), 2401–2427.

Golub, A. and Martens, K. (2014). Using principles of justice to assess the modal equity of regional transportation plans. *Journal of Transport Geography*, 41, 10–20.

Gössling, S. and Cohen, S. (2014). Why sustainable transport policies will fail: EU climate policy in the light of transport taboos. *Journal of Transport Geography*, 39, 192–207.

Handy, S. (2002). Accessibility vs. mobility-enhancing strategies for addressing automobile dependence in the US. Report, European Conference of Ministers of Transport (ECMT), Paris.

Hansen, W.G. (1959). How accessibility shapes land use. *Journal of American Institute of Planners*, 25(1), 73–76.

Harvey, D. (1973). *Social Justice and the City*. Arnold, London.

Harvey, D. (1992). Social justice, postmodernism and the city. *International Journal of Urban and Regional Research*, 16(4), 588–601.

Imrie, R. (2000). Disability and discourses of mobility and movement. *Environment and Planning A*, 32, 1641–1656.

Jamar, D. and Lannoy, P. (2011). Idéaux et troubles d'un droit à la mobilité (ou comment faire de la mobilité un territoire politique). In *Mobile/Immobile. Quels choix, quels droits pour 2030/Choices and Rights for 2030*, Gay, C., Kaufmann, V., Landriève, S., Vincent-Gueslin, S. (eds). L'Aube - Forum Vies Mobiles, La Tour d'Aigues, 63–73.

Jouffe, Y. (2007) Précaires mais mobiles. Tactiques de mobilité des travailleurs précaires flexibles et nouveaux services de mobilité, PhD Thesis, École Nationale des Ponts et Chaussées, Paris.

Kain, J.F. (1968). Housing segregation, negro employment and metropolitan decentralization. *Quarterly Journal of Economics*, 82, 175–197.

Kain, J.F. (1992). The spatial mismatch hypothesis: Three decades later. *Housing Policy Debate*, 3(2), 371–460.

Kaufmann, V. (2002). *Rethinking Mobility: Contemporary Sociology*. Ashgate, Aldershot.

Kaufmann, V. (2005). Mobilités et réversibilités : vers des sociétés plus fluides ? *Cahiers internationaux de sociologie*, 118(1), 119–135.

Kaufmann, V., Pflieger, G., Jemelin, C., Barbey, J. (2007). Inégalités sociales d'accès : quels impacts des politiques locales de transport ? *EspacesTemps* [Online]. Available at: https://www.espacestemps.net/articles/inegalites-sociales-acces/ [Accessed 25 November 2019].

Kesselring, S. (2014). Mobility, power and the emerging new mobilities regimes. *Sociologica* [Online]. Available at: https://www.rivisteweb.it/doi/10.2383/77047 [Accessed 7 January 2020].

Kesselring, S. and Vogl, G. (2013). The new mobilities regimes. In *New Mobilities Regimes in Art and Social Sciences*, Witzgall, S., Vogl, G., Kesselring, S. (eds). Ashgate, Farnham.

Koenig, J.G. (1974). Théorie économique de l'accessibilité urbaine. *Revue Économique*, 25(2), 275–297.

Koenig, J.G. (1980). Indicators of urban accessibility: Theory and applications. *Transportation*, 9, 145–172.

Korsu, E. and Wenglenski, S. (2009). Jobs accessibility, residential segregation and risk of long-term unemployment in the Paris region. *Urban Studies*, 47(11), 2279–2324.

Kotef, H. (2015). *Movement and the Ordering of Freedom: On Liberal Governances of Mobility*. Duke University Press, Durham/London.

Kymlicka, W. (1999). *Les théories de la justice : une introduction*. La Découverte, Paris.

Langan, C. (2001). Mobility disability. *Public Culture*, 13(3), 459–484.

Larsen, J. and Jacobsen, M.H. (2009). Metaphors of mobility. Inequality on the move. In *Mobilities and Inequalities*, Ohnmacht, T., Maksim, H., Bergman, M.M. (eds). Ashgate, Farhnam/Burlington.

Lefebvre, H. (1968). *Le droit à la ville*. Anthropos, Paris.

Leivestad, H.H. (2016). Motility. In *Keywords of Mobility. Critical Engagements*, Salazar, N.B. and Jayaram, K. (eds). Berghahn, New York/Oxford.

Levine, J., Grengs, J., Merlin, L. (2019). *From Mobility to Accessibility: Transforming Urban Transportation and Land-Use Planning*. Cornell University Press, New York/London.

Levinson, D. (2010). Equity effects on road pricing: A review. *Transport Reviews*, 30(1), 33–57.

Lévy, J.-P. (2000). Les nouveaux espaces de la mobilité. In *Les territoires de la mobilité*, Bonnet, M. and Desjeux, D. (eds). Presses Universitaires de France, Paris.

Lévy, J.-P. (2009). Mobilités urbaines : des pratiques sociales aux évolutions territoriales. In *Les mondes de la mobilité*, Dureau, F. and Hily, M.-A. (eds). Presses Universitaires de Rennes, Rennes.

Litman, T. (2002). Evaluating transportation equity. *World Transport Policy and Practice*, 8(2), 50–65.

Lucas, K., van Wee, B., Maat, K. (2016). A method to evaluate equitable accessibility: Combining ethical theories and accessibility-based approaches. *Transportation*, 43(3), 473–490.

Martens, K. (2006). Basing transport planning on principles of social justice. *Berkeley Planning Journal*, 19(1), 1–17.

Martens, K. (2016). *Transport Justice. Designing Fair Transportation Systems*. Routledge, New York/London.

Martens, K., Golub, A., Robinson, G. (2012). A justice-theoretic approach to the distribution of transportation benefits: Implications for transportation planning practice in the United States. *Transportation Research A*, 46, 684–695.

Massey, D. (1991). A global sense of place. *Marxism Today*, 24–29.

Massey, D. (2005). *For Space*. Sage, London.

Massot, M.-H. and Orfeuil, J.-P. (2005). La mobilité au quotidien, entre choix individuel et production sociale. *Cahiers internationaux de sociologie*, 118, 81–100.

Metz, D. (2008). The myth of travel time saving. *Transport Reviews*, 28(3), 321–336.

Nahmias-Biran, B., Martens, K., Shiftan, Y. (2017). Integrating equity in transportation projects assessment: A philosophical exploration and its practical implications. *Transport Reviews*, 37(2), 192–210.

Neutens, T., Schwanen, T., Witlox, F., de Maeyer, P. (2010). Equity in urban service delivery: A comparison of different equity measures. *Environment and Planning A*, 42, 1613–1635.

Nicolas, J.-P., Verry, D., Longuar, Z. (2012). Évolutions récentes des émissions de CO_2 liées à la mobilité des Français : analyser les dynamiques à l'œuvre grâce aux enquêtes nationales. Transports de 1994 et 2008. *Économie et Statistique*, 457–458, 161–183.

Noiriel, G. (1998). Surveiller les déplacements ou identifier les personnes ? Contribution à l'histoire du passeport en France de la Ire à la IIIe République. *Genèses. Sciences sociales et histoire*, 30, 77–100.

Nussbaum, M.C. (2011). *Creating Capabilities: The Human Development Approach*. Belknap Press of Harvard, Cambridge.

Ohnmacht, T., Maksim, H., Bergman, M.M. (2009). *Mobilities and Inequality*. Ashgate, Aldershot.

Orfeuil, J.-P. and Ripoll, F. (2015). *Accès et mobilités : les nouvelles inégalités*. Infolio, Gollion.

Pereira, R.H.M., Schwanen, T., Banister, D. (2017). Distributive justice and equity in transportation. *Transport Reviews*, 37(2), 170–191.

Rawls, J. (1971). *A Theory of Justice*. Harvard University Press, Cambridge.

Reynaud, A. (1981). *Société, espace et justice*. PUF, Paris.

Roche, D. (2003). *Humeurs vagabondes. De la circulation des hommes et de l'utilité des voyages*. Fayard, Paris.

Sager, T. (2006). Freedom as mobility: Implications of the distinction between actual and potential travelling. *Mobilities*, 1(3), 465–488.

Sanchez, T. (2008). Poverty, policy, and public transportation. *Transportation Research A*, 42, 833–841.

Savidan, P. (ed.) (2018). *Dictionnaire des inégalités et de la justice sociale*. Presses Universitaires de France, Paris.

Séchet, R. (1989). *Mythes égalitaires et pauvretés, une approche géographique*. CNRS, Paris.

Sen, A. (1985). *Commodities and Capabilities*. North Holland, Amsterdam.

Sen, A. (2009). *The Idea of Justice*. Allen Lane, London.

Shamir, R. (2005). Without borders? Notes on globalization as a mobility regime. *Sociological Theory*, 23(2), 197–217.

Sheller, M. (2018). *Mobility Justice: The Politics of Movement in an Age of Extremes*. Verso, London/Brooklyn.

Smith, D.M. (1987). *Geography, Inequality and Society*. Cambridge University Press, Cambridge.

Soja, E.W. (2010). *Seeking Spatial Justice*. University of Minnesota Press, Minneapolis.

Thomopoulos, N., Grant-Muller, S., Tight, M.R. (2009). Incorporating equity considerations in transport infrastructure evaluation: Current practice and a proposed methodology. *Evaluation and Program Planning*, 32(4), 351–359.

Urry, J. (2007). *Mobilities*. Polity Press, Cambridge.

Vanoutrive, T. and Cooper, E. (2019). How just is transportation justice theory? The issues of paternalism and production. *Transportation Research A*, 122, 112–119.

Vanoutrive, T. and Ziljstra, T. (2018). Who has the right to travel during peak hours? On congestion princing and "desirable" travelers. *Transport Policy*, 63, 98–107.

Viegas, J.M. (2001). Making urban road pricing acceptable and effective: Searching for quality and equity in urban mobility. *Transport Policy*, 8(4), 289–294.

Wachs, M. and Kumagai, T.G. (1973). Physical accessibility as a social indicator. *Socio-Economic Planning Sciences*, 7, 437–456.

Walzer, M. (1983). *Spheres of Justice: A Defense of Pluralism and Equality*. Basic Books, New York.

van Wee, B. and Geurs, K. (2011). Discussing equity and social exclusion in accessibility evaluations. *European Journal of Transport and Infrastructure Research*, 11(4), 350–367.

Wenglenski, S. (2004). Une mesure des disparités sociales d'accessibilité au marché de l'emploi en Île-de-France. *Revue d'économie régionale et urbaine*, 4, 539–550.

Wenglenski, S. (2013). Is daily mobility good or bad? *Global Conference on Mobility Futures*, Lancaster, 4–6 September.

Young, I.M. (1990). *Justice and the Politics of Difference*. Princeton University Press, Princeton.

4

Appropriations and Uses of Travel Time: How to Inhabit Mobility

Juliana GONZÁLEZ

Laboratoire de sociologie urbaine (LaSUR), École polytechnique fédérale de Lausanne, Switzerland

4.1. Introduction

Time has always been a central factor in understanding the challenges of daily mobility. For a long time, and still today, methods of economic evaluation of transport projects have monetized time savings so that they can be included in the cost–benefit analysis. This is done under the assumption that, on the one hand, travel is a "derived demand" of the activities that take place at each destination (Banister 2018). On the other hand, and generally under the injunction of the capitalist economy, where increasing speed is directly linked to saving time – and thus productivity (Lyons and Urry 2005; Banister 2011) – it is also assumed that individuals seek to spend less time on their daily travel (Mokhtarian and Salomon 2001). Because of its "useless" nature *a priori*, travel time is considered a cost to be reduced in models (Mokhtarian and Salomon 2001; Lyons and Urry 2005; Jain and Lyons 2008). Nevertheless, for more than a decade, research in the field of mobility has challenged the apparent uselessness of travel time and highlighted some of the changes that are taking place in relationships with time and space.

This chapter presents the current state of knowledge concerning the qualitative dimension of travel time. Firstly, it reviews the renewed interest of researchers in the question of the experience of travel time in the field of transport and mobility. Secondly, it seems necessary to place this research work in a broader perspective that reveals a certain number of issues for contemporary societies, particularly with regard to the consequences of a possible hedonistic use of travel time in a context of climatic emergency. Thirdly, we will discuss the methods used to measure the use of travel time, emphasizing the importance of mixed methods in the construction of the theoretical bases that constitute the subject. In a fourth step, we will review the state of the art to present the major works on the use of travel time. Finally, we will present the latest debates and research perspectives that are emerging on the subject of travel time in the study of mobility.

4.2. The emergence of a research field in search of a position

Since the late 1990s, much of the work in the field of transport and mobility has challenged a series of generally accepted ideas: on the one hand, the idea that transport is only a demand derived from the activities taking place at each destination (Mokhtarian and Salomon 2001); and, on the other hand, the idea that the choice of modes of travel is only dictated by the instrumental rationality of individuals who seek to optimize their time or the cost of their mobility (Kaufmann 1998).

In fact, individual behaviors cover various factors that respond to the individual's social, spatial, and temporal experience (Bailly et al. 1980). By focusing on human orientation in space (Bailly 1985), the geography of representations has paved the way to work on the perception of travel time by considering the complexity of the perception of movement (Bailly 1974). In the case of trains, there are significant discrepancies between the individual's evaluation of time and the time actually spent on public transport (O'Farrell and Markham 1947; Bailly 1979; Moreau 1992; Wardman 1998), particularly in relation to the mode of transport or the choices available to the user (O'Farrell and Markham 1974). The studies that show a relationship between the quality of spaces and the overestimation of waiting time in train stations (Moreau 1992) go against the idea that these spaces are nonplaces, with no identity, no relationships, and no history (Augé 1990). More recent works put into perspective the symbolic richness of the station as an experienced space with which individuals have an affective relationship (Audas 2008) and the importance of the analysis of waiting at several scales to describe the territories of mobility (Vidal and Musset 2015).

Although different in their approach, these works highlight the importance of questioning the way in which the value of time is considered in the field of transport. Since the 1960s, and still today, the value of time has been fundamental to the justification of transport investments, since – from an economic perspective – travel time, optimized by transport infrastructure, became productive time, particularly dedicated to the transportation of goods. Nevertheless, at an aggregate level, it has been shown that the time budget devoted to travel remains stable (Shafer 2000; Crozet and Joly 2003; Lyons 2003; Mokhtarian and Chen 2004), particularly as the speed of the various means of transport increases and, consequently, the distances travelled increase.

As a result, the experience of travel time has challenged researchers in the field of transportation and mobility for several years, across a multiplicity of disciplines (Keseru and Macharis 2018). Although the question of the utility of travel time has been addressed by several authors over the past two decades (Mokhtarian and Salomon 2001; Lyons 2003; Lyons and Urry 2005), it is still a field of research in a consolidation phase. Initially interested in the experience of mobile workers travelling by car (Laurier 2002; Brown and O'Hara 2003; Laurier 2004), research on travel time use has quickly focused on public transport, particularly on the train and its virtues for travel time use (Khan and Sundstrom 2007; Lyons et al. 2007; Axtell et al. 2008; Ohmori and Harata 2008; Gripsrud and Hjorthol 2012; Susilo et al. 2012; Lyons et al. 2013).

Most of the work in this area has come from the English language academic world, with empirical results in developed countries. Because of the heterogeneity of the methods and approaches proposed, it seems difficult to characterize the body of work produced on the use of travel time from a single perspective.

However, as has been pointed out by some authors, the subject brings to the forefront the need to ask the right questions about mobility today, but also the need to assess the societal impact that the use of travel time could have on contemporary societies, and on the mobility of the future (Mokhtarian 2018).

4.3. The basis for exploring the uses of travel time

The observation that a series of activities are carried out during travel time is not new. Since people have had the possibility of crossing space, they have invested their travel time according to the objects they have at their disposal (Lyons 2003). On the other hand, the development of the various means of transport is accompanied by a fact that is, to say the least, unexpected for transport economists: the increase in speed goes hand in hand with an increase in the distances covered and is not necessarily intended to compensate for the time spent travelling, but rather to give individuals the possibility of making more journeys, or of covering greater distances (Metz 2008). In this sense, the behavioral aspects of travel need to be reconsidered.

This question has been the basis of much work arguing for the existence of a constant average travel time budget per day per individual, i.e., that individuals have a fixed amount of time per day that they are willing to invest in travel (Mokhtarian and Chen 2004).

At the end of the 1970s, Yacov Zahavi took this issue further by noting that transport time budgets are relatively constant, but that the spatial scope of travel is increasing as a result of technical improvements in the various means of transport and their travel speed (Zahavi 1979; Zahavi and Ryan 1980; Zahavi and Talvitie 1980; Mokhtarian and Chen 2004; Kaufmann 2005).

The concept of travel time budget and its evolution are still controversial topics today because its variations are more or less evident depending on the survey methods used, the level of aggregation of available data, and the regions of the world (Stopher et al. 2017). While in the 1990s throughout Switzerland, travel time per person per day was 117.5 minutes, it increased to 183.4 minutes in 2010 (Kaufmann 2008). However, cross-sectional analyses in Great Britain (Metz 2008) or in several countries (Schafer 2000; Joly 2004; Harms et al. 2018) show a transport time budget that varies very little and is around 1 or 1.1 hours per day.

The importance of the debate on travel time budgets lies in the possibility of going beyond conventional methods of mobility prediction by taking into account the subtleties of individual behavior. For example, it has been argued that people's preferences for travel vary according to three criteria of travel utility: the reasons for travel, the activities that take place during travel, and the travel itself (Mokhtarian and Salomon 2001).

A field of research has also been built around travel time in the prism of perception, not only of travel time in a vehicle but also in relation to transit and waiting time associated with the use of public transport, and in particular the overestimation of perceived waiting time compared to the perceived time in a vehicle (Wardman 1998). In this regard, more recent studies investigate the role of the design of waiting spaces in the perception, which is realistic to varying degrees, of waiting time in a station or on the street (Watkins et al. 2011; Fan et al. 2016).

Lyons and Urry argue that the development of information and communication technologies can reinforce certain uses of time, which can have both positive and negative consequences for contemporary societies (Lyons 2003; Lyons and Urry 2005). On the positive side, the change in the relationship with different modes of transport would benefit public transport operators who could use the productivity argument to encourage a modal shift from car to public transport. On the negative side, the ability to deploy activities, enhanced by the use of ICT, could further increase the scope for travel, thereby further exacerbating transport-related social inequalities (Lyons and Urry 2005).

4.3.1. *What are the uses of travel time for each mode of transport?*

The analysis of travel time usage is developed to various degrees depending on the country and the data available. In this sense, work on the United Kingdom and recently on the United States is probably the most recurrent, given the regularity of the studies over the last two decades.

Among the studies carried out in different countries, the first to formally address the activities deployed, the spatial arrangements and the strategies put in place to guarantee a certain experience of travel are characterized by their exploration of a specific profile: "mobile" workers travelling by car (Laurier 2002; Brown and O'Hara 2003; Bull 2004; Laurier 2004). Far from questioning the value of travel time, the aim of these studies was not to question the value of travel time but to highlight the potential for transforming the car into a mobile office, and the role that certain tools, such as cell phones, could play in distancing or bringing the work environment closer.

This work, which relies mainly on qualitative methods, has made it possible to put into perspective the fact that travel time, especially for business trips, constitutes an important part of productivity, which is more or less present depending on the strategies and objects available. With an ethnographic eye, some of these works allow us to reconstruct the process of assembling the mobile office. The routines that constitute this assembly, banal at first sight, are constructed with the aim of giving more stability to the daily routine (Laurier 2002) and can show how the experience of travel reflects the abstract theories of time and space (Watts 2008).

This early work concerning the car and also the more recent work on the use of travel time on the train (Kenyon and Lyons 2007; Lyons et al. 2007; Axtell et al. 2008; Fickling et al. 2008; Lyons et al. 2008) have also raised the central role of information and communication technologies in the experience of travel time. For mobile workers who travel by car or train, for example, cell phones allow them to defer requests from their colleagues or superiors (Laurier 2002; Axtell et al. 2008). For train users, network outages will also structure the activities deployed during the trip due to the impossibility of communicating by phone or sending emails (Axtell et al. 2008). Some authors attribute to communication tools the permeability of the family, professional, and personal spheres, which allows, for example, highly mobile people to create a certain degree of familiarity (Vincent et al. 2015) or to bring the personal sphere into proximity during the journey (Cailly and Fourny 2013).

In the scientific literature on the use of travel time, it is possible to observe a shift from the study of car space to the study of public transport, particularly the train. Still interested in the productivity potential of travel time, researchers were exploring more – about 10 years ago – about the practices of business travelers or mobile workers. This is probably due to the possibility of attributing an economic value to time that is directly related to work.

Among the findings about the use of travel time, the train is indeed a mode of travel suitable for a large number of activities. Activities such as reading, working, writing, eating, telephoning, or sleeping appear in different proportions according to contextual characteristics such as the type of individuals surveyed, the distance, or the duration of the trip.

In order to better understand the experience of travel, some authors propose to approach these activities from three aspects: the constraints for "mobile" work, the type of activity deployed, and the technology used (Axtell et al. 2008). Regarding the constraints for work, they identify spatial constraints, but also sensory constraints associated with the train. These constraints are then discussed in more detail in interviews, where the workers interviewed refer to constraints related to the configuration of the vehicles, such as the availability of a table to put a computer on, and the competition that arises between passengers to reach them (Axtell et al. 2008). Other authors also show that individuals implement strategies such as putting their computers or notebooks on their knees to cope with the vibration levels of the train or the inadequate height of the tables available (Khan and Sundstrom 2007).

But beyond contextual factors, sociodemographic characteristics may also influence the activities deployed during the trip. Empirical results for train users in San Francisco show a correlation between gender and certain activities. Women are more active in discussion than men (Timmermans and Van der Waerden 2008). This is particularly interesting since, due to norms of conduct, behavior may differ from country to country. In a survey in Tokyo, for example, the authors emphasize that there are activities that are not recommended or that are even prohibited on the train, such as talking on the phone or singing (Ohmori and Harata 2008).

The various travel experiences and the activities that take place during the trip change throughout the journey, depending on the conditions that make them possible. This is also the case with regard to the perceived usefulness of travel time. For example, in Table 4.1, which summarizes the results of research on travel time use in the United Kingdom (Lyons et al. 2008), the proportion of people who perform different activities throughout the trip is lower than the proportion who perform the different activities part of the time (1st and 2nd columns, respectively).

These results are consistent over time, as in a 2010 survey in the UK, activities such as looking at the landscape/other people or reading for leisure remain prevalent on the train (Lyons et al. 2013).

Empirical investigations of this topic also make comparisons between travel motives, and even between "outbound" and "return" trips. For business travelers, their preferred activities on the train would be working and looking at the landscape or the people around them (Lyons et al. 2007; Holley et al. 2008; Gripsrud and Hjorthol 2012), even though they generally invest just as much time in other leisure activities such as making private phone calls or reading (Gripsrud and Hjorthol 2012). Going into more detail, some authors also show that activities considered as "leisure" are deployed more by business travelers on their return trip, probably as a way of decompressing after the trip has been completed. In this sense, some attempt to attribute some kind of productivity to travel time by mobilizing the notion of taskscape, developed by Tim Ingold in the 1990s (Holley et al. 2008).

Activity	Most of the time	Part of the time	People who consider that they have used their time very successfully	People who consider that they have made some use of their time	People who consider it a waste of time
Work/study	31%	51%	42%	54%	2%
Reading for leisure	25%	47%	23%	63%	12%
Looking out the window/people watching	13%	53%	12%	58%	28%
Talking with other passengers	5%	13%	24%	56%	19%
Sleeping/napping	3%	13%	15%	57%	27%
SMS/phone calls – Work-related	2%	22%	39%	58%	2%
SMS/phone calls – Personal	1%	15%	26%	50%	12%
Eating/drinking	1%	21%	19%	80%	1%

Table 4.1. *Statistics on travel time use from the UK National Rail Passenger Survey (2004) (source: (Lyons et al. 2008), Table 6.1, p. 78)*

For commuters who travel by train, the results show that they use their travel time more to look out the window, listen to music, or read (Lyons et al. 2007; Gripsrud and Hjorthol 2012) or to perform leisure activities that take place both on the outward and return journey (Lyons et al. 2007). Some more recent studies also confirm that the activities considered by the authors as "anti-activities" or "passive" activities such as looking out the window, texting, or sleeping are the activities that concern bus and train travelers in Sweden the most (Vilhelmson et al. 2011). However, we will see later that describing activities alone is not enough. The analysis of the experience of time must be embedded in a reflection on the affective experience created by travel and the cognitive processes associated with it (Flamm 2005a).

In addition, and among the results of the approaches analyzed above, it seems interesting to note that, for example, in Tokyo, a significant proportion (83%) of high-level train users specifically choose a specific train not to optimize their time but because they can get a seat or because the train spaces will not be overcrowded. The authors thus refer to the fact that people are even willing to pay more for this activity potential associated with a more comfortable environment (Ohmori and Harata 2008).

Research on the use of travel time has also focused on high mobility, which is increasing as a consequence of the mobility injunction that characterizes contemporary societies (Ravalet et al. 2014). In their approach through the appropriation of travel time, results from six European countries (France, Germany, Poland, Belgium, Spain, and Switzerland) suggest that the highly mobile, particularly those who are away from home for a few days, operate more processes of appropriation of spaces that, beyond travel, are unfamiliar spaces that require the implementation of specific strategies to manage their "foreignness" (Vincent-Geslin et al. 2015).

In a study using a similar approach to reclaiming travel time (Flamm 2005b), differences in activity potential appear between the modes. While the train represents a large activity potential – especially in the productive reappropriation of time – the bus, streetcar, or even more significantly walking and cycling are characterized by a smaller activity potential, at least in terms of the number of activities. Walking and cycling have a distinct productivity for their users, which is that of exercise (Flamm 2005b).

Among the elements studied in relation to travel time, waiting time constitutes a central research axis. It is addressed from the point of view of perception versus actual time, but also from the point of view of the influence of waiting on modal practices. Research on the subject has shown that, in general, individuals tend to overestimate waiting time and transit time (O'Farrell and Markham 1974; Wardman 1998; Dziekan and Kottenhoff 2007). Perceived time is on average 1.2 times longer than actual observed time for public transportation (Watkins et al. 2011; Fan et al. 2016). This work has highlighted that space improvements (real-time information, benches, shelters) can reduce this discrepancy between perceived and actual waiting time.

With regard to representations of waiting time, a survey conducted in New Zealand shows that a significant proportion of respondents (more than a quarter of the sample) consider that waiting time is a waste of time (Russell 2012). This is also true for analyses in Switzerland among users of different modes, who reportedly experience waiting at bus stops, train stations, but also in traffic jams in a negative way (Flamm 2005b; Higgins et al. 2018).

In a second New Zealand study, based on observations of passengers on buses and trains, the authors note some differences in the activities performed during travel. The proportion of people looking out of the window, for example, is higher on buses than on trains, while the proportion of people reading is higher on trains than on buses (Russell et al. 2011).

Studies conducted on buses explore Goffman's notion of civil inattention, proposing a behavioral category referred to as non-social transient behavior (Kim 2012). On the bus, individuals are more "active" in their goal of being unnoticed and not acknowledging the presence of the other. In her survey across the United States, the author highlights the multiple strategies that are put in place by travelers to avoid or to invite others onto the bus. The performance takes place through body language (avoiding eye contact, pretending to be asleep), but also through personal objects (headphones, a charging phone, luggage, etc.).

This non-social behavior is explained in the study as the consequence of factors such as uncertainty about others, delays in travel, and physical and psychosocial fatigue. Furthermore, it highlights the relationship of permeability between the station and the vehicles through specific situations where, for example, the station toilets are used by individuals to prepare themselves to spend the night in the vehicle: brushing their teeth, putting on pajamas, or even washing themselves (Kim 2012).

4.3.2. *What theoretical frameworks should be used to address the qualitative dimension of travel time?*

In section 4.1, we discussed the value of time and – very briefly – new theoretical frameworks for overcoming the current view of travel time in transport and mobility as unnecessary and costly.

It is clear that travel time provides a number of benefits to individuals. However, the way in which the experience of travel time is taken into account in scientific research is not yet methodologically and empirically standardized. The dialogue between theoretical foundations and empirical results still needs to be consolidated.

Among the first authors to consider the conceptualization of the utility of travel time, it has been suggested that there are three criteria of utility that individuals consider when travelling: activities at the destination of the trip, activities during the trip, and the trip itself (Mokhtarian and Salomon 2001). The authors suggest that the combination of these three aspects would allow for a better assessment of the utility of travel time. More recently, work in this area has assumed that the travel time budget that individuals are willing to spend on each trip involves a series of utilitarian evaluation processes that involve cognitive and affective aspects of travel that have developed over the course of the individual's life (Milakis et al. 2015).

One way to study travel time is to consider it as a gift. This would move beyond "economic" exchange to an approach to time as a gift, which the authors argue produces and sustains social relationships (Jain and Lyons 2008). From this perspective, the authors argue that the utility of travel time is not only about the gain that individuals obtain from the destination (through exchange, participation, and moments of co-presence). This utility can also be associated with the trip itself, as it is a time given to them to reflect, prepare, decompress, etc. They also define two categories to qualify this time:

– travel time as transition time;

– travel time as free time.

For his part, Michael Flamm proposes an approach that consists of classifying the activities that take place during travel according to their belonging to three logics of meaning, attributed by individuals to travel time. These are the logic of productivity, the logic of relaxation and transition, and the logic of sociability (Flamm 2005b). Through this categorization, it is possible to attribute more or less activity to each mode of travel, and thus to determine the meaning of these modes for individuals. The perspective of this work is to include the valuation of travel time as one of the factors constituting the "optimal solution" for mode of travel choice.

Among the ways of taking into account the uses of travel time that have the most potential today, especially with regard to possible applications in the field of transport, multitasking appears to be an important conceptualization. The first proposals in this direction emphasize that behavioral research has neglected the ability of individuals to conduct multiple activities simultaneously. According to the authors, the idea that we all have 24 hours available per day can be partially challenged because multitasking allows individuals to optimize the use of their time on a daily basis (Kenyon and Lyons 2007).

From the perspective of multitasking, the empirical work focuses not only on the activities that are performed during the trip but also on the order of importance that they occupy. The "secondary" activities are also treated from the perspective of Internet access, where they testify to an active participation of individuals in the different spheres of life. Some authors argue that these "secondary" activities have an impact on people's quality of life, although they are often underreported (Kenyon 2010), as is the case for activities that take place during travel, which have often been considered unimportant because travel itself is the main activity.

The study of time usage in transport in the form of multitasking has grown considerably in the last 10 years. Depending on the authors and the survey instruments used, the variables that determine the type and intensity of multitasking differ. Overall, seven categories of variables have been identified as having a relationship with multitasking: sociodemographic variables, trip-related variables (duration, mode, or distance), attitudinal variables, comfort and equipment-related variables, spatial attributes, and non-trip time usage variables (Keseru and Macharis 2018).

Some authors, interested in the uses of travel time, propose to approach the subject through the notion of the taskscape (Holley et al. 2008), proposed by Ingold (2002) in relation to the perception of the environment and in relation to the activities that constitute living. Referring to temporality, which according to the author is neither chronology nor history, Ingold (2002, p. 194) considers that events "encompass a pattern of retentions from the past and protensions for the future."

Thus, Ingold argues that each activity is significant in its position in relation to a set of activities. If we return to the use of travel time, the notion of the taskscape makes sense insofar as certain activities, considered to be "useless" or "unproductive" *a priori*, would ultimately have a beneficial role for individuals (Holley et al. 2008). Moreover, this schematization of the use of travel time is applied particularly to business travel, and its importance is therefore linked to the value that can be attributed to this type of travel and therefore to the consequences for the employee and the employer.

In Francophone literature on the meaning of travel time, some authors explore the experience of movement from the perspective of inhabiting. Dwelling, in the Heideggerian sense of the term, corresponds to "the existential dimension of man's presence on earth" (Paquot 2005). The authors who defend the proposal of "inhabiting mobility" assume that the forms of appropriation of a moving vehicle are all manifestations of inhabiting (Frétigny 2011). In this sense, the train possesses a flexible territoriality that is constantly renegotiated through the place that the individual occupies in the "mobile" space. Moreover, some geographers propose to move away from the opposition between mobility and anchoring, where only the latter would be representative of inhabiting. Thus, they propose the hypothesis of "polytopic inhabitation," which considers the notion of inhabitation as "the practice of places" (Stock 2005).

The potential risk of this approach is to consider that it is sufficient to describe the activities that individuals carry out to refer to inhabitation. However, epistemological reflections in geography concerning inhabiting from the perspective of phenomenology (Hoyaux 2002) make it possible to go beyond the ways of doing things associated with a particular space to consider inhabiting through two dimensions that are specific to it: that of the individual in relation to their world, and that of the individual in relation to themselves.

From an empirical point of view, and despite the small amount of work on this subject, the analysis of the experience of travel time from the point of view of inhabiting, it is possible to highlight types of "proximity", for example, in the context of the daily mobility of inhabitants of peri-urban areas (Cailly and Fourny 2013). These "proximities" are constitutive of the territorialization that the individual carries out permanently, and which refers us to the first dimension of inhabiting. The second dimension, concerning the ontological constitution of being, nevertheless still seems to escape the empirical analysis devices mobilized by geographers in the field of mobility.

4.4. Inhabiting travel time: at what cost to the environment?

Among the questions that emerge about the possibility of "inhabiting travel time", the most recurrent concerns the harmful consequences of unlimited mobility. It is about the diversification of lifestyles, which is also indicative of changes in the social and economic organization of our time (Thomas and Pattaroni 2012).

On the one hand, on a planetary scale, the contemporary context is marked by the climate emergency. Although climate change is at the forefront of speeches and demonstrations, concrete action is struggling to emerge. Some authors (Soubeyran and Berdoulay 2012) suggest that adaptation must be truly integrated into the vocabulary of land-use planning in order to face the already visible consequences of climate change. On the other hand, the consequences of the ecological and social crisis are felt at the individual level through a sense of spillover into their lifestyles. According to a survey conducted by the Vie Mobiles Forum (2016) on people's aspirations in terms of mobility and pace of life in six countries, 74% of respondents consider the current pace of life to be too fast, and 50% say they lack time to carry out their daily activities (Descarrega and Moati 2016). This feeling of being overwhelmed seems to confirm the negative effects of the "excess" that characterizes the postmodern society, and which is reflected in the injunction to perform, to be flexible, and to react quickly (Aubert 2008; Drevon 2019).

The development of information technologies is not without consequences in this regard. Today's information flows create a "situation of plethoric supply" in the face of which individuals feel they lack the time to "keep up to date" (Citton 2014). Added to this is the fact that the boundaries separating the different spheres of life are increasingly blurred, as individuals have to manage the immediacy of social relationships. These extreme situations are, among other things, at the origin of stress-related illnesses, such as anxiety or depression. Some authors insist in particular on the "violence of time" with which individuals in postmodern societies are permanently confronted (Aubert 2008).

From the perspective of mobility, the empirical studies cited above highlight the strategies of individuals with respect to their time resources (Drevon et al. 2020). Some use their travel time not because of a contractual obligation but in order to be able to dedicate time at home to their private and family sphere. The development of ICT opens up the possibilities for a productive experience of travel time, which can be problematic in relation to urban sprawl. Increased improvements in the experience of travel time would therefore be directly related to increasingly fluid, comfortable, and accessible mobility. The gain in comfort would be at the expense of a reflection on the location of the activities of daily life.

4.5. The relevance of mixed methods for building a common survey base

The new interest in scientific research on the qualitative dimension of travel time poses a number of challenges with respect to methods of data collection, processing, and analysis that can consolidate the theoretical frameworks proposed so far by some authors and presented in section 4.4.

Firstly, the finding suggesting that travel time is useful, which would challenge transport project appraisal models, needs to be supported by precise empirical results. Obviously, this requires dedicated surveys that capture the usefulness of travel time. This usefulness is addressed in the surveys in two forms:

– directly, by asking individuals about the status they give to travel time;

– by highlighting those activities that show some utility. As a result, the empirical results present a portrait of travel time that, in some cases, confronts a positive or negative representation of travel time with the "reality" of reported practices. Several limitations are identified in relation to these devices.

Firstly, some authors refer to the bias of the memory effect. The reliability of the statements is therefore determined by the individual's reflexivity, by the time that has elapsed between the trip and the moment of filling in a questionnaire, or by the singularity of the trip mentioned in the questionnaire.

Secondly, as in mobility surveys, some surveys cover only the day on which the questionnaire is applied. While this may reduce the effect of individuals' memories, it does so at the expense of the variability that may exist depending on the day or the reason for travel.

Thirdly, although the latest devices try to answer this question, because of the "newness" of this type of research, there is still no unanimity as to how to consider the activities. While some will aggregate activities into broad types, others will favor a disaggregated approach.

Finally, the mere description of these practices and the representations of travel time as useful or useless is not sufficient to assess the "value" that should be attributed to travel time. This raises the question of the "alternative" models that the transport field seeks to propose, where travel time would have a lower cost.

Another way of approaching the qualitative dimension of travel time from a methodological perspective is to focus on qualitative approaches, namely participant observation and interviews. Both methods are relevant to the detailed understanding of the experience of travel time and the place that this experience occupies in daily life. In addition to showing that people carry out activities, these approaches make visible a series of subtleties that are constituent with behavior and that allow us to consider travel in a life course. That said, some observational approaches that aim at a quantitative analysis of the prevalence of activities are problematic because they (too) often make assumptions about the meaning of gestures.

In view of the methodological limitations of travel time use, mixed methods appear to be the most appropriate alternative for obtaining empirical results. Researchers in this field agree that – although this is beginning to evolve – there is no common basis for the use of travel time at present. From the point of view of data collection and analysis methods, it seems necessary to emphasize the qualities of each type of method. On the one hand, quantitative analysis seems necessary in considering the value of time in the transport domain. On the other hand, qualitative analysis helps to refine and delimit the spectrum of behaviors, attitudes, and relationships with the space–time of travel.

4.6. Major research studies

Works on the use and appropriation of travel time take different directions depending on the disciplines and approaches used. In relation to the field of transport, the subject is gaining momentum through the prism of "perception" and multitasking.

Introduced in 2007 in relation to the use of information and communication technologies while on the move, multitasking has become a leading concept when referring to the use of travel time (Kenyon and Lyons 2007). A significant proportion of the studies presented above are studies that approach the uses of travel time from the perspective of the simultaneity of the activities that make up the trip. In this sense, the latter is often considered as the main activity (Kenyon 2010) to which secondary activities are added, depending on the motives and individuals, their characteristics, or the characteristics of the environment in which the trip is made.

In terms of empirical studies, the work in Great Britain is well consolidated due to the availability of a time-use survey module that has been integrated into the national survey of train users and has allowed for the comparison of time series (Lyons et al. 2013). The analysis of these data allows us to go beyond the transportation theme to better understand the conditions that make multitasking possible but also to link travel time to other temporal constraints that constitute individuals' daily lives (Lyons 2003; Kenyon and Lyons 2007; Lyons et al. 2008; Lyons et al. 2013; Lyons et al. 2016). Other work explores the link between multitasking and modal choice. According to the authors, travel time use is linked to travel mode through three coefficients: a coefficient of perception of the mode, a coefficient of the importance of multitasking for individuals, and finally, a coefficient of predisposition to the use of an electronic device (laptop, tablet, e-reader, etc.) (Malokin et al. 2019).

Research on the perception of travel time can be traced back to the interest of geographers, from the 1970s onward, in the representation of space and distance in relation specifically to movement (Appleyard et al. 1964; Tobler 1976; Bailly 1979; Bailly 1985; Miller 2004), or to the concrete planning of urban spaces (Cauvin 1999). These works explore the factors that influence the perception of distance and reveal the existing distortions between waiting time and the time perceived by individuals.

The analysis of these differences for the different means of transportation considers the different stages of travel: waiting, transit, and travel in a vehicle (O'Farrell and Markham 1974; Wardman 1998; Dziekan and Kottenhoff 2007; Watkins et al. 2011; Fan et al. 2016; Wardman et al. 2016). Through appropriation and mental representations, some works have shown the existence of an affective relationship with the station that goes beyond the functional character of the designed space (Audas 2008). The same observation has been made in relation to the possibilities of designing the space of airports, which, by calling upon the visual and tactile memory of the body, testify to the multiple uses of waiting time (Tiné 2012). Although some of these infrastructures are representative of globalization and its effects (Roseau 2012), these different meanings given to spaces of mobility contrast with the hypothesis of *non-places* that is still evoked in urban planning.

4.7. Discussions and research perspectives

As mentioned earlier, the interest in studying the use and appropriation of travel time goes beyond the simple description of activities that have basically not changed since the appearance of the different modes of travel. From a transport perspective, for example, the challenge of current research is to determine the utility, prevalence, and impact of travel time use in mobility practices and the rationales underlying people's modal choice.

To do this, it is still necessary to refine the methodological apparatus with which the researchers study these uses. On the one hand, this is a qualitative dimension of time that had not been formally considered in the construction of the surveys. In this sense, some suggest continuing to explore the subject with mixed methods that make it possible to gain both finesse and robustness in the collection and analysis of data (Keseru and Macharis 2018). Some authors have very recently recognized the inadequacy of questionnaires based on a single survey day to determine, for example, the influence of Internet access in modal practices, but also the costs and difficulty of conducting surveys over several days (Lachapelle and Jean-Germain 2019).

While the challenge is methodological, it is also important to consider why the subject is central to behavioral changes in contemporary and future societies. The transportation field seems to want to finally integrate the "usefulness" of travel time in predictive models of future mobility. However, although the available studies address the value of time from different perspectives and across a wide range of conditions, more work is needed on a more "formal" definition of what constitutes utility (Shaw et al. 2019) in order to be able to predict future mobility in order to incorporate this utility derived from current predictive models.

Among the debates and research perspectives in the field of transport, some raise the importance of taking into account the fragmentation of time – the fact of being able to relocate and detemporize certain activities – in the construction of mobility scenarios. They are consistent with our hypothesis that mobility is enhanced by an improved travel experience, which would have very negative consequences for the environment (Mokhtarian 2018).

4.8. References

Appleyard, D., Lynch, K., Myer, J. (1964). The view from the road. transportation. *Research Board*, 21–31.

Aubert, N. (2008). Violence du temps et pathologies hypermodernes. *Cliniques méditerranéennes*, 78(2), 23 [Online]. Available at: https://doi.org/10.3917/cm.078.0023.

Audas, N. (2008). De l'espace conçu à l'espace vécu : les modes d'appropriation affective d'un archétype du non-lieu, la gare. PhD thesis, Université Rennes 2, Rennes.

Augé, M. (2015). *Non-lieux. Introduction à une anthropologie de la surmodernité.* Le Seuil, Paris.

Axtell, C., Hislop, D., Whittaker, S. (2008). Mobile technologies in mobile spaces: Findings from the context of train travel. *International Journal of Human-Computer Studies*, 66(12), 902–915 [Online]. Available at: https://doi.org/10.1016/j.ijhcs.2008.07.001.

Bailly, A.S. (1974). Perception de la ville et déplacement. L'impact de la mobilité sur le comportement. *Cahiers de géographie du Québec*, 18(45), 525 [Online]. Available at: https://doi.org/10.7202/021228ar.

Bailly, A.S (1979). La perception des transports en commun par l'usager. *T.E.C.*, 32, 23–29.

Bailly, A.S. (1985). Distances et espaces : vingt ans de géographie des représentations. *Espace géographique*, 14(3), 197–205 [Online]. Available at: https://doi.org/10.3406/spgeo.1985.4033.

Bailly, A.S., Raffestin, C., Reymond, H. (1980). Les concepts du paysage : problématique et représentations. *Espace géographique*, 9(4), 277–285 [Online]. Available at: https://doi.org/10.3406/spgeo.1980.3575.

Banister, D. (2011). The trilogy of distance, speed and time. *Journal of Transport Geography*, 19(4), 950–959 [Online]. Available at: https://doi.org/10.1016/j.jtrangeo.2010.12.004.

Banister, D. (2018). *Inequality in Transport*. Alexandrine Press, Marcham.

Brown, B. and O'Hara, K. (2003). Place as a practical concern of mobile workers. *Environment and Planning A: Economy and Space*, 35(9), 1565–1587 [Online]. Available at: https://doi.org/10.1068/a34231.

Bull, M. (2004). Automobility and the power of sound. *Theory, Culture & Society*, 21(4/5), 243–259 [Online]. Available at: https://doi.org/10.1177/0263276404046069.

Cailly, L. and Fourny, M.-C. (2013). Gérer les proximités et franchir les distances. L'agencement des proximités dans la mobilité quotidienne périurbaine. *Géo-Regards*, 6.

Cauvin, C. (1999). Pour une approche de la cognition spatiale intra-urbaine. *European Journal of Geography, Political, Cultural and Cognitive Geography* [Online]. Available at: https://doi.org/10.4000/cybergeo.5043.

Citton, Y. (2014). *Pour une écologie de l'attention*. Le Seuil, Paris.

Descarrega, B. and Moati, P. (2016). Modes de vie et mobilité, une approche par les aspirations. Study, Forum Vies Mobiles [Online]. Available at: https://fr.forumviesmobiles.org/projet/2016/05/23/aspirations-liees-mobilite-et-aux-modes-vie-enquete-internationale-3240.

Drevon, G. (2019). *Proposition pour une rythmologie de la mobilité et des sociétés contemporaines*. Alphil/Presses universitaires Suisses, Neuchâtel.

Drevon, G., Gerber, P., Kaufmann, V. (2020). Dealing with daily rhythms: Families' strategies to tackle chronic time pressure. *Sustainability*, 12(17), 7193 [Online]. Available at: https://doi.org/10.3390/su12177193.

Dziekan, K. and Kottenhoff, K. (2007). Dynamic at-stop real-time information displays for public transport: Effects on customers. *Transportation Research Part A: Policy and Practice*, 41(6), 489–501 [Online]. Available at: https://doi.org/10.1016/j.tra.2006.11.006.

Fan, Y., Guthrie, A., Levinson, D. (2016). Waiting time perceptions at transit stops and stations: Effects of basic amenities, gender, and security. *Transportation Research Part A: Policy and Practice*, 88, 251–264 [Online]. Available at: https://doi.org/10.1016/j.tra.2016.04.012.

Fickling, R., Gunn, H., Kirby, H.R., Bradley, M., Heywood, C. (2008). Productive use of rail travel time and the valuation of travel time savings for rail business travellers. Report, Department for Transport, London.

Flamm, M. (2005a). Le vécu des temps de déplacement : cadres d'expérience et réappropriations du temps. In *Mobilités et temporalités*, Montulet, B. (ed.). Presses de l'Université Saint-Louis, Brussels.

Flamm, M. (2005b). A qualitative perspective on travel time experience. In *5th Swiss Transport Research Conference*, Ascona.

Frétigny, J.-B. (2011). Habiter la mobilité : le train comme terrain de réflexion. *L'Information géographique*, 75(4), 110 [Online]. Available at: https://doi.org/10.3917/lig.754.0110.

Gripsrud, M. and Hjorthol, R. (2012). Working on the train: From "dead time" to productive and vital time. *Transportation*, 39(5), 941–956.

Harms, T., Gershuny, J., Olaru, D. (2018). Using time-use data to analyse travel behaviour: Findings from the UK. *Transportation Research Procedia*, 32, 634–648 [Online]. Available at: https://doi.org/10.1016/j.trpro.2018.10.007.

Higgins, C.D., Sweet, M.N., Kanaroglou, P.S. (2018). All minutes are not equal: Travel time and the effects of congestion on commute satisfaction in Canadian cities. *Transportation*, 45(5), 1249–1268 [Online]. Available at: https://doi.org/10.1007/s11116-017-9766-2.

Holley, D., Jain, J., Lyons, G. (2008). Understanding business travel time and its place in the working day. *Time & Society*, 17(1), 27–46 [Online]. Available at: https://doi.org/10.1177/0961463X07086308.

Hoyaux, A.-F. (2002). Entre construction territoriale et constitution ontologique de l'habitant : introduction épistémologique aux apports de la phénoménologie au concept d'habiter. *Cybergeo* [Online]. Available at: https://doi.org/10.4000/cybergeo.1824.

Ingold, T. (2002). *The Perception of the Environment: Essays on Livelihood, Dwelling and Skill*. Routledge, London [Online]. Available at: https://doi.org/10.4324/9780203466025.

Jain, J. and Lyons, G. (2008). The gift of travel time. *Journal of Transport Geography*, 16(2), 81–89.

Joly, I. (2004). Travel time budget – Decomposition of the worldwide mean. In *International Association of Time-Use Research* (IATUR). Rome, 27–29 October [Online]. Available at: https://halshs.archives-ouvertes.fr/halshs-00087433.

Kaufmann, V. (1998). *Sociologie de la mobilité urbaine : la question du report modal*. École Polytechnique Fédérale de Lausanne, Lausanne [Online]. Available at: http://infoscience.epfl.ch/record/32236.

Kaufmann, V. (2005). La conjecture de Zahavi, un mécanisme régulateur. *Car Free – La vie sans voiture(s)* [Online]. Available at: http://carfree.fr/index.php/2005/09/13/la-conjecture-de-zahavi-un-mecanisme-regulateur.

Kaufmann, V. (2008). *Les paradoxes de la mobilité : bouger, s'enraciner*. Presses polytechniques et universitaires romandes, Lausanne [Online]. Available at: https://books.google.fr/books?id=GD8EfZl9TogC.

Kenyon, S. (2010). What do we mean by multitasking? – Exploring the need for methodological clarification in time use research. *Electronic International Journal of Time Use Research*, 7(1), 42–60 [Online]. Available at: https://core.ac.uk/download/pdf/6372186.pdf.

Kenyon, S. and Lyons, G. (2007). Introducing multitasking to the study of travel and ICT: Examining its extent and assessing its potential importance. *Transportation Research Part A: Policy and Practice*, 41(2), 161–175 [Online]. Available at: https://doi.org/10.1016/j.tra.2006.02.004.

Keseru, I. and Macharis, C. (2018). Travel-based multitasking: Review of the empirical evidence. *Transport Reviews*, 38(2), 162–183.

Khan, M.S. and Sundstrom, J. (2007). Effects of vibration on sedentary activities in passenger trains. *Journal of Low Frequency Noise, Vibration and Active Control*, 26(1), 43–55 [Online]. Available at: https://doi.org/10.1260/026309207781487448.

Kim, E.C. (2012). Nonsocial transient behavior: Social disengagement on the Greyhound bus. *Symbolic Interaction*, 35(3), 267–283 [Online]. Available at: https://doi.org/10.1002/symb.21.

Lachapelle, U. and Jean-Germain, F. (2019). Personal use of the Internet and travel: Evidence from the Canadian Social Survey's 2010 time use module. *Travel Behaviour and Society*, 14, 81–91.

Laurier, E. (2002). The region as a socio-technical accomplishment of mobile workers. In *Wireless World*, Brown, B., Green, N., Harper, R. (eds). Springer, London [Online]. Available at: https://doi.org/10.1007/978-1-4471-0665-4_4.

Laurier, E. (2004). Doing office work on the motorway. *Theory, Culture & Society*, 21(4–5), 261–277 [Online]. Available at: https://doi.org/10.1177/0263276404046070.

Lyons, G. (2003). Future mobility – It's about time. *35th Universities Transport Study Group Conference*, June.

Lyons, G. and Urry, J. (2005). Travel time use in the information age. *Transportation Research Part A: Policy and Practice*, 39(2/3), 257–276 [Online]. Available at: https://doi.org/10.1016/j.tra.2004.09.004.

Lyons, G., Jain, J., Holley, D. (2007). The use of travel time by rail passengers in Great Britain. *Transportation Research Part A: Policy and Practice*, 41(1), 107–120 [Online]. Available at: https://doi.org/10.1016/j.tra.2006.05.012.

Lyons, G., Jain, J., Holley, D. (2008). The business of train travel: A matter of time use. In *Mobility and Technology at the Work Place*, Hislop, D. (ed.). Routledge, London.

Lyons, G., Jain, J., Susilo, Y., Atkins, S. (2013). Comparing rail passengers' travel time use in Great Britain between 2004 and 2010. *Mobilities*, 8(4), 560–579 [Online]. Available at: https://doi.org/10.1080/17450101.2012.743221.

Lyons, G., Jain, J., Weir, I. (2016). Changing times – A decade of empirical insight into the experience of rail passengers in Great Britain. *Journal of Transport Geography*, 57, 94–104.

Malokin, A., Circella, G., Mokhtarian, P.L. (2019). How do activities conducted while commuting influence mode choice? Using revealed preference models to inform public transportation advantage and autonomous vehicle scenarios. *Transportation Research Part A: Policy and Practice*, 124, 82–114 [Online]. Available at: https://doi.org/10.1016/j.tra.2018.12.015.

Metz, D. (2008). The myth of travel time saving. *Transport Reviews*, 28(3), 321–336 [Online]. Available at: https://doi.org/10.1080/01441640701642348.

Milakis, D., Cervero, R., van Wee, B., Maat, K. (2015). Do people consider an acceptable travel time? Evidence from Berkeley, CA. *Journal of Transport Geography*, 44, 76–86 [Online]. Available at: https://doi.org/10.1016/j.jtrangeo.2015.03.008.

Miller, H.J. (2004). Tobler's first law and spatial analysis. *Annals of the Association of American Geographers*, 94(2), 284–289 [Online]. Available at: https://doi.org/10.1111/j.1467-8306.2004.09402005.x.

Mokhtarian, P.L. (2018). The times they are a-changin': What do the expanding uses of travel time portend for policy, planning, and life? *Transportation Research Record: Journal of the Transportation Research Board*, 2672(47), 1–11 [Online]. Available at: https://doi.org/10.1177/0361198118798602.

Mokhtarian, P.L. and Chen, C. (2004). TTB or not TTB, that is the question: A review and analysis of the empirical literature on travel time (and money) budgets. *Transportation Research Part A: Policy and Practice*, 38(9/10), 643–675 [Online]. Available at: https://doi.org/10.1016/j.tra.2003.12.004.

Mokhtarian, P.L. and Salomon, I. (2001). How derived is the demand for travel? Some conceptual and measurement considerations. *Transportation Research Part A: Policy and Practice*, 35(8), 695–719 [Online]. Available at: https://doi.org/10.1016/S0965-8564(00)00013-6.

Moreau, A. (1992). Public transport waiting times as experienced by customers: Marketing research involving the Grenoble system. *Public Transport International*, 41(3), 52–71.

O'Farrell, P.N. and Markham, J. (1974). Commuter perceptions of public transport work journeys. *Environment and Planning A: Economy and Space*, 6(1), 79–100 [Online]. Available at: https://doi.org/10.1068/a060079.

Ohmori, N. and Harata, N. (2008). How different are activities while commuting by train? A case in Tokyo. *Tijdschrift voor economische en sociale geografie*, 99(5), 547–561.

Paquot, T. (2005). Habitat, habitation, habiter. Ce que parler veut dire... *Informations sociales*, 123, 48–54.

Ravalet, E., Dubois, Y., Kaufmann, V. (2014). Grandes mobilités et accès à l'emploi. *Reflets et perspectives de la vie économique*, LIII(3), 57 [Online]. Available at: https://doi.org/10.3917/rpve.533.0057.

Roseau, N. (2012). Habiter la grande échelle. In *Habiter les aéroports – Paradoxes d'une nouvelle urbanité*, Urlberger, A. (ed.). MétisPresses, Geneva.

Russell, M.L. (2012). Travel time use on public transport: What passengers do and how it affects their wellbeing. PhD thesis, University of Otago, Dunedin.

Russell, M.L., Price, R., Signal, L., Stanley, J., Gerring, Z., Cumming, J. (2011). What do passengers do during travel time? Structured observations on buses and trains. *Journal of Public Transportation*, 14(3), 7.

Schafer, A. (2000). Regularities in travel demand: An international perspective. *Journal of Transportation and Statistics* [Online]. Available at: https://doi.org/10.21949/1501657.

Shaw, F.A., Malokin, A., Mokhtarian, P.L., Circella, G. (2019). It's not all fun and games: An investigation of the reported benefits and disadvantages of conducting activities while commuting. *Travel Behaviour and Society*, 17, 8–25 [Online]. Available at: https://doi.org/10.1016/j.tbs.2019.05.008.

Soubeyran, O. and Berdoulay, V. (2012). L'adaptation aux changements climatique : perspectives historiques sur son cadrage théorique en aménagement. Report, Programme CDE.

Stock, M. (2005). Les sociétés à individus mobiles : vers un nouveau mode d'habiter ? *EspacesTemps* [Online]. Available at: https://www.espacestemps.net/articles/societes-individus-mobiles/.

Stopher, P.R., Ahmed, A., Liu, W. (2017). Travel time budgets: New evidence from multi-year, multi-day data. *Transportation*, 44(5), 1069–1082 [Online]. Available at: https://doi.org/10.1007/s11116-016-9694-6.

Susilo, Y.O., Lyons, G., Jain, J., Atkins, S. (2012). Rail passengers' time use and utility assessment: 2010 findings from Great Britain with multivariate analysis. *Transportation Research Record: Journal of the Transportation Research Board*, 2323(1), 99–109 [Online]. Available at: https://doi.org/10.3141/2323-12.

Thomas, M.-P. and Pattaroni, L. (2012). Choix résidentiels et différenciation des modes de vie des familles de classes moyennes en Suisse. *Espaces et sociétés*, 148–149(1), 111–127 [Online]. Available at: https://doi.org/10.3917/esp.148.0111.

Timmermans, H. and Van der Waerden, P. (2008). Synchronicity of activity engagement and travel in time and space: Descriptors and correlates of field observations. *Transportation Research Record: Journal of the Transportation Research Board*, 2054(1), 1–9 [Online]. Available at: https://doi.org/10.3141/2054-01.

Tiné, G. (2012). Faire avec le regard et le corps. In *Habiter les aéroports – Paradoxes d'une nouvelle urbanité*, Urlberger, A. (ed.). MétisPresses, Geneva.

Tobler, W. (1976). The geometry of mental maps. In *Spatial Choice and Spatial Behavior: Geographic Essays on the Analysis of Preferences and Perceptions*, Golledge, R.G. and Rushton G. (eds). Ohio State University Press, Columbus.

Vidal, L. and Musset, A. (2015). L'attente comme état de la mobilité. In *Les territoires de l'attente : migrations et mobilités dans les Amériques (XIXe–XXIe siècle)*. Presses Universitaires de Rennes, Rennes.

Vilhelmson, B., Thulin, E., Fahlén, D. (2011). ICTs and activities on the move – People's use of time while traveling by public transport. In *Engineering Earth: The Impacts of Megaengineering Projects*, Stanley, D.B. (ed.). Springer, Amsterdam.

Vincent, S., Ravalet, E., Kaufmann, V. (2015). L'appropriation des temps et des espaces de la grande mobilité à l'ère du numérique. *Géo-regards*, 7, 17–35.

Wardman, M. (1998). The value of travel time: A review of British evidence. *Journal of Transport Economics and Policy*, 32, 285–316.

Wardman, M., Chintakayala, V.P.K., de Jong, G. (2016). Values of travel time in Europe: Review and meta-analysis. *Transportation Research Part A: Policy and Practice*, 94, 93–111 [Online]. Available at: https://doi.org/10.1016/j.tra.2016.08.019.

Watkins, K.E., Ferris, B., Borning, A., Rutherford, G.S., Layton, D. (2011). Where is my bus? Impact of mobile real-time information on the perceived and actual wait time of transit riders. *Transportation Research Part A: Policy and Practice*, 45(8), 839–848 [Online]. Available at: https://doi.org/10.1016/j.tra.2011.06.010.

Watts, L. (2008). The art and craft of train travel. *Social & Cultural Geography*, 9(6), 711–726 [Online]. Available at: https://doi.org/10.1080/14649360802292520.

Zahavi, Y. (1979). UMOT project. Report, U.S. Department of Transportation/Ministry of Transport, Washington/Berlin.

Zahavi, Y. and Ryan, J. (1980). Stability of travel components over time. *Transport Research Record*, 750, 19–26.

Zahavi, Y. and Talvitie, A. (1980). Regularities in time and money expenditures. *Transportation Research Record*, 750, 13–19.

5

Designing Space for Walking as the Primary Mode of Travel

Sébastien LORD[1] and Mathilde LOISELLE[2]

[1] École d'urbanisme et d'architecture de paysage, Université de Montréal, Canada
[2] Faculty of Planning, Université de Montréal, Canada

5.1. Introduction

Walking and urban spaces are now a matter of course, in the era of so-called soft, sustainable, or active mobility, planners, city planners, architects, landscape architects, and other actors who create the city, attributing many virtues to this way of moving or getting around. This is why walkability is today one of the essential criteria when analyzing the quality of urban projects or of the renovation of built environments in the past. In many cases, this is because walkability has not always received the attention it deserves, especially in the development said to be *by* and *for* the automobile in past decades.

When walking becomes an argument against motorized mobility, it must be considered beyond the simple dimension of movement and rather considered as a primary mode of mobility in person–environment interactions. Thus, the walker moves, opposing sedentariness but also animates neighborhoods, streets, and terraces, creating different atmospheres. When arriving in a place by car, bus, or subway, the person who moves will then be a walker, and this walker will walk more in an environment considered pleasant, comfortable, and stimulating, in short a space congruent with their needs, aspirations, and preferences. In this sense, walking can bring and diversify socioeconomic activities in urban environments, such as shopping streets or tourist destinations, but also natural or developed places for walking as a destination activity. It is then in the image of the place and in the social link that the walker arouses the interest of the actors and decision-makers of the city, as well as of the shopkeepers, the artists, or the other participants in urban life.

To be interested in and question the practice of walking and the place of the walker in the city is to criticize and challenge, as Jacobs (1961) did in the 1960s, modern town planning that has prevailed and participated in the development of the functional city. It is the city of segregated uses, of metropolitan specialization, of suburban and peri-urban sprawl. It is the space of all comforts for the motorist and of difficult accessibility for the other modes of travel. Some will speak of inequalities, for the non-motorized, but especially for the walker. Some important works, in line with this current of thought, such as those of Lynch (1960, 1981), or Appleyard (1981), who followed him, have laid the theoretical and empirical foundations for the analysis and discussion of the space of the walker in its morphological, functional, and psychosocial dimensions. The first gave the codes and methods of fundamental analysis, still used today by urban planners and architects (Bosselman 2019) for the understanding and appropriation of urban space by the walker. The second put into perspective the quality of urban forms and the essential dimensions of an urban design capable of serving the walker well (Alcântara de Vasconcellos 2004). Professionals integrating these methods and principles of urban design today would also be the best equipped to repair the modern city (Bosselman 2019).

As Gehl (2016) has been repeating for several decades now, with a constantly renewed actuality, this is a perspective that falls under the umbrella of the developed city in the era of cheap gasoline and the absence of environmental concerns. This perspective has led to the car reflex, which many define as a pathology, the car addiction (Dupuy 1999), which is difficult to cure. Urban and regional planners are the first to be challenged and are trying to find alternatives that are accessible and appropriate for several population profiles (Lord et al. 2015). While things are evolving slowly, with oil becoming scarcer and climate change entering the political discourse, planning must nevertheless deal with a spread-out city and spaces where walking is an unpleasant, difficult, and even unrealistic experience if one moves away from the central sectors.

In the face of this, with the updating of modern cities to a form of mobility where walking finds its place in transport options, walking mobility occupies a distinct place in recent mobility research, but also in urban planning practice and in the discourse of city policies. This attention gives it a new position and a special status in urban renewal and development. But its integration into postmodern urban thinking is complex. Considered as a means of travel hidden within the mainstream modes of transport, walking can be approached as a physical activity, a leisure activity, or a sport, rather than as a mode of travel. Its place in the city will be optional for some, as an alternative to the usual motorized mobility for others. A first part of the complexity of walking comes from the fact that it is the common denominator of most ways of getting around, whether by car, train, metro, tram, bus, bicycle, etc. In addition, it may be relevant to distinguish walking from active mobility. In this sense, all modes of travel involve walking.

The fundamental characteristics of the urban form are in many ways the hidden determinants of walkability of living environments. Cervero and Kockelman (1996), Handy (1992), or Ewing (1994) put forward, almost 30 years ago now, the "3 Ds" perspective: density, diversity, and design. As Torres (2012) points out, the first two "Ds" are rather simple. They are also characteristics of central neighborhoods, of the European-style city, but also of several North American urban centers. These characteristics imply a close relationship between walking and short distances, diversity of destinations, and good connectivity of the urban form. This last morphological characteristic will join the third "D": design. This is a link in the organization of space, particularly with the road network, which gives different urban forms to this density and diversity. Ewing et al. (2005) bring to this design perspective five qualities of walking environment design: imageability (character of the environment), spatial framing (vertical and horizontal architectural and green elements of the place), human scale (scale, speed, and adaptation of the place), transparency (visibility beyond the physical limits of the place), and complexity (number and diversity of activities in the place). The underlying assumption here is that so-called central environments are more walkable than so-called suburban or even peri-urban environments because the latter are more spread out, dispersed, and fragmented.

These perspectives on the morphology and functional organization of the walking environment, built on the same theoretical bases, but also on experiential and relative referents, lead us to a second dimension of complexity. The differentiated urban forms, placing the walker in conditions that can be contrasted, force us to consider the possibility of a plurality of walking experiences. The works of Joseph (1984), Thomas (2004), Amar (2010), and Thibaud (2015), among others, place the focus on the interaction, sometimes objectified, sometimes subjectivized, between the walker and his walking environment, or even more closely on his lived and interiorized experience, as done by Sansot (1996), Paquot (2006), or Rousseau and Husserl (1992) (cited in Thomas (2007)). Walking thus allows us to approach movement and mobility as they are experienced in everyday life, in terms of familiarity and intimacy, in terms of people's interactions with their environments.

However, these experiences vary considerably in intensity and meaning according to the age of life, the social and cultural contexts, and, inevitably, the territory.

This chapter is therefore a part of these debates, which have their origins in the idea of a better understanding of what makes people walk and what environments would be conducive to walking, for different reasons and different feelings. The following sections aim to contribute to this reflection on walking, the walker, and the walkability of spaces by discussing three perspectives present in Northern American and European scientific and professional debates in planning and urban design. The first part discusses the diversity of research approaches to walking. The second part focuses on the physical–spatial determinants of walkability in relation to the perceptions and emotions of walkers. The third and concluding part highlights some of the challenges of scales of analysis in a perspective of intervention on living environments.

5.2. A diversity of approaches to the objective conditions of walking, first of all a question of scale?

Objective approaches to walking have contributed to the development of knowledge about the morphofunctional determinants of walking. These approaches posit that the characteristics of urban form and function influence, and even determine, people's walking behavior – and their propensity to combine or use other modes of travel. Among the first to examine the impact of the built environment on walking were Lynch (1960), Jacob (1961), and Ghel (1987). It is precisely in this effort at objectivity that Cervero and Kockelman (1997) discuss the "3 Ds" discussed in section 5.1, criteria widely used as determinants of walking. The methods used to objectify built environments, whether at the city or neighborhood level or at the level of the individual walker, all emphasize the description of walking environments. They are particularly based on geography and public health, and come mainly from countries where walking has a limited modal share with an urbanization that has materialized with the car and which promote active mobility to some extent, namely the United States, Australia, and Canada (Wang and Yang 2019).

5.2.1. *Walkability of the city and the neighborhood*

The emergence of geographic information systems favors the operationalization of walkability criteria on a large scale. These data are now made available and accessible to many local government organizations and generally contain information on land roles, the location of various amenities or facilities, and sometimes even the condition of municipal infrastructure such as sidewalks, street furniture, bike paths, trees, vegetation in the public domain, etc. In addition to these, statistical agencies can link data on urban form and function with a range of demographic information, providing a wide range of research possibilities (Handy et al. 2002; Frank et al. 2009) and enabling analysis beyond urban areas. Most often used as an aggregate of elements accessible by a walker's metrics or by a major origin/destination when discussing multimodality, the criteria are defined, for example, by the number of dwellings per hectare (density), the number of retail, commercial, and park facilities per hectare (density and diversity), the number of residential areas within 400 meters of a commercial area (diversity), and the number of intersections where four directions intersect (design) (Cervero and Kockelman 1997). The Walkscore[1] in the United States and Local Logic[2] in Quebec are good examples of private companies opening some of their analyses or indices of territorial accessibility to walking, either directly or as a complement to other modes of travel.

These perspectives, which are on a macroscale, seek to identify the morphofunctional characteristics of environments deemed to be conducive to walking. The development of indices or good practices to better inform the development of public policies in the areas of health or planning appears to be recurrent (Leslie et al. 2007). We can then speak of a common denominator in the primary conditions for walking, the accessibility of the territory to the walker, the feasibility of walking to a destination, and the presence of urban destinations. Without these conditions, walking is not possible or useful. Thus, research methods that favor a macro and objective approach to walking environments have the advantage of covering large territories and taking into account an imposing number of variables, including sociodemographic or socioeconomic ones, in their analysis. However, these advantages are countered by the impossibility of integrating the criteria of relevant built environments that can be perceived only at the level of the walker. Moreover, this type of approach is more or less useful for informing the transformation of existing walking environments, a change that is often slow to materialize in the available databases.

5.2.2. *The urban quality and the walking environment*

In order to take into account the scale of walking environments, other approaches will also favor objective perspectives, but this time to characterize the attributes of the environment. The development and validation of analysis tools that can be

---

1 www.walkscore.com/.
2 www.locallogic.co/.

applied at the scale of the walker are therefore fundamental. A considerable number of walkability audits have been developed for this purpose by Americans, Australians, and Canadians (Pikora et al. 2002; Cunningham et al. 2005; Boarnet et al. 2006; Clifton et al. 2007). Urban audit approaches go beyond the walking accessibility discussed above, in that they allow the characteristics of the environment to be objectified in the logic of walking mobility and not of land accessibility.

Audits most often take the form of a grid of criteria that can be observed directly in the field and are designed to assess the attributes of the walking environment against standards. They include categories of criteria that are very similar from one audit to another: urban form and function, the condition of walking infrastructure, the presence of benches and other street furniture, the interaction between different road users, and the safety and attractiveness of the street segments or pedestrian routes audited. The development of new audits is usually motivated by the need to adapt existing tools to a particular territorial context (Clifton et al. 2007). Other walkability audits have also been developed to analyze the suitability of walking environments for different profiles of walkers. This is the case, for example, of the Senior Walking Environmental Audit Tool (SWEAT) (Cunningham et al. 2005) and the Walkability Audit for the Elderly (*Marchabilité pour les personnes âgées*, MAPPA) (Negron-Poblete and Lord 2014), which were developed to inform the particular needs of older walkers in relation to walking environments.

The analyses developed around the walkability audits are in almost all cases *in situ*. However, as a complement to these field surveys that must be conducted on multiple criteria and entire urban neighborhoods or suburban areas, the reuse of video capture (Osmond 2005; Ewing and Handy 2009) and online Google Street View-like imagery is gaining popularity in recent work. The Street Walkability Audit Tool for Pedestrian Route Choice Analysis (SWATCH) (Shatu and Yigitcanlar 2018) and the Virtual Systematic Tool for Evaluating Pedestrian Streetscapes (Virtual-STEPS) (Steinmetz-Wood et al. 2019) have thus been developed specifically for conducting walkability audits using Google Street View. Tested in Brisbane, Australia and Montreal, Canada, respectively, these audits experience a sufficient level of compliance with *in situ* assessments to claim the validity of virtual methods. However, these virtual tools depend on updating databases that do not necessarily correspond to the times of the observations to be made. More fundamentally, the Google Street View images are taken from a car in the center of the street, which is not consistent with the walker's environment, making it difficult to validly characterize the walker's environment.

The complexity of administering walkability audits is due to the need to ensure consistency in the interpretation of criteria, which leads to the search for standardized shortcuts or the use of online resources that struggle to capture the complexity of walking environments. Indeed, urban audits are typically conducted by teams of trained auditors using validated tools (Pikora et al. 2002; Boarnet et al. 2006; Clifton et al. 2007; Negron-Poblete and Lord 2014). The use of expert panels and trained auditors limits the subjectivity of the results. This concern is reinforced when the work incorporates subjective criteria about different urban qualities of the walk space in addition to the objective attributes of the walking environments analyzed, as is the case in the work of Ewing and Handy (2009), for example.

5.2.3. Applications for the development of walking environments

The works objectifying walking and walkability of spaces have been prolific since the late 1990s. Moreover, in the context of growing concerns about climate change, research on walking as the first link in active mobility is abundant. There is work in the Gehl and Jacobs stream of thought for the design of quality walking environments, but also perspectives put forward by geographers or public health officials that aim to establish correlations and modeling of the attributes of the most walkable environments. From all of this, the establishment of a reference framework on the knowledge of walkability and its determinants emerges. The major current works associated with an objective approach to walking fall into two categories: those concerned with walking for public health reasons (Box 5.1) and those concerned with walking as a primary mode of travel in land-use planning and development (Box 5.2).

> The growing concern with sedentary behavior and the associated health risks is motivating many research projects to look at the forms to be given to the city, including ways of renovating and requalifying (sub- and peri-)urban spaces that are recognized as being unfriendly to walking. While suburban environments are designed with automobile accessibility in mind (functional segregation, functional barriers (highways, boulevard), distance to destinations, etc.), peri-urban spaces exacerbate the constraints even more (absence of destinations, absence of public transport, etc.). The impacts of the city and the mobility it generates on sedentariness are central here. Among the authors in this field, the work of James F. Sallis, Lawrence D. Frank, Delfien Van Dyck, and others is of particular interest. Frank, Van Dyck, and their numerous collaborators appear as essential references (Frank et al. 2004; Frank et al. 2006; Owen et al. 2007; Adams et al. 2015; Grasser et al. 2016).
>
> For example, a large study in the Atlanta area of the United States, involving over 10,000 participants, found a link between the walkability of an area and the obesity rate of its population. The results of this type of study suggest that time spent in a vehicle is a key

risk factor for obesity and is linked to the walkability of an area through low functional mix and sprawling urban form (Frank et al. 2004). In another study conducted in King County, Washington, USA, the walkability of an area was positively associated with active travel time among its population (Frank et al. 2006). Similar work in Australia also concludes that the walkability of an area has an impact on the rate of active mobility among its residents, including walking (Owen et al. 2007). A study conducted in Graz, Austria, validated the appropriateness of the walkability criteria used in Canadian, American, and Australian research in the European context (Grasser et al. 2016). Finally, the work of Feuillet et al. (2018) has made it possible to qualify the impact of densification interventions on the walking experience. The effect of these interventions would be most beneficial in low- or medium-density settings. While this work merely validates many of the observations already made by many urban planners and architects, it has the advantage of quantifying and measuring the effect of significant determinants of walkable environments, thereby revealing the extent of the work involved in redesigning sprawling New World metropolises to be more walkable.

Box 5.1. *Risks of sedentary lifestyles and health risks avoided by walking*

The second category of work puts forward the perspective of territorial planning and development with regard to walkability. This work conceptualizes walkability as an "index" or "indicator" that makes it possible to assess and evaluate the impacts of the morphofunctional organization of living environments on health, but also on the inclusion of people, the social and economic vitality of territories, their heritage, or the viability of their dominant mobility models. This work aims to inform the development of new living environments, but also, and above all, to guide the adaptation of existing environments to the new and evolving issues they face.

A first perspective looks at the place of the pedestrian in relation to other road users. In a study conducted in Mexico City, Perez Lopez (2015) highlights the discomfort of pedestrian-hostile environments such as crossings that require bypassing, dropped kerbs, or introduce a level of endangerment. In addition to inhospitable infrastructure, the study's findings point to the behavior of other road users, particularly motorists, as the primary source of pedestrian insecurity. A second perspective looks at mobility behavior in relation to people's socioeconomic profiles. This is notably the case with the work of Ravalet (2007) and Ravalet et al. (2014). They qualify the impact of morphofunctional determinants of walking by indicating that the analysis of walkability must also take into account the different profiles of walkers. Not everyone is equal when it comes to the level of walkability of urban spaces, which is not without issues for categories of populations such as the elderly, children, and people facing a disability (Sugiyama and Ward Thompson 2008, 2017; Negron-Poblete 2012; Brookfield et al. 2017; Raulin et al. 2020).

Finally, Sonia Lavadinho's work is one of the few examples, because it is based on evidence, to offer solutions for operationalizing walkability criteria in an urban intervention perspective on the quality of walking environments (Lavadinho 2011a; Lavadinho and Winkin 2012). The work carried out from a territorial planning and development perspective, while incorporating the correlative and moderating analyses described above, goes beyond this, because such findings on the determinants of the walkability of urban environments must be translated into planning criteria and not remain in the form of general principles or "good practices" that are difficult to transfer from one context to another. Thus, they sometimes use more exploratory research methods such as *in situ* observations, walking interviews and focus groups (Lavadinho 2011a, 2011b; Lord and Negron-Poblete 2014; Brookfield et al. 2017; Després et al. 2019). They thus incorporate subjective dimensions into their analysis, therefore sharing certain theoretical and methodological affinities with the work we have hereafter grouped under sensitive approaches.

Box 5.2. *Territorial development for walking*

5.3. The conditions of operation, what is the place for the walker's experience?

Walking, the walking environment, and the walker themselves involve a wide variety of fields of study. The major works that approach walking in its sensitive conditions, particularly from the point of view of mobility, focus on the analysis of the person–environment relationship. Research on the modes of appropriation or the various practices of public spaces has been abundant for several decades. The works mobilized today on the subjectivity of walking have their theoretical origins from two main perspectives.

On the one hand, we note authors such as Irwin Altman, a pioneer of environmental sociology and psychology. On the other hand, we note authors close to the practice of planning, such as Jacob (1961) and Gehl (1987), mentioned above, on the importance of taking into account the social dimensions and the atmosphere in urban intervention. Of this group, Kevin Lynch was among the first to oppose the importance of sensitive components of public spaces to modern planning. Whyte's (1980) observation of New York public spaces is also a good example of a major work that contributed significantly to the development of *in situ* methodological approaches. On the basis of these two perspectives, recent work continues in many cases to develop the analysis of walking in its subjective complexity.

5.3.1. *The subjectivity of walking in its social and sensory dimensions*

A body of research is interested in walking from a perspective of inhabiting, especially in its social dimensions and the opportunities it allows (Joseph 1984;

Sansot 1996; Bordreuil 2000; Amar 2010; Lord 2012). It is the person–environment relationship that receives the attention of researchers here. We are particularly interested in the social dimensions linked to micromobility and the opportunities differentiated according to the walker's profile. Amar (2010) identifies, for example, the concept of "environment grip" (or the French concept of "adhérence") to talk about the opportunities encountered during a journey.

Also, in relation to the opportunities and accessibility of walking environments from a person–environment perspective, Bordreuil (2000) proposes the neighborhood concept to emphasize the social experiences that are offered to the walker as they travel. As an example, a vast pedestrianization project carried out in downtown Brussels, documented by the Brussels Studies Institute–Brussels Centre Observatory (BSI-BCO) (2020), highlights the redefinition of the relationship with the city engendered by the reconfiguration of the hierarchy between modes of travel. The affective constructs resulting from this person–environment relationship are also studied in Feildel (2013) with questions of pleasure and displeasure, but also of memory, anchoring, and the feeling of belonging. The richer the environment is in human and sensitive experiences, the more it is perceived as walkable. Results in this sense can be cited from a research project comparing the walking environments of a suburb south of Montreal (Longueuil) in Quebec with those of a central district of the metropolis. A mixed-method approach combining a walkability audit and focus groups revealed that the experiential quality of the walking environment is sometimes more important than the simple morphofunctional quality of the territory in terms of the choice of walking destinations among older walkers (Lord and Negron-Poblete 2014).

The social experience of walking is juxtaposed with the sensory experience. The sensory dimensions of the experience of the moving body are analyzed in an original perspective in the work of Thomas (2004). It is the body and its reactions to the experience that is given to it that constitute the pillar of this approach. The analysis of the sensitive qualities of walking environments can be carried out according to the states of the body aroused by the experience of the city, the street, and the environment of proximity. More technically, the sensory experience of walking can also be studied, as in Apparicio et al. (2019), in terms of the level of pollution inhaled according to the mode of transport preferred. Walking is then approached as part of the other modes studied, including cycling, public transport, and the automobile.

Together, social and sensory experiences constitute the sensitive experience of walking. Knowledge of this complexity also allows for a better understanding of the design criteria – from the person walking to the city – capable of enhancing the walker's experience. These criteria are not fundamentally different from the walkability criteria of the urban audits seen earlier, but are integrated not as norms or determinants but rather as elements to be combined through urban design by planners, to create an atmosphere, etc.

5.3.2. *The atmosphere and its components*

Aesthetics has strongly influenced work on the subjectivity of walking, which addresses the atmosphere as a central notion (Augoyard 1998; Thibaud 2013). In these approaches focused on the individual and collective experience of the city, the environment does not determine the walking experience as objective approaches. Nor is the body, in its sensory and interpretive response to walking, the anchor of the analysis. Rather, it is the balance of all these material, immaterial, ephemeral, interpretative, personal, cultural, etc. dimensions that together form the third object of study that is the urban environment. The richness of the concept lies in its complexity and its encompassing character.

Works such as those of the Cresson laboratory offer several examples of analysis of the constituent elements of the architectural and urban atmosphere. Augoyard (1990) was among the first to take an interest in the constituents of urban atmosphere, notably through his work on urban lighting in relation to the feeling of insecurity or the sound comfort of urban spaces (1992). Central to the question of urban atmospheres, the question of contextuality raises the analysis beyond the accumulation of technical statements on the perceptible signals to integrate the personal, cultural, temporal, and spatial contexts of the sensitive experience. Augoyard (1995) speaks about recurrent contextuality to describe this singularity of the lived experience of the same sensitive signal according to the individual, the moment, and the place where it is experienced. The sensitive signals that constitute the urban atmosphere can be mobilized in the analysis, but the pertinence of their measurement can be contested according to the context and the intention. Taking the example of noise complaints in an urban context, Delétré (2004) points out that the measurements are complex to carry out and often costly. They do not necessarily provide more information than the testimony of the complainants, which, unlike the technical measurement, also provides information on the subjectivity of the situation and its context. At the crossroads of individual, social, and physical experience of the territory, the atmosphere offers an interesting analytical scope for informing urban planning in both its sensitive and more objective dimensions (see Box 5.3).

> Approaches that take the subjectivity of the walker and his sensory reactions as the focal point of analysis, as well as those that are interested in the atmosphere as a third object between the walker and the environment, have the originality of the analysis

methods used in common. To the classical and often sedentary methods that are interested either in the sensory criteria of the environments or in their perception by the walkers, a diversity of *in situ* approaches is added.

Classical methods for analyzing the walker's experience

Walking is experienced in a singular way according to the individual's personal and cultural experience. The question of perception in the appreciation of walking environments has attracted the attention of both researchers who favor objective approaches and those who are interested in the sensitive dimensions of the experience. Many authors share the view that the walker's perception influences his appreciation of the quality and feasibility of the walking environment and, ultimately, his decision to walk or not (Thomas 2004; Alfonzo 2005; Ewing and Handy 2009; Lavadinho 2011a; Lord and Negron-Poblete 2014; Troped et al. 2016; Brookfield et al. 2017). Among the traditional methods used to consider walkers' perceptions, the survey and focus group appear to be the most commonly used.

The survey is used to take into account people's perception of (pre)evaluated walking environments – in particular through urban audits. These surveys incorporate a series of walkability criteria that can be established as statistically significant. Potential respondents are asked to complete their assessment, in the majority of cases, from their homes via a postal, telephone, or online questionnaire (Saelens et al. 2003; Dyck et al. 2013; Bracy et al. 2014). Alternatively, the focus group is used to capture the perceptions and attitudes of walkers, especially in urban planning and development studies. The focus group can be used as a complement to walkability audits to take into account the perspective of the walker with respect to the morphological and functional characteristics of walking environments or activities and destinations that make different population profiles walk (or not) (Negron-Poblete and Lord 2014).

This approach in walking analysis can then incorporate video capture or photographic media. In this way, participants comment on a known or proposed environment, including through simulation (Brookfield et al. 2017). These methods focus on the person's experience in its perceived and reflected forms, but the decontextualized nature of their analysis does not allow access to the experience truly felt by the walker.

In situ **analysis methods**

In situ analysis proves particularly useful to take into account the sensitive dimensions of the environments, other than in its form reported by the walker. The book by Michèle Grosjean and Jean-Paul Thibaud (2001), *L'espace urbain en méthodes*, can be a reference in French-speaking literature. It reviews a good number of original methods available to researchers and professionals for studying urban public space from a perspective of complexity. Without giving an exhaustive account of them, we have grouped together some of these approaches here, particularly concerning observation methods and mobile methods.

Observation of the environment

Observation is widely used in research as well as in more professional perspectives of intervention on the city. The technique essentially consists of observing the behavior of walkers in the space. The positioning of bodies and their reactions to environmental cues or to other walkers, the route taken, and the empathic relationship with the people who share the walking experience are all variables usually observed when dealing with walking behavior. These, depending on the context, provide information, for example, on the state of the walker's body (Thomas 2004), on the social inclusion and opportunities they encounter (Amar 2010; Bigo 2018), on the modes of appropriation of spaces (Whyte 1980), on the conditions of safety (Lord et al. 2018), and on so many other observable phenomena of interest to researchers and planners. Observation strategies vary according to the objectives pursued. They include descriptive narrative, descriptive note-taking, and more analytical forms. Current technologies also allow the use of photo and video capture, with or without geo-referencing of the observed phenomena.

Mobile methods

Particularly useful in the context of research on walking, many researchers opt for *in situ* and mobile survey or analysis methods. These have the advantage of taking into account the experience of walking in its pathological dimensions, intrinsic to the action of walking. It is a perspective that also serves to approach multimodality, reloads, and the multifunctionality of walking locations.

The researcher sometimes adopts a mobile observer position. In this case, he keeps the walker's observation within the limits established by the methodological strategy adopted, as Bigo (2018) does with wandering in recreational and tourist spaces. The methods of accompanying the walker also take the form of the commented route, as Chaudet (2009) develops with the elderly or even voluntary accompaniment with Levy (2001) who walks in spaces and places frequented daily, i.e., stations.

Again, researchers use a variety of data collection strategies, but most favor audio and video capture that allows for repeated listening or viewing that is conducive to a stratified analysis of the data collected. In the same vein, and in a similar way to sociological approaches to walking, some works use walking as a survey tool to highlight or mobilize the immersive and experiential relationship of individuals with an environment. This is the case of the deliberative walk used in the work of Lindell and Ehrstroem (2020). In a consultative process on a social and territorial issue, sensory immersion promotes, through walking, the democratic investment of the participants and the feeling of inclusion in the consultative process. This immersive approach through walking is also used in education (Stickney 2020).

To enrich the research approach and maximize the scope, or even the representativeness, of the results, some researchers opt for mixed methodological strategies that combine, for example, observations with accompanied methods or

> sedentary interviews with walking interviews (Després et al. 2019). This is notably the case in the work of Chelkoff (2001), who combines observations with exploratory walks and acoustic and light measurement operations. This work aims to capture the subjectivity of the built environments by an analysis centered on the atmospheres of the place and not only on the physicospatial criteria discussed previously.

Box 5.3. Methods of sensitivity analysis

5.3.3. *On the hermeneutic significance of atmospheres in the practice of walking*

In connection with the technical applications of sensitive conditions, involved in Chelkoff's definition, there is also an insistence on the importance of the context in which the components of the atmosphere are articulated, but also of their perceptual dimensions:

> Reducing an existing context to a material, spatial, and technical device obliterates the part of the investment of the beings who walk through it, feel it, and live it while staying or working in it. (Chelkoff 2006, p. 5)

This criticism is not unrelated to that raised by researchers engaged in objectivist approaches to walking, on the importance of taking into account the perceptual dimension of walkers in the analysis of morphofunctional determinants of walking environments.

The advantage of the urban atmosphere analysis is that it allows a comparison between purely objective approaches that analyze the morphofunctional determinants of the walking environment and subjective analyses that focus on either the sensory reactions of the body or the sociological dimensions associated with the walking experience. From a planning perspective, however, subjective approaches face the challenge of the scale of intervention that they presuppose. Analysis based on the components of the urban atmosphere or on the sensitive reaction of bodies to the walking environment poses the challenge of informing intervention projects on the scale of the city or the neighborhood.

Moreover, the "making" or "creating" of atmospheres is often the primary objective of architects and urban planners, especially when it comes to public spaces. This is all the more crucial when walking is approached in a multimodal manner, as the primary mode of travel. However, the levers used by planning professionals often only concern physical and functional attributes, leaving little concrete influence on lifestyles and the way they are deployed. How then can we create meaningful environments capable of getting people to walk more and longer in the course of their lives?

5.4. What are the challenges of the scales of analysis for intervention in living environments?

As we have outlined in this chapter, research and studies on walking environments are flourishing, even though their subjects date back several decades, particularly in relation to the consequences of functional town planning. However, the new technologies and technical possibilities of today allow these perspectives to be renewed. Thus, various commonplace aspects of everyday urban environments, such as the difficulties posed by steps or thresholds that are difficult to access, the poor configuration of areas shared with other road users, or the presence of sidewalks that are in varying degrees of condition, can, in combination with factors related to the individual, considerably complicate mobility, especially for the elderly or people with disabilities. At the same time, this same combination can represent a different walking environment, or even a stimulating atmosphere sought after by different profiles of walkers, such as younger people or teenagers in search of a challenge.

How then can we approach walking and create environments that make people want to walk, or even make them walk more without being aware of it? This is the goal of most of the actors in urban planning, public health, and the multitude of actors associated with sustainable development. The overview of research, approaches, and methods to approach walking, the walker, and the walking environment, even if fundamental determinants are identified, shows that the influence of perceptions on walking or other mobility choices should not be ignored. Walking may be a choice, but the opportunity provided by another mode of transport to "walk" during the trip or at the destination should not be overlooked. The distinction between walking and other active modes of transport then becomes meaningful, as does the accessibility and quality of the destinations available to the population. We emphasize here the complexity associated with developing urban interventions capable of supporting walking.

On the one hand, a number of criteria of the built environment favorable to walking at the city scale are present and can even be unanimously agreed upon. These criteria, which overlap with the so-called "3 Ds" (diversity, density, and design), are relatively well articulated for urban designers and other planners. Urban walkability audits are exemplary in this respect for creating knowledge to improve specific criteria – or combinations of criteria. They are detailed and often very specific, as they incorporate microlevel criteria at the level of the walker. That said, the number of criteria and their relevance in isolation limit their scope for planning intervention, this time at the urban scale.

Moreover, such approaches conceptualize walking and the walking environment on a scale where it is difficult to take into account the walker and what can constitute for him, in all its diversity, an atmosphere favorable to walking. Many spaces have been designed with exemplary walkability, without having any real impact on walking itself, such as several residential developments that are based on the principles of new town planning. These environments incorporate all of the criteria for walkability on paper, but in practice can be living environments lacking in character and atmosphere, with few utilitarian destinations, such as retail, meeting services, or recreation.

On the other hand, we try, often with great technical or subjective precision, to approach and reproduce the components of the walker's experience on their scale. But this poses a double challenge. Firstly, a microscale, which is inevitable in the analysis of familiar and intimate relationships of person–environment interactions, prevents these approaches from being used on a large territory such as the neighborhood scale, or even on the scale of large urban projects and their interfaces in their environment of insertion. Secondly, the factors taken into account in the analyses of the subjectivity of the walker are contextualized (e.g., culturally, socially, temporally, etc.). Their usefulness in informing intervention in different, varied, or contrasting settings raises issues of transferability or potential social acceptance.

Many good urban design projects, especially those that focus on pedestrianization or on sharing the street between different users, do not resonate with the preferences of many Canadian or American residents, even for those living in central areas, even though they are often the norm for European cities. The commitment to alternative forms of travel, especially the difficulties posed by sprawling urban forms or topographical and climatic constraints, poses the limits of what planners, often constrained by political and democratic imperatives, can actually accomplish.

What then is the role of developers and planners in relation to walking? A number of perspectives can be put forward, including that of considering walking as the primary mode of travel. Walking is everywhere, in all modes of travel, but, as we have seen in this chapter, its integration into the city is often carried out in opposition to other ways of getting around. Environments are analyzed for walkers, they are now designed for walking, or they are concerned with the aspirations and preferences of exclusive pedestrians. However, car drivers could walk more at their destination, as could cyclists and public transit users, the latter walking along the way. It would seem appropriate to incorporate walking, and the environments that result from it, into analyses of walkability. It is therefore in the search for opportunities to walk along the mobility chain that it seems worthwhile to look, particularly for the sprawling cities of the New World, and even for several of the new European suburban dwellings. While walking and the walker are increasingly well known, what about walking opportunities from the point of view of environments and temporalities?

Should developers and planners, through their development projects, seek to produce contexts that encourage the emergence of rich walking spaces offering a variety of walking experiences? The challenge is not so much to understand the technical dimensions as to understand the diversity of points of view on mobility and the city. The perspective of the co-construction of space, contributing to the walker's experience, appears relevant here. We should then be interested in how to integrate different profiles of walkers into urban projects, rather than producing environments that will probably make people walk. It is a question of encouraging the emergence of a diversity of experiences, by taking into account what is perceived and felt, in development projects. This is certainly present in the design concepts of the projects, but the contribution of citizens, all walkers to varying degrees, bringing both an experiential perspective and evidence could improve the perspective.

The recent work on urban atmosphere and its consideration in the development projects offers a stimulating framework for addressing the sensitive dimensions of the walking experience and for encouraging their translation into criteria or development methods that are conducive to walking. This could be achieved by developing a field of knowledge on mixed approaches to walkability, favoring interdisciplinarity, in order to develop planning solutions based on problems to be solved in their context. It would be a question of increasing the exploration of strategies for taking into account the atmosphere, perhaps more than the search for determinants, so as to develop urban intervention projects consistent with the walker.

5.5. References

Alcântara de Vasconcellos, E. (2004). The use of streets: A reassessment and tribute to Donald Appleyard. *Journal of Urban Design*, 9(1), 3–22.

Amar, G. (1993). Pour une écologie urbaine des transports. *Les Annales de la Recherche Urbaine*, 141–151.

Apparicio, P., Gelb, J., Mathieu, M.E. (2019). Un atlas-web pour comparer l'exposition individuelle aux pollutions atmosphérique et sonore selon le mode de transport. *Cybergeo : European Journal of Geography*, 903 [Online]. Available at: http://journals.openedition.org/cybergeo/32391.

Augoyard, J.-F. (1995). L'environnement sensible et les ambiances architecturales. *Espace géographique*, 24(4), 302–318.

Augoyard, J.-F., Delétré, J.-J., Blauert, J., Jouenne, P., Dabat, M.-A., Mathys, J., Bénichou, F., Kilberge, M., Lunven, T., Efthymiatos, D. (eds) (1992). La qualité sonore des espaces habités/Sonic quality in the living environment. *HAL*, 379.

Boarnet, M.G., Day, K., Alfonzo, M., Forsyth, A., Oakes, M. (2006). The Irvine-Minnesota inventory to measure built environments: Reliability tests. *American Journal of Preventive Medicine*, 30(2), 153–159 [Online]. Available at: doi:10.1016/j.amepre.2005.09.018.

Bosselmann, P. (2018). Kevin Lynch and his legacy on teaching professional planners and designers. *Journal of the American Planning Association*, 84(3/4), 284–292.

Brookfield, K., Ward-Thomson, C., Scott, L. (2017). The uncommon impact of common environmental: Details on walking in older adults. *International Journal of Environmental Research and Public Health*, 14 [Online]. Available at: doi:10.3390/ijerph14020190.

Cervero, R. and Kockelman, K. (1997). Travel demand and the 3Ds: Density, diversity, and design. *Transportation Research*, 2(3), 199–219.

Chelkoff, G. (2001). Formes, formants et formalités : catégories d'analyse de l'environnement urbain. In *L'espace urbain en méthodes*, Grosjean, M. and Thibaud, J.-P. (eds). Éditions Parenthèses, Marseille.

Clifton, K.J., Smith, A.D.L., Rodriguez, D. (2007). The development and testing of an audit for the pedestrian environment. *Landscape and Urban Planning*, 80, 95–110.

Delétré, J.-J. (2004). Quel rôle les mesures physiques peuventelles jouer dans la compréhension des ambiances architecturales et urbaines? In *Ambiances en débats*, Amphoux, P., Chelkoff, G., Thibaud, J.-P. (eds). Éditions à la Coiseé, Paris.

Dupuy, G. (1999). *La dépendance automobile*. Economica, Paris.

Ewing, R. (2008). Characteristics, causes, and effects of sprawl: A literature review. In *Urban Ecology*, Marzluff, J.M., Shulenberger, E., Endlicher, W., Alberti, M., Bradley, G., Ryan, C., Simon, U., ZumBrunnen, C. (eds). Springer, Boston.

Ewing, R., Clemente, O., Handy, S.L., Brownson, R.C., Winston, E. (2005). Identifying and measuring urban design qualities related to walkability. *J. Phys. Act. Health*, 3(s1).

Fenton, G., Glorieux, A., Letesson, Q., Minnen, J. (2020). *Centre-ville, piétonnisation et modes de vie*. Brussels Studies Institute/Brussels Centre Observatory, Brussels.

Frank, L.D., Andresen, M.A., Schmid, T.L. (2004). Obesity relationships with community design, physical activity, and time spent in cars. *Am. J. Prev. Med.*, 27(2), 87–96. DOI: 10.1016/j.amepre.2004.04.011.

Frank, L.D., Sallis, J.F., Saelens, B.E., Leary, L., Cain, K., Conway, T.L., Hess, P.M. (2009). The development of a walkability index: Application to the Neighborhood Quality of Life Study. *Br. J. Sports Med.*, 44, 924–933. DOI: 10.1136/bjsm.2009.058701.

Grasser, G., Van Dyck, D., Titze, S., Stronegger, W.J. (2016). A European perspective on GIS-based walkability and active modes of transport. *The European Journal of Public Health*, 27(1), 145–151.

Handy, S. (1992). *How Land Use Patterns Affect Travel Patterns*. Council of Planning Librarians, Chicago.

Husserl, E. (1992). *Méditations cartésiennes : introduction à la phénoménologie*. Vrin, Paris.

Joseph, I. (1984). *Le passant considérable : essai sur la dispersion de l'espace public*. Meridiens, Paris.

Lavadinho, S. (2013). Les hubs de vie : quelles opportunités pour faire la ville au-delà de la mobilité ? *Les cahiers du développement urbain durable*, 13, 93–120.

Leslie, E., Coffee, N., Frank, L.D., Owen, N., Bauman, A., Hugo, G. (2007). Walkability of local communities: Using geographic information systems to objectively assess relevant environmental attributes. *Health & Place*, 13, 111–122.

Lindell, M. and Ehrström, P. (2020). Deliberative walks: Citizen participation in local-level planning processes. *Eur. Polit. Sci.*, 19, 478–501 [Online]. Available at: https://doi.org/10.1057/s41304-020-00243-4.

Lord, S., Negron-Poblete, P., Torres, J. (eds) (2015). *Mobilité et inclusion, quelles relations ?* Presses de l'Université Laval, Quebec.

Lynch, K. (1981). *A Theory of Good City Form*. MIT Press, Cambridge.

Negron-Poblete, P. and Lord, S. (2014). Marchabilité des environnements urbains autour des résidences pour personnes âgées de la région de Montréal : application de l'audit MAPPA. *Cahiers de géographie du Québec*, 58(164), 233–257.

Osmond, P. (2005). Evaluating urban ambience: An investigation into quantifying the qualities of the walkable city. *The 6th International Conference on Walking in the 21st Century*, Zurich.

Paquot, T. (2006). *Des corps urbains : sensibilités entre béton et bitume*. Autrement, Paris.

Pérez López, R. (2015). Quand le piéton défie la ville : traverser la chaussée à Mexico. *Environnement urbain/Urban Environment*, 9 [Online]. Available at: https://doi.org/10.7202/1036213ar.

Raulin, F., Butzbach, C., Negron-Poblette, P., Poldma, T., Lord, S. (2020). Vers l'amélioration de la marchabilité de la ville pour tous. Retour d'expérience sur l'aménagement de l'accessibilité autour d'un centre commercial à Montréal. *Géocarrefour*, 94(4) [Online]. Available at: https://doi.org/10.4000/geocarrefour.13323.

Ravalet, E., Christie, D., Munafò, S., Kaufmann, V. (2014). D'un quartier à l'autre : analyse quantitative de la marche dans la Suisse urbaine. Report, École Polytechnique Fédérale de Lausanne, Lausanne.

Saelens, B.E., Sallis, J.F., Black, J.B., Chen, D. (2003). Neighborhood-based differences in physical activity: An environment scale evaluation. *American Journal of Public Health*, 93(9), 1552–1558.

Shatu, F. and Yigitcanlar, T. (2018). Development and validity of a virtual street walkability audit tool for pedestrian route choice analysis – SWATCH. *Journal of Transport Geography*, 70, 148–160.

Stickney, J. (2020). Philosophical walks as place-based environmental education. *Journal of Philosophy of Education*, 54, 1071–1086 [Online]. Available at: https://doi.org/10.1111/1467-9752.12469.

Thibaud, J.-P. (2013). L'énigme des ambiances en partage. *Ambiances urbaines en partage. Pour une écologie sociale de la ville sensible*, Thibaud, J.-P. and Duarte, C.R. (eds). Métis Presses, Geneva.

Thomas, R. (2004). Quand le pas fait corps et sens avec l'espace. Aspects sensibles et expressifs de la marche en ville. *European Journal of Geography Cybergeo*. DOI: 10.4000/cybergeo.4304.

Torres, J. (2012). Mobilité quotidienne et design urbain : la transposition du modèle Quartiers verts à Montréal. *VertigO* [Online]. Available: http://journals.openedition.org/vertigo/11773.

6

Residential Trajectories and Ways of Living: An Overview of France and Europe

Samuel CARPENTIER-POSTEL

Laboratoire ThéMA, CNRS, Université Bourgogne Franche-Comté, Besançon, France

6.1. Introduction

Contemporary social, economic, and spatial dynamics, such as the individuation of lifestyles (Viard 2012), the flexibilization of career paths, and the process of metropolization (Scott 2001), have contributed to significant changes in societies' relationship with space. These changes are reflected in the increasing complexity of mobility and residential trajectories of households, gradually giving rise to new ways of living, and notably new relationships with the places that individuals visit (Stock 2004). The recent period has thus seen the development of multiple spatial practices that reflect these changes: long commutes, dual residences, teleworking, and coworking, to name just a few (Gerber and Carpentier 2013).

While the emergence of new residential practices and new mobilities is part of the process of individuation and diversification of household trajectories, it is not without collective determinations, whether social or spatial. In this respect, the ability of an individual or household to position itself in the residential space partly conditions access to the economic and social resources of a territory and thus to the related opportunities. Residential trajectories and the associated daily mobility are thus more than ever a discriminating factor in social and life trajectories, particularly in a context of metropolitanization. Considered as a process of sociospatial selection, mobility partly reifies social positions in geographic space (Thomas 2013). Level of education, type of employment, age, household composition, and other social characteristics thus help define a set of preferences and possibilities that lead to residential choices that are largely constrained by generally tense urban real-estate markets, which exacerbate competition for the "best" places.

The contemporary societal challenges related to these residential trajectories are numerous. The most emblematic is probably that of the social fragmentation of spaces, particularly urban spaces, which raises the question of the coherence of the social fabric. Another major issue concerns intergenerational relations, insofar as the conditions of access to the housing market, and in particular to home ownership, have become more difficult in many cities due to the sharp rise in land and property prices. Finally, the articulation between career and residential trajectories raises questions about the new relationships between social and spatial mobility.

In this context, this chapter proposes an overview of contemporary dynamics relating to the residential trajectories of households and the resulting ways of living. To do so, we will first review the main theoretical and conceptual achievements of research on residential mobility, defined as "the change in a household's place of residence within a living area" (Rérat 2016). In particular, we will see how the classic models for analyzing socioresidential spaces, which stem from the pioneering work of the Chicago School sociologists (Park and Burgess 1925, pp. 47–62), must now be reexamined in the light of a new analytical grid that takes into account the diversity of individual and household configurations. Secondly, we will focus on an empirical analysis of residential mobility in France and Europe using data from population censuses to identify the main trends. In order to take this analysis further, we will then discuss emerging practices that articulate new forms of residential and daily mobility within new ways of living, as well as the conceptual and methodological challenges that their analysis implies.

6.2. Residential choice as social positioning

Because of the societal issues involved, residential mobility is currently attracting renewed interest in the social science research community. However, the question of residential locations and their evolution is an old issue, particularly in urban areas, which, because of their size, lead to the constitution of areas socially marked by the over- or underrepresentation of certain social groups.

6.2.1. *Classical models...*

Work on the residential organization of cities is generally traced back to the sociologists of the Chicago School. As early as the 1920s, they developed conceptual[1] models that sought to identify the structures and processes leading to the formation of what Timms (1971) described years later as an urban mosaic, i.e., the juxtaposition of socially differentiated neighborhoods.

Burgess (1925) was responsible for formulating the first explicative model. This was based on a concentric logic in which the categories of population were distributed unequally according to the distance from the center. This structuring by concentric zones was based in particular on a context of demographic growth, fueled at the time by the high level of immigration in their study area: the city of Chicago. This demographic growth and the urban sprawl that accompanied it led the sociologists of the Chicago School to quickly consider the dynamic nature of these residential structures. While, in the mind of Burgess, his concentric model aimed to explain the overall socioresidential structure, the numerous empirical studies that followed showed that this type of structuring is generally based on sociofamily characteristics, mainly reflecting the position in the life cycle and illustrating, in particular, the logics of urban growth that lead young families to look for available land in the suburbs.

In 1939, Homer Hoyt proposed a second model following a sectoral logic. Based on a critique of Burgess's model, he wanted to improve it by taking into account the effect of infrastructures and structuring axes linking the center to the peripheries, and thus the differentiated accessibilities that result from them. Once again, despite the attempts at a global explanation of this model, the statistical studies that have tested it have shown that it very often reflects the unequal socioresidential distribution of households according to their socioeconomic status, often approached by income and level of education. The structuring by sector thus reflects social inequalities in which the contact zones between the most distant categories on the social scale are minimized.

Later, in 1945, Chauncy Harris and Edward Ullman put forward a third model, this time based on the existence of multiple nuclei, in other words, secondary centralities in the surroundings of large cities. In many cases, this type of structuring of socioresidential space reflects, in addition to these secondary centralities, the existence of minorities who find a valuable social resource in the form of spatial grouping.

---

1 For a synthesis, an interested reader can consult Reymond (1997) and Antoni (2009).

While the pioneering work of the Chicago School sociologists was based on the collection of mainly qualitative data, particularly from the life stories of residents (Grafmeyer and Joseph 1979), the 1950s saw the emergence of the first quantitative work based on these theoretical foundations. Under the name of Social Area Analysis (Shevky and Bell 1955), and then factorial urban ecology (Berry and Kasarda 1977), numerous empirical analyses based on census data were conducted throughout the world to test the models of the Chicago sociologists. These analyses, repeated in different places and for different periods of time, have not validated a universal model of the social organization of cities. However, beyond the numerous regional variations, this research has revealed recurrent socioresidential structures that often combine the three basic models mentioned above (Abu-Lughod 1969; Reymond 1997).

By emphasizing the social specialization of neighborhoods according to socioprofessional categories, age groups, or ethnic groups, these studies highlight the unequal distribution of social categories in urban space. However, it is important to remember that "a natural area is never completely homogenous, and the city dweller's neighbor is not really his fellow man. In these conditions, physical proximity does not exclude social distance" (Park 1929). The unequal spatial distribution of social categories does not, therefore, usually reflect true segregation, although this term has been frequently used in this field (Apparicio 2000). However, recent research has identified that residential mobility currently often contributes to the reinforcement of socioresidential inequalities (Baker et al. 2016).

While the major models of socioresidential structuring are still relevant in explaining the distribution of the main population categories, the recent period has nevertheless been marked by a diversification of lifestyles leading to an increase in the variability of residential behavior (Thomas 2013, 2016). The diversification of family models and the flexibilization of professional careers are leading to an increase in the complexity of residential trajectories in which mobility is becoming a resource, if not an injunction, for social positioning (Scheiner and Kasper 2003).

6.2.2. ... to mobility turn

Following the linguistic turn, the cultural turn, and the spatial turn, the mobility turn proposes a new interdisciplinary analytical framework involving sociology, history, anthropology, geography, transport economics, and urban studies, to name but a few of the most involved disciplines (Faist 2013). Based on the observation of the rapid increase in all kinds of mobility, marking the advent of a network society (Castells 1996), many social science researchers are now advocating a renewed approach to social phenomena. The challenge is to understand the co-production of space and societies through the frequentation, the virtual or real co-presence of places.

Emblematic of this shift in mobility, the new mobility paradigm[2] (Sheller and Urry 2006) is in line with the work of Castells (1996) on the information and network society and the research of Zygmunt Bauman. Through the concept of "liquid modernity" (Bauman 2000), the latter describes societal evolutions that are more and more focused on the individual. For him, the progressive substitution of structures by networks reflect the weakening of social ties; society is thus moving from "solid" structures to "liquid" networks. This weakening of large collective structures in favor of an individuation of lifestyles is a major social fact, which has an impact on all dimensions of social life (family, employment, social participation, etc.) and especially on mobility.

In this respect, mobility, especially long-distance mobility, and enrolment in networks become a powerful instrument of social distinction, with hypermobile elites when the rest of the population remains more strongly circumscribed to a local base. This trend is in line with the writings of Giddens (1990) on the consequences of modernity, where the postmodern society implies a new relationship with time and space (whose friction tends to be reduced).

Although it originated in sociology, the new mobilities paradigm intends to go beyond classical disciplinary divisions by deploying an interdisciplinary approach that takes into account the social dimension (particularly social inequalities), the spatial dimension (mobility territories), and the sociocognitive dimension (particularly values). In doing so, it tends to blur the analytical categories separating social and geographic mobility, short- and long-distance mobility, and linear and cyclical mobility. From this perspective, the question of residential mobility should be placed in a broader set of practices, norms, and values, and in relation to other forms of mobility, whether spatial, such as daily mobility, or social.

Based on this conceptual foundation, section 6.3 will first present empirical analyses of residential mobility in French and European cases. Firstly, it will illustrate the general trends in the structuring of these mobilities according to the geographical, sociodemographic, and socioeconomic determinants linked to individuals.

---

2 For a synthesis of the work from this research stream, the interested reader can consult Belton-Chevallier et al. (2019).

6.3. Elements of analysis of residential mobility in France and Europe

The residential mobility data used in this section to illustrate the French case are taken from the detailed residential migration files (*Migrations résidentielles*) for the year 2016 provided by INSEE[3]. These files, derived from the population census, provide for a sample of more than 18 million individuals, the municipality of residence in 2016, the municipality of residence in 2015, as well as a set of descriptors relating to the individual, households, and their residential trajectory. A weighting variable is used to obtain an estimate of the variables for the entire French population (nearly 66 million individuals). To put the French case in perspective, Eurostat data, which is based on the various national statistical institutes, is used. On the subject of residential mobility, the latest date for which harmonized data between countries are available, at the time of writing, is 2012.

6.3.1. *General spatial dynamics of residential mobility*

Between 2015 and 2016, approximately 7.2 million people (or 11% of the population) moved home, according to INSEE data. This mobility rate puts France slightly above the European average of 9%, established for the year 2011 (CGET 2018).

From a geographical point of view, the first structuring logic of these mobilities, in the French case, is that of a form of stability, insofar as 34% of people who moved did not change their municipality of residence (Figure 6.1). An analysis of these residential moves, according to the INSEE's urban area zoning[4], makes it possible to identify the underlying geographical logic from the point of view of urban[5] structure. The main finding is, once again, that there was a form of stability insofar as many moves took place within the same urban area.

---

3 See www.insee.fr/fr/statistiques/4171543?sommaire=4171558.
4 For a description of the urban area zoning methodology, the reader may consult: www.insee.fr/fr/statistiques/1281191#documentation.
5 There are also logics of regional differentiation of residential mobility that will not be addressed here. The interested reader can consult the CGET report (2018) on this subject.

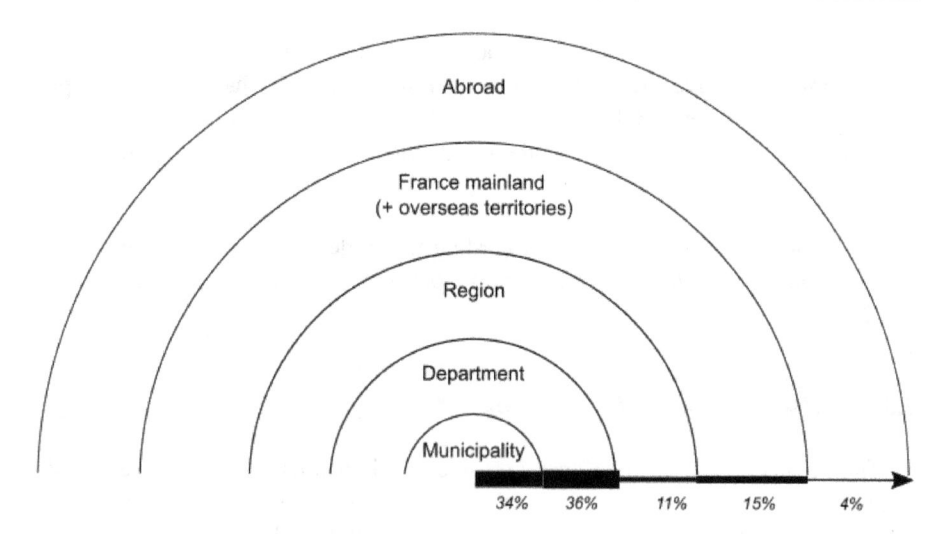

Residential Trajectories and Ways of Living: An Overview of France and Europe 113

[Diagram: Concentric arcs labeled from outer to inner: Abroad, France mainland (+ overseas territories), Region, Department, Municipality. Below, percentages along an arrow: 34%, 36%, 11%, 15%, 4%.]

Figure 6.1. *Distribution of residential migration of the French population by destination (source: (INSEE 2016), author's calculations)*

Beyond this finding, it appears that many individuals preferred to move to the same type of municipality as the one where they previously resided. For example, nearly 84% of inhabitants of major centers (municipalities with 10,000 or more jobs) who moved between 2015 and 2016 did so within a municipality belonging to a major center, whether it was the same urban area or a move between two separate urban areas (Table 6.1). However, this proportion tends to decrease for peripheral areas, with 54% for residential mobility involving a municipality belonging to the periphery of a major center as both the municipality of origin and the municipality of destination, and 43% for the multipolarized municipalities of urban area centers.

	Share of moves between municipalities in the same category
Urban area center	83.7%
Urban periphery	54%
Multipolarized municipality of large urban areas	43%

Table 6.1. *Proportion of moves within each type of type of municipality (source: (INSEE 2016), author's calculations)*

In Europe, residential mobility also varies according to the type of municipality. The largest cities have the highest mobility rate, with more than 21% of people having moved between 2008 and 2012 (Eurostat), compared with just over 17% for secondary cities and the surroundings of cities and only 13.5% for rural municipalities.

This gradation of mobility rates according to the degree of urbanization is also true for France, with 30.2% for large cities, 26.4% for secondary cities and suburbs, and 23.1% for rural municipalities (Eurostat 2012).

6.3.2. *Differentiation by life course*

The census data used here does not give any indication of life-course events. Otherwise, age classes can be used as a proxy for this dimension. Firstly, when we look simply at the propensity to move by age, we see that the share of individuals who have moved in the past year varies strongly with age (Figure 6.2). Young adults have the highest rates (the maximum is 27.6% for 20–24 year olds, followed closely by 25–29 year olds with 27%), illustrating the major role of life-course events related to this age: parental decohabitation, entering a relationship, entry into working life, etc. At 2.8%, the minimum is reached for the 75–79 age group, but in older age, this rate rises slightly, illustrating this time mobilities linked to the gradual loss of autonomy that affects a significant number of individuals.

In Europe, analysis of residential mobility rates by age group shows results similar to those observed for France. Focusing on the working-age population, we see that working people aged 15 to 29 accounted for 44% of workers who moved in 2012. This proportion drops to 39% for those aged 30–49 and to less than 11% for those aged 50–64. The decreasing gradation of values according to age observed in France is thus confirmed at the EU level.

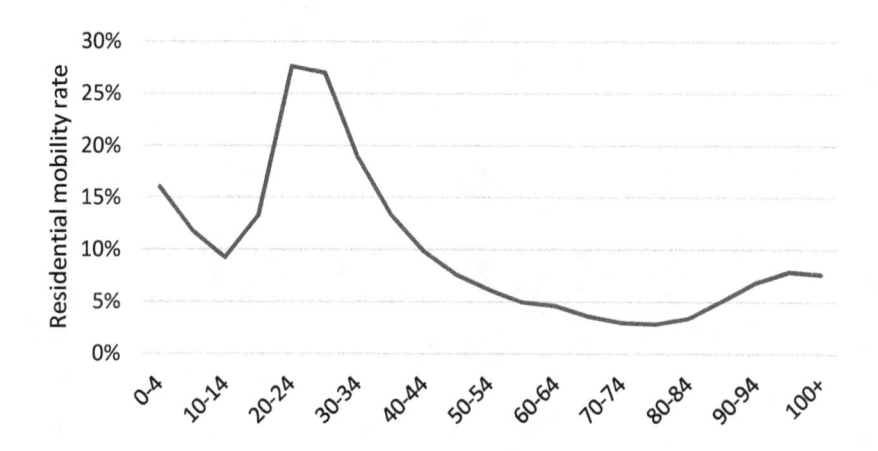

Figure 6.2. *Residential mobility by age group (source: (INSEE 2016), author's calculations)*

Beyond levels of mobility, there are also strong age differences in where people move to (Figure 6.3). Young people are much more attracted to urban areas than older people, either due to preference or necessity. For example, nearly 74% of 15–24 year olds who moved in the previous year moved to a municipality belonging to a major center[6], compared with only 53% of 60–64 year olds (the least urban category in this respect). Conversely, only 2.6% of 20–24 year olds moved to an isolated municipality outside the influence of the centers, while this rate rose to 7.7% for 60–64 year olds. This last age category illustrates residential choices frequently linked to retirement, which, as has already been shown elsewhere, coincide for a significant proportion of individuals with a change of region (CGET 2018).

---

6 It is worth noting that some of them were already living there previously.

Figure 6.3. *Settlement area by five-year age groups (source: (INSEE 2016), author's calculations). For a color version of this figure, see www.iste.co.uk/drevon/mobility.zip*

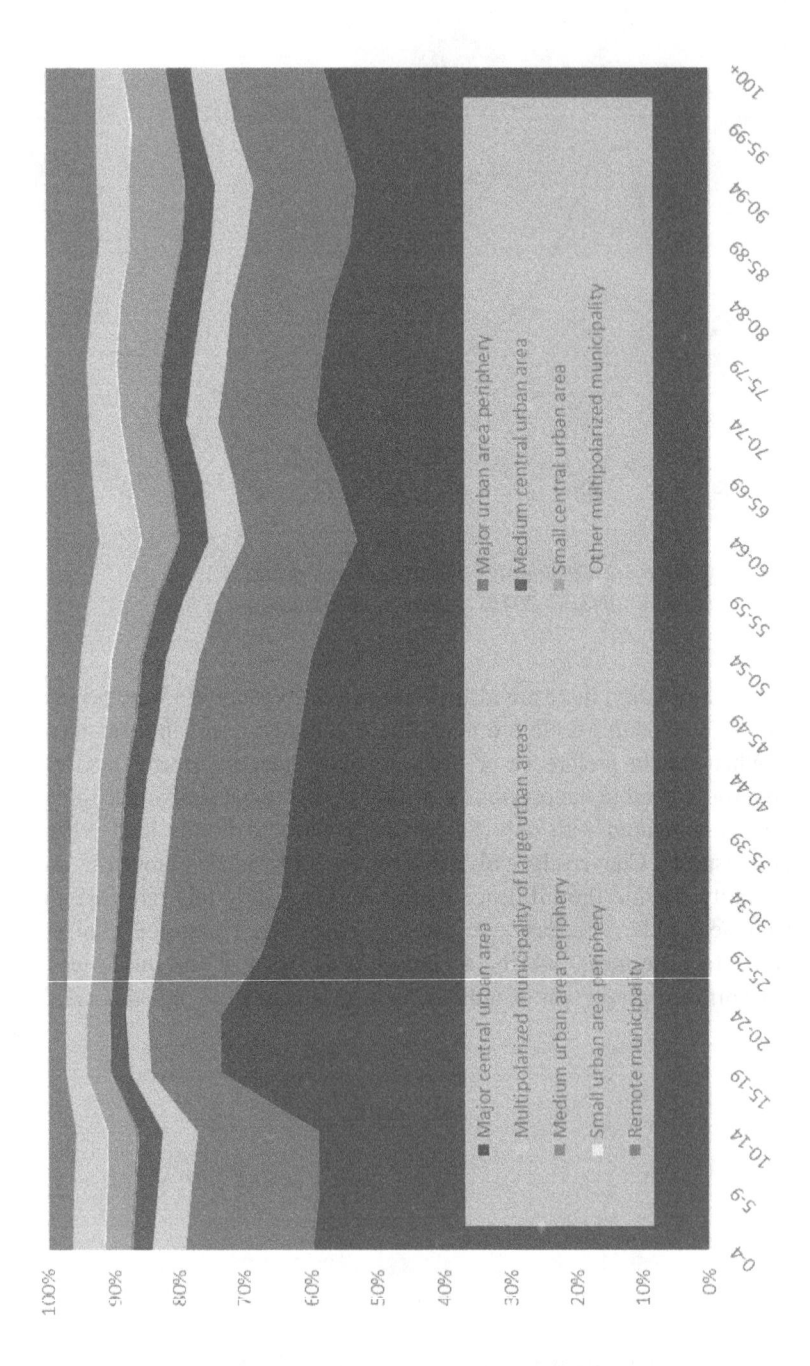

Such an approach by age group allows us to draw up a general overview within which, however, some blind spots remain from the point of view of life courses. From this point of view, we can cite, for example, the case of single-parent families, whose residential trajectories have been characterized as "imposed" by recent surveys conducted in seven Ile-de-France neighborhoods undergoing renovation (Lelévrier 2016).

6.3.3. *Differentiation by social position*

The observation of residential mobility levels according to the typology of socioprofessional categories (Figure 6.4) shows a differentiation of profiles. The highest rates, with nearly 14%, correspond to the categories of executives, intermediate professions, and employees, followed by laborers at nearly 13%. This rate is higher than the national average (11%), thus showing the impact of salaried employment on mobility.

The self-employed, on the other hand, have significantly lower rates. With 4.3%, farmers are the category with the fewest moves, as suggested by the very nature of their activity, which is linked to localized operations. Craftsmen, merchants, and business owners also have a lower rate than employees, at just under 10%.

People who are not in the labor force reflect sharply contrasting situations. On the one hand, retirees have a low residential mobility rate of less than 4%, as the previous analysis by age group suggested. On the other hand, the rate for other nonworking people is relatively high (12.6%), which is close to the rates observed for employees.

In a complementary manner, the intersection of levels of education and residential mobility rates also shows a clear differentiation of profiles (Figure 6.5).

Here, the observation is simple: the higher the level of education, the greater the mobility for the group in question. This finding is consistent with the interpretations concerning residential trajectories linked to less linear career paths, particularly for the most highly educated. It also illustrates the fact that the most highly educated seem more inclined or more forced to move than the rest of the population.

118   Mobility and Geographical Scales

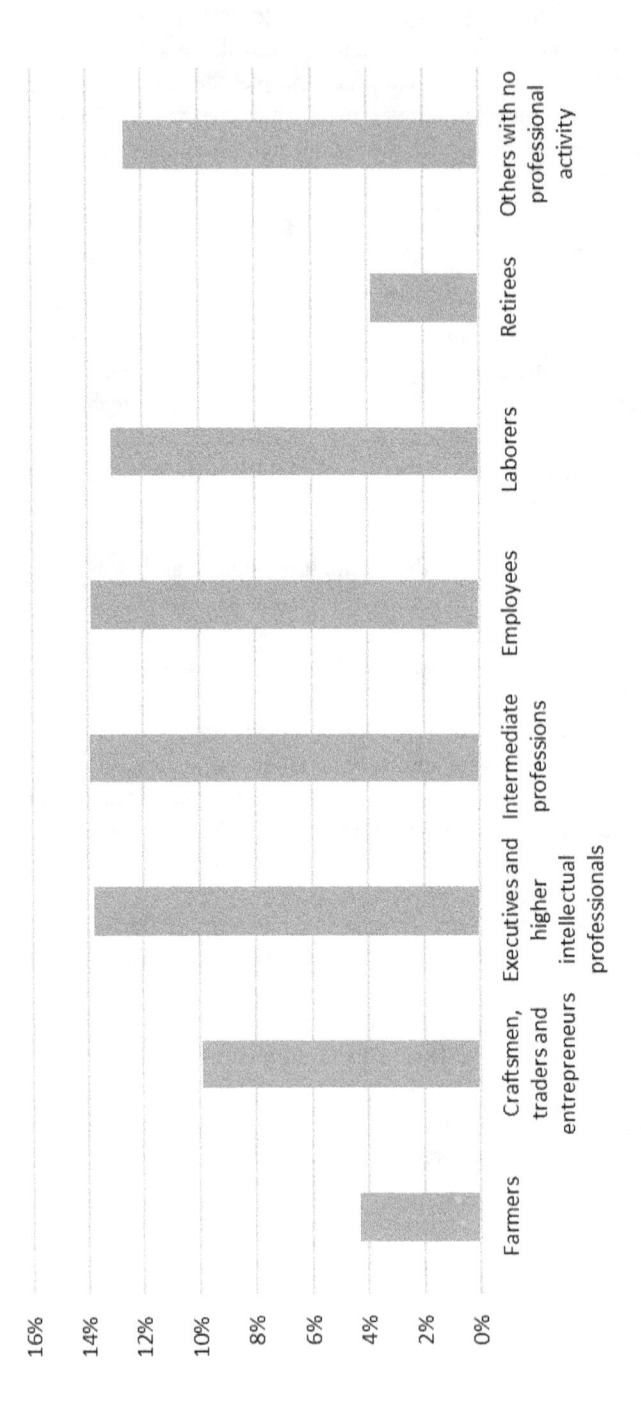

Figure 6.4. *Residential mobility rates by socio-professional category (source: (INSEE 2016). author's calculations)*

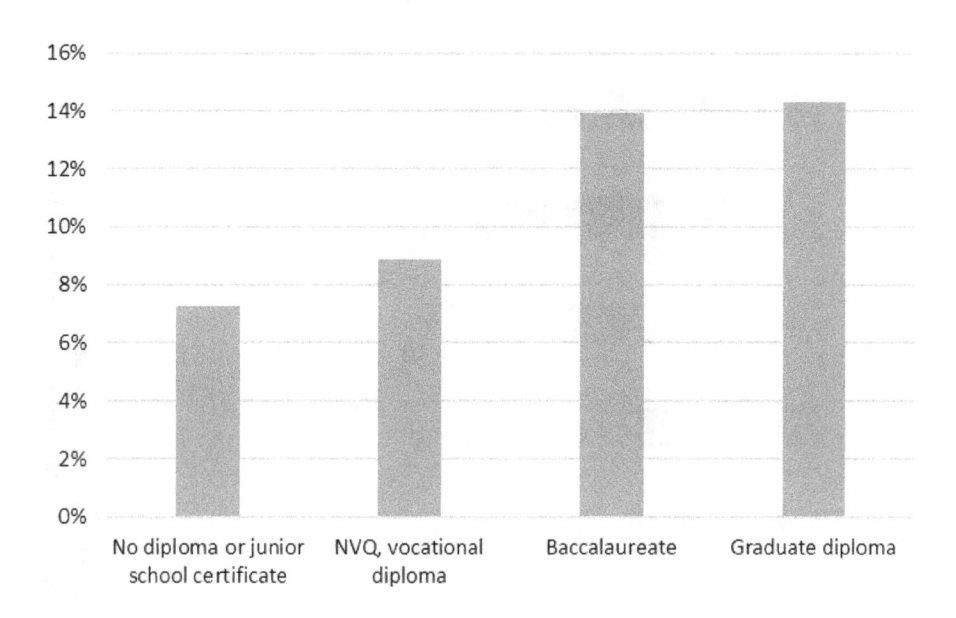

Figure 6.5. *Residential mobility rates by level of education (source: (INSEE 2016), author's calculations)*

If we now look at the sectors of activity of the individuals, the figures available for Europe show a differentiation of mobility rates. Some sectors of activity have an overrepresentation of their workers among those who moved in the previous year. For example, while individuals working in trade, transport, hotels, and restaurants represented 23% of the workforce in 2012, they accounted for nearly 25% of the workforce that moved in the previous year. Conversely, people working in the industrial sector represented nearly 17% of the active population but only 13% of those who moved (Eurostat 2012).

In France, the social differentiation of mobility, like what we observed for age groups, is expressed beyond mobility levels alone. Residential trajectories also differ according to the type of living places involved (Figure 6.6). Managers and university graduates are the categories that prefer to move to the major urban centers. Here, the impact of metropolization, which concentrates a certain number of tertiary activities in the largest urban areas, is clearly felt. Conversely, blue-collar workers and individuals with few qualifications are less likely to move to the city. These figures provide a good illustration of the contribution of residential mobility to the unequal distribution of social categories in geographic space.

120 Mobility and Geographical Scales

Figure 6.6. *Settlement area by socio-professional categories and degree levels (source: (INSEE 2016), author's calculations). For a color version of this figure, see www.iste.co.uk/drevon/mobility.zip*

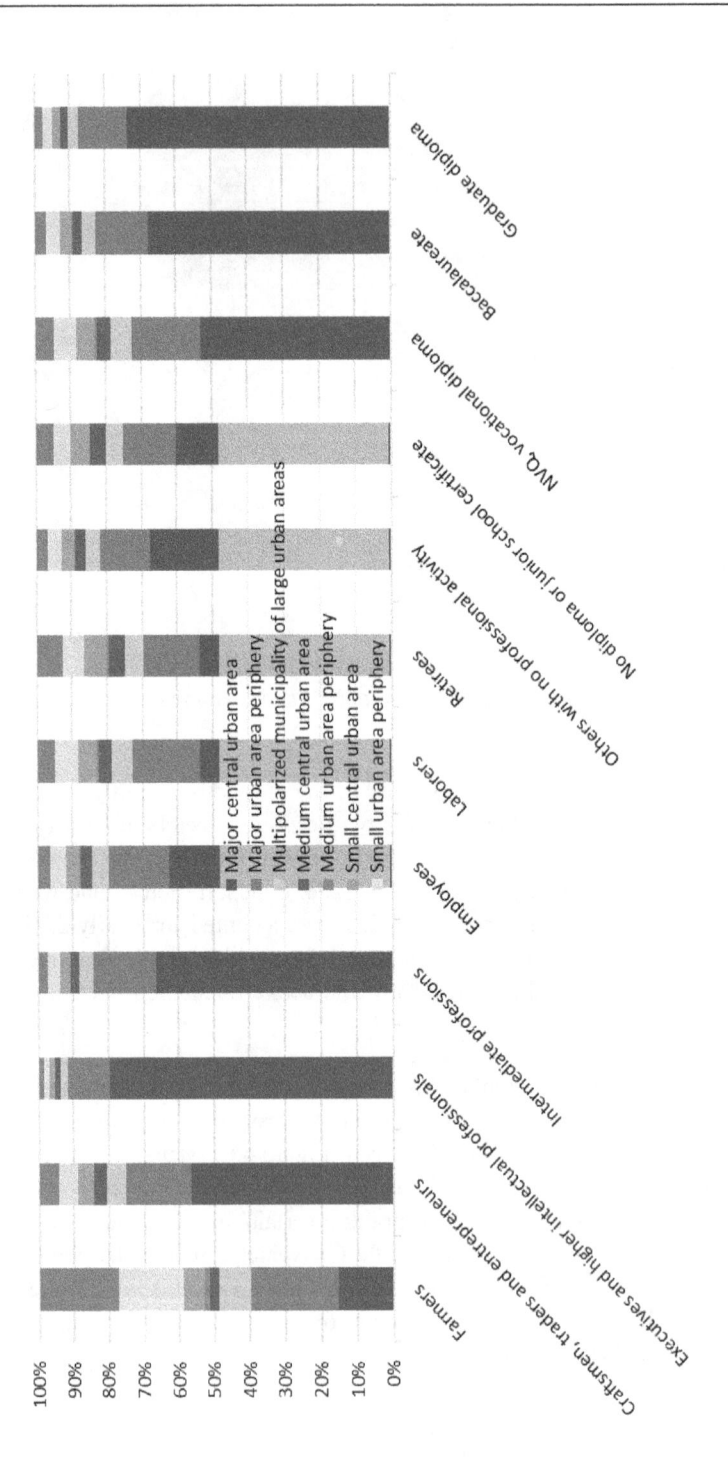

At the end of this section, the use of census data has enabled us to produce a brief overview of the major spatial, demographic, and social dynamics linked to residential mobility, thus highlighting the various logics of the social segmentation of geographic space. While useful, this overview is far from exhaustive. Indeed, while census data have the advantage of being highly representative (and even locally exhaustive), they have several drawbacks in the analysis of contemporary residential movements. The first is the limited number of variables describing individuals and households, which are all possible determinants of mobility behavior. The use of variables such as socioprofessional categories may, in fact, raise questions in a context where the feeling of belonging to a social class tends to decrease (Rémy and Voyé 1992). The second is the absence of surveys of opinions and preferences that would make it possible to move away from approaches that are still very objectivist from this point of view. The third, and not least, is that the census data do not allow for very detailed monitoring of the spatial, professional, and personal trajectories of individuals.

However, given the importance of life-course events in the choice of location, a biographical and therefore longitudinal approach, like the one initiated in the 1980s at the French Institute for Demographic Studies – Ined (Courgeau 2020), is needed to extend and deepen these global analyses.

6.4. Discussion and perspectives: toward new ways of living

This last section aims to present recent advances as well as current theoretical and methodological debates in the study of residential mobility behaviors. Starting with a review of recent works and emerging practices, we will conclude with an opening on the need to develop comprehensive and biographical approaches.

6.4.1. *Multifaceted emerging practices*

The previous analysis, using census data, does not, as we have seen, make it possible to grasp the overall context that leads a household to make a particular residential choice. That being said, it masks, behind the major trends, the multiplicity of personal situations and the resulting residential trajectories. To go further, an examination of recent literature on mobility makes it possible to identify few variations of these emerging ways of living. This work is in line with the new mobility paradigm, mentioned in the first part of this chapter, and thus contributes to a decompartmentalization of the analysis of the various forms of mobility. They allow for a better understanding of the relationships between residential and daily mobility, as well as between spatial and social mobilities.

Among the developing phenomena, long commutes are undoubtedly the most well-documented. As part of the development of rapid modes of transport, and very often accompanied by a significant increase in travel time budgets, this type of living is based on the consent to travel long distances each day to reach a distant workplace. In the literature, we find various terms to describe this category of people whose daily commuting time often exceeds two hours: long commuters or mega-commuters (Rapino and Fields 2013), to name just a few. This type of arrangement is based on a singular transaction where very intense daily mobility serves to maintain a stable residential location. This is the case, for example, for many cross-border workers who accept long commutes in order to benefit from better salaries abroad while enjoying lower real-estate prices in their home country, as can be observed around Luxembourg or Switzerland (Pigeron-Piroth and Wille 2019).

More generally, the development of long commutes is partly related to a form of insecurity in contemporary career paths, making relocation for professional reasons too uncertain in terms of the constraints it may impose, particularly in terms of disruption of the socialization network (Vincent-Geslin and Ravalet 2016). Quantitatively, the share of long commuters in France has tended to increase significantly (+35% between 2008 and 2013 according to the French National Institute of Statistics and Economic Studies (INSEE) for individuals with commutes of more than 200 km)[7], but the individuals concerned rarely make this a long-term practice (Ravalet et al. 2015). Sociologically, a variety of profiles exist, although an overrepresentation of men and managers can be identified (Ravalet et al. 2015). At the European level, the average duration of daily trips varies greatly between countries. Overall, Western and Northern European countries have higher travel times, with, for example, 89 minutes per day in Luxembourg, 83 minutes in France and the Netherlands, compared with only 52 minutes in Romania and 62 minutes in Greece (Harmonised European Time Use Survey 2010). If the analysis is reduced to commuting time only, France has the longest commuting time (CGET 2019).

Another form of contemporary way of living results in the occupancy of two (biresidentiality) or more dwellings (multiresidentiality) (Imbert et al. 2014). This situation translates into a variety of configurations ranging from the recreational use of a second home, the "pied-à-terre" located in the municipality of a place of work that is too far from the main home, or the "student room." In the latter two cases, it is also a matter of preserving a previous residential base, but, unlike the long commuters, by using a second residence rather than by travelling long distances every day. Relatively recent figures show significant differences by region and social[8] category. For example, retirees and students are most affected by the

---

[7] www.insee.fr/fr/statistiques/2019022.
[8] www.insee.fr/fr/statistiques/1285854.

phenomenon: the former for study reasons and the latter for recreational purposes. Geographical differences are also apparent. People living in the other regions who have a second home in Île-de-France do so mainly for work reasons; conversely, people living in Île-de-France who have a second home in the other regions do so mainly for leisure reasons (INSEE 2011).

Another form of emerging practice, aiming at better reconciling residential choice and daily mobility, is illustrated by telework, defined in France by law n° 2012-387 of March 22, 2012 as *"any form of work organization in which work that could also have been carried out on the employer's premises is carried out by an employee away from these premises on a regular and voluntary basis, using information and communication technologies within the framework of an employment contract or an amendment thereto."* The strategy implemented this time is based on the minimization of the volume of mobility by substituting it with virtual mobility (telework). If the home is the main place for teleworking (64%[9]), other places are mobilized, such as offices provided by the employer (21%), coworking spaces (7%), or proximity networks (8%). Like the other forms of mobility mentioned so far, telework is a socially discriminated practice. While this phenomenon concerns 3% of working people at least 1 day a week, this rate rises to 11.1% among executives, compared to only 1.4% among employees and 0.2% among laborers (Dares-DGT-DGAFP 2017[10]). A Eurostat[11] study from 2018 shows great disparities in the practice of telework in Europe. Virtually absent in Romania or Bulgaria, for example, it concerns 14% of workers in the Netherlands and more than 13% in Finland. France is, according to the definition adopted by Eurostat, slightly above the European average (5.2%) with a value identical to that of Belgium (6.6%).

Beyond these generic situations, these different phenomena can of course be combined in complex forms. A frequent commuter may thus telework partly at home or on the train, as may a "multiresident." This hybridization of practices shows the limits of sectoral approaches to daily and residential mobility. Ways of living are part of spatial, social, and temporal dynamics that require them, as they become more complex, to adapt the conceptual and methodological frameworks for their analysis (Büscher and Urry 2009).

---

9 www.cget.gouv.fr/chiffres-teletravail-2016.
10 www.insee.fr/fr/statistiques/4238573.
11 www.ec.europa.eu/eurostat/fr/web/products-eurostat-news/-/DDN-20200206-1.

6.4.2. *Toward comprehensive and biographical approaches*

Recent work on daily and residential mobility has highlighted the need for approaches that take into account the various aspects of the daily life of households. Indeed, the factors that explain mobility behavior are numerous and relate to the different spheres of daily life: professional, social, family, and personal. These studies are therefore confronted with the question of whether geographical or social determinants are responsible for differences in travel behavior associated with residential locations.

In other words, are the observed behaviors mainly the result of various spatial configurations or of the unequal distribution of social categories in the residential space, inducing differences in lifestyles, preferences, and representations? This interdependence of explanatory factors, known as residential self-selection (Scheiner 2007; Van Acker et al. 2014), thus refers to the interweaving of sociospatial determinants. Recent studies adopting a multifactorial approach, integrating spatial, sociodemographic and sociocognitive attributes, show in particular that the weight of factors relating to daily mobility is relatively low in the residential choices of a large part of the population (Ettema and Nieuwenhuis 2017). In other words, behavioral differentiations are not mechanically due to individual and social differences alone, but rather reflect ecological dynamics specific to each type of residence. To overcome the conceptual and methodological pitfall of residential self-selection, theoretical proposals have recently been formulated that suggest considering mobility behaviors in their temporal depth, that of the life course, and no longer only in terms of cross-sections that reify positions (social, spatial) without taking trajectories into account. In particular, it is a question of going beyond a static approach to residential choice by substituting a dynamic approach to residential mobility (Dureau and Imbert 2014; Coulter et al. 2016).

The first theoretical framework, called the life-oriented approach (Zhang 2014, 2017), considers that residential mobility choices and the related daily mobility are the expression of more global life choices whose aim is to improve quality of life. In doing so, it tends to advocate a decompartmentalization of the various domains involved in the concept of quality of life (housing, transport, health, environment, etc.). Mobility behaviors, especially residential and daily, must then be understood not only in their interrelationships but also in a broader set of "life choices." This conceptual model implies a broad approach to the issue of residential self-selection, taking into account longer-term life choices involving all aspects of daily life.

From a methodological point of view, this implies adapting current surveys by not restricting them to mobility behaviors only. For example, Zhang et al. (2011)

have proposed nine main domains that allow for a comprehensive understanding of life choices and related quality of life: residence, household budget, health, neighborhood, education, employment, family life, leisure time, and mobility behaviors. Such a perspective makes it possible to address the compensatory effects of the various dimensions in the face of mobility choices that may sometimes appear restrictive. For example, recent studies have shown that strong overall residential satisfaction can compensate for marked dissatisfaction in terms of daily travel (Gerber et al. 2017). The notions of equilibrium, on which many economic models are based, appear to be in question. Indeed, analyzing mode choice for its own sake, for example, is to make that choice an end in itself. However, comprehensive studies show that these behaviors are the consequence of choices related to other spheres of daily life, including, but not limited to, the place of residence. This argues in favor of a transversal analysis of the different dimensions of living.

In parallel with the life-oriented approach, a convergent perspective called mobility biographies has developed in Germany, embodied in the work of Lanzendorf (2003) and Scheiner (2007). These works propose to place the analysis of mobilities in a longitudinal approach corresponding to the events of individuals' lives. The concept of the life cycle is no longer linked solely to residential mobility, but more broadly to all geographic mobility. This work is based particularly on the observation that the routinized dimension of a large part of daily mobility behaviors (Gärling et al. 1998) implies strong inertia. Since the constitution of routines is made necessary by the logic of cognitive load reduction, the question of behavioral change becomes difficult to address for this type of behavior. The various changes linked to the life cycle or to the career path of individuals are then considered as events conducive to the creation of conditions favorable to behavior change (Carpentier 2010; Scheiner 2014), insofar as they often coincide with residential movements that can modify the context in which lifestyles are deployed.

The interest of the biographical approach is thus catalyzed by the increasing complexity of individual trajectories linked to the societal transformations mentioned above: individuation of lifestyles, changes in family structures, flexibility of work, etc. The result is an increase in the number of events likely to trigger residential mobility and thus affect other mobility behaviors. The analysis of the determinants of mobility behavior must therefore be considered according to the periods of life and the events that mark them. Three complementary dimensions come into play to determine trajectories: events relating to household composition (marriage, birth, separation, death, etc.), events relating to the career path (finding and changing jobs, training, etc.), and the residential history (parental decohabitation, home ownership, etc.). Such a temporal approach to individual biographies (Drevon 2019) paves the way to identifying not only behavioral determinants but more specifically the determinants of behavioral changes.

6.5. Conclusion

Residential mobility is a concrete expression in geographic space of major socioeconomic changes that affect societies and individuals. In this respect, they constitute a valuable tool for analyzing contemporary societies, since they provide a tangible picture of the processes involved in the constitution of differentiated socioresidential areas and, through a form of homology, of the underlying social relationships. In this respect, the major sociodemographic and socioeconomic categories still partly condition residential histories and thus the social trajectories linked to them, as the analysis of French census data has shown. For example, the residential trajectories of the most highly educated people, especially those in managerial jobs, are influenced by the high concentration of service sector activities in the largest metropolitan areas. Conversely, a higher-than-average number of retirees leave cities for rural areas, where they aspire to find the kind of quality of life inherent to sparsely populated areas.

While, to a certain extent, classical models maintain a form of relevance for the analysis of global structures, the emergence of new ways of living has highlighted the need to change conceptual and methodological frameworks. The evolution of family structures or the flexibilization of professional careers tends to produce new ways of living in which the relationship with the place(s) of residence evolves. Thus, long commutes, dual residences, coworking, and telework are ways of spatializing lifestyles that question traditional analytical grids. While some forms, such as the long commute, tend to give an important part to daily mobility, others, such as coworking or telecommuting, tend on the contrary to minimize it. In both cases, the trade-offs break out of the classical pattern in which the choice of residence and the choice of workplace (when there is a choice) are made in a form of proximity, more or less respecting the time budget of one hour identified by Zahavi (1979).

Beyond the identification of more or less new ways of living, recent research has shown the changing nature of these configurations. The biographical and global analysis of geographical mobility – emphasizing the articulation of different trajectories: social, professional, family, spatial – is a promising theoretical perspective. It presupposes the evolution of methodological frameworks toward longitudinal biographical surveys, whose methods of implementation remain complex.

6.6. References

Abu-Lughod, J.L. (1969). Testing the theory of social area analysis: The ecology of Cairo, Egypt. *American Sociological Review*, 34(2), 198–212 [Online]. Available at: https://doi.org/10.2307/2092177.

Antoni, J.-P. (2009). *Lexique de la ville*. Ellipses, Paris.

Apparicio, P. (2000). Les indices de ségrégation résidentielle : un outil intégré dans un système d'information géographique. *Cybergeo : European Journal of Geography* [Online]. Available at: http://cybergeo.revues.org/12063.

Baker, E., Bentley, R., Lester, L., Beer, A. (2016). Housing affordability and residential mobility as drivers of locational inequality. *Applied Geography*, 72, 65–75 [Online]. Available at: https://doi.org/10.1016/j.apgeog.2016.05.007.

Bauman, Z. (2000). *Liquid Modernity*. Polity Press/Blackwell, Cambridge/Malden.

Belton-Chevallier, L., Oppenchaim, N., Vincent-Geslin, S. (2019). *Manuel de sociologie des mobilités géographiques*. Presses Universitaires François Rabelais, Tours.

Berry, B.J.L. and Kasarda, D. (1977). *Contemporary Urban Ecology*. Macmillan Publishing, New York.

Burgess, E.W. (1925). The growth of the city. An introduction to a research project. In *The City*, Park, R.E. and Burgess, E.W. (eds). The University of Chicago Press, Chicago.

Büscher, M. and Urry, J. (2009). Mobile methods and the empirical. *European Journal of Social Theory*, 12(1), 99–116 [Online]. Available at: http://doi.org/10.1177/1368431008099642.

Carpentier, S. (ed.) (2010). *La mobilité résidentielle transfrontalière entre le Luxembourg et ses régions voisines*. Saint-Paul, Luxembourg.

Castells, M. (1996). *The Information Age: Economy, Society and Culture: The Rise of the Network Society*, volume 1. Wiley-Blackwell, Malden.

CGET (2018). Les mobilités résidentielles en France : tendances et impacts territoriaux. Report, Observatoire des territoires.

CGET (2019). Se déplacer au quotidien : enjeux spatiaux, enjeux sociaux. Report, Observatoire des territoires.

Coulter, R., van Ham, M., Findlay, A.M. (2016). Re-thinking residential mobility. *Progress in Human Geography*, 40(3), 352–374 [Online]. Available at: http://doi.org/10.1177/0309132515575417.

Courgeau, D. (2020). L'enquête "Triple biographie : familiale, professionnelle et migratoire". In *Biographies d'enquêtes : Bilan de 14 collectes biographiques*, GRAB (ed.). Ined, Paris [Online]. Available at: http://books.openedition.org/ined/6573.

Drevon, G. (2019). *Proposition pour une rythmologie de la mobilité et des sociétés contemporaines*. Alphil/Presses Universitaires Suisses, Neuchâtel.

Dureau, F. and Imbert, C. (2014). L'approche biographique des mobilités résidentielles. In *D'une métropole à l'autre. Pratiques urbaines et circulations dans l'espace européen*, Imbert, C., Dureau, F., Dubucs, H., Giroud, M. (eds). Armand Colin, Paris.

Ettema, D. and Nieuwenhuis, R. (2017). Residential self-selection and travel behaviour: What are the effects of attitudes, reasons for location choice and the built environment? *Journal of Transport Geography*, 59, 146–155 [Online]. Available at: http://doi.org/10.1016/j.jtrangeo.2017.01.009.

Faist, T. (2013). The mobility turn: A new paradigm for the social sciences? *Ethnic and Racial Studies*, 36(11), 1637–1646 [Online]. Available at: http://doi.org/10.1080/01419870.2013.812229.

Gärling, T., Gillholm, R., Gärling, A. (1998). Reintroducing attitude theory in travel behavior research: The validity of an interactive interview procedure to predict car use. *Transportation*, 25(2), 129–146 [Online]. Available at: http://doi.org/10.1023/A:1005004311776.

Gerber, P. and Carpentier, S. (eds) (2013). *Mobilités et modes de vie : vers une recomposition de l'habiter*. Presses Universitaires de Rennes, Rennes [Online]. Available at: https://doi.org/10.4000/books.pur.34471.

Gerber, P., Ma, T.-Y., Klein, O., Schiebel, J., Carpentier-Postel, S. (2017). Cross-border residential mobility, quality of life and modal shift: A Luxembourg case study. *Transportation Research Part A: Policy and Practice*, 104, 238–254 [Online]. Available at: https://doi.org/10.1016/j.tra.2017.06.015.

Giddens, A. (1990). *The Consequences of Modernity*. John Wiley & Sons, New York.

Grafmeyer, Y. and Joseph, I. (1979). *L'école de Chicago. Naissance de l'écologie urbaine*. Aubier, Paris.

Harris, C.D. and Ullman, E.L. (1945). The nature of cities. *The Annals of the American Academy of Political and Social Science*, 242(1), 7–17 [Online]. Available at: http://doi.org/10.1177/000271624524200103.

Imbert, C., Deschamps, G., Lelièvre, É., Bonvalet, C. (2014). Vivre dans deux logements : surtout avant et après la vie active. *Population & Sociétés*, 507(1), 1–4.

Lanzendorf, M. (2003). Mobility biographies. A new perspective for understanding travel behaviour. In *10th International Conference on Travel Behaviour Research "Moving through nets: The physical and social dimensions of travel"*, Lucerne [Online]. Available at: http://webarchiv.ethz.ch/ivt/news/archive/20030810_IATBR/lanzendorf.pdf.

Lelévrier, C. (2016). La trajectoire, une autre approche des effets de la rénovation. In *Mobilités résidentielles, territoires et politiques publiques*, Fol, S., Miot, Y., Vignal, C. (eds). Presses universitaires du Septentrion, Lille [Online]. Available at: http://books.openedition.org/septentrion/3192.

Park, R.E. (1929). The city as a social laboratory. In *Chicago. An Experiment in Social Science Research*, Smith, T.V. and White, L.D (eds). The University of Chicago Press, Chicago.

Park, R.E. and Burgess, E.W. (1925). *The City*. The University of Chicago Press, Chicago.

Pigeron-Piroth, I. and Wille, C. (2019). Les travailleurs frontaliers au Luxembourg et en Suisse : emploi, quotidien et perceptions. Thematic notebook 2, Borders in Perspective [Online]. Available at: https://doi.org/10.25353/ubtr-xxxx-2824-db4c.

Rapino, M.A. and Fields, A.K. (2013). Mega commuters in the U.S.: Time and distance in defining the long commute using the American Community Survey. In *Association for Public Policy Analysis and Management Fall 2013 Conference*. 13.

Ravalet, E., Vincent-Geslin, S., Kaufmann, V., Viry, G., Dubois, Y. (2015). *Grandes mobilités liées au travail. Perspective européenne*. Economica, London.

Remy, J. and Voyé, L. (1992). *La ville : vers une nouvelle définition*. L'Harmattan, Paris.

Rérat, P. (2016). Mobilité résidentielle. *Forum Vies Mobiles* [Online]. Available at: https://fr.forumviesmobiles.org/reperes/mobilite-residentielle-3203.

Reymond, H. (1997). L'écologie urbaine factorielle : ce qu'elle est, ce qu'elle n'est pas. In *L'espace géographique des villes*, Reymond, H., Cauvin, C., Kleinschmager, R. (eds). Anthropos, Chippenham.

Rüger, H., Pfaff, S., Skora, T., Schneider, N.F. (2016). Job mobilities and family lives in Europe – Second wave: Panel data set & oversampling. *BiB Daten- und Metho-denbericht*, 3 [Online]. Available at: https://nbn-resolving.org/urn:nbn:de:bib-dmb-2016-036.

Scheiner, J. (2007). Mobility biographies: Elements of a biographical theory of travel demand. *Erdkunde*, 61(2), 161–173 [Online]. Available at: http://www.jstor.org/stable/25647982.

Scheiner, J. (2014). Residential self-selection in travel behavior: Towards an integration into mobility biographies. *Journal of Transport and Land Use*, 7(3), [Online]. Available at: http://doi.org/10.5198/jtlu.v7i3.439.

Scheiner, J. and Kasper, B. (2003). Modes de vie, choix de l'emplacement de l'habitation et déplacements quotidiens. *Revue internationale des sciences sociales*, 176, 355–369 [Online]. Available at: https://doi.org/10.3917/riss.176.0355.

Scott, A.J. (ed.). (2001). *Global City-Regions: Trends, Theory, Policy*. Oxford University Press, New York.

Sheller, M. and Urry, J. (2006). The new mobilities paradigm. *Environment and Planning A*, 38(2), 207–226 [Online]. Available at: http://doi.org/10.1068/a37268.

Shevky, E. and Bell, W. (1955). *Social Area Analysis*. Stanford University Press, Stanford.

Stock, M. (2004). L'habiter comme pratique des lieux géographiques. *Espacetemps* [Online]. Available at: http://www.espacestemps.net/articles/habiter-comme-pratique-des-lieux-geographiques/.

Thomas, M.-P. (2016). Les choix résidentiels : une approche par les modes de vie. In *Mobilités résidentielles, territoires et politiques publiques*, Fol, S., Miot, Y., Vignal, C. (eds). Presses Universitaires du Septentrion, Lille.

Timms, D. (1971). *The Urban Mosaic – Towards a Theory of Residential Differenciation*. Cambridge Geographical Studies, Cambridge.

Van Acker, V., Mokhtarian, P.L., Witlox, F. (2014). Car availability explained by the structural relationships between lifestyles, residential location, and underlying residential and travel attitudes. *Transport Policy*, 35, 88–99 [Online]. Available at: http://doi.org/10.1016/j.tranpol.2014.05.006.

Viard, J. (2012). *Nouveau portrait de la France : la société des modes de vie*. Éditions de l'Aube, La Tour d'Aigues.

Vincent-Geslin, S. and Ravalet, E. (2016). Determinants of extreme commuting. Evidence from Brussels, Geneva and Lyon. *Journal of Transport Geography*, 54, 240–247 [Online]. Available at: https://doi.org/10.1016/j.jtrangeo.2016.06.013.

Zahavi, Y. (1979). The UMOT project. Report, US Department of Transportation/ Ministry of Transport Fed. Rep. of Germany, Washington/Berlin [Online]. Available at: http://www.surveyarchive.org/Zahavi/UMOT_79.pdf.

Zhang, J. (2014). Revisiting residential self-selection issues: A life-oriented approach. *Journal of Transport and Land Use*, 7(3) [Online]. Available at: http://doi.org/10.5198/jtlu.v7i3.460.

Zhang, J. (ed.) (2017). Life-oriented approach. In *Life-Oriented Behavioral Research for Urban Policy*. Springer, Berlin [Online]. Available at: http://doi.org/10.1007/978-4-431-56472-0_1.

Zhang, J., Tsuchiya, Y., Fujiwara, A., Chikaraishi, M. (2011). Citizens' life decisions and behavior survey: Proposal and application to the evaluation of quality of life. *Proceedings of Infrastructure Planning*, 43.

7

City, State, Transnational Space: Scales and Multidisciplinary Approaches of Migrations

Garance CLÉMENT[1] and Camille GARDESSE[2]

[1] *Laboratoire de sociologie urbaine (LaSUR), École polytechnique fédérale de Lausanne, Switzerland*
[2] *Lab'Urba, École d'urbanisme de Paris, Champs-sur-Marne, France*

7.1. Introduction

In 1908, Georg Simmel described the "stranger" as one "who arrives one day and the next stays" (Simmel 2019, p. 13). For Amelina and Horvath (2017), it is through these two dimensions identified by the German sociologist – migration as movement and immigration as anchorage – that the field of migration studies was structured throughout the 20th century. Moreover, while some works focus on migration dynamics and their social effects, others deal primarily with migration policies and the control exercised over foreign populations (Amelina and Horvath 2017).

Without excluding one approach or another, this chapter allows us to move through landmark research in migration studies while pointing out more recent references and still emerging approaches. In doing so, it sheds light on the scientific issues that lead to the choice of one scale of analysis over another. The first part of the book takes stock of contemporary migration by breaking with a few myths and by distinguishing between interregional and international migration. The second part shows how new research paradigms have relativized the importance of the state as the preferred framework for analyzing migration. The third part is based on works that put the urban scale back at the center of their concerns in order to grasp migration phenomena, in a different perspective from the approach developed more than a century ago by the Chicago school of thought. Finally, the last part discusses the survey methods used to understand the different sociospatial facets of migratory phenomena.

7.2. Myths and realities of contemporary migration

Dictionaries generally define migration as a process by which individuals move to a new place to live[1]. While this can be seen as a "total social fact" (Bassand and Brulhardt 1983), its forms and the conditions in which it takes place vary greatly according to the regions of the world and the times. Demography and sociology have long distinguished between different types of migration according to the administrative and political boundaries crossed: those of the neighborhood, the city, the region, or international borders (Keely 2000). Far from being a history of migration, this section provides an overview of the major trends that marked the second half of the 20th century and came to characterize the contemporary "migration landscape" (Wihtol de Wenden 2001), distinguishing between interregional and international migration. This categorization, which considers that the crossing of state borders involves specific logics, is discussed in section 7.3, in the light of research paradigms that criticize precisely this statocentric approach.

7.2.1. *A majority of interregional migration*

Contrary to popular belief, on a global scale, international migration is four times smaller than regional migration (Bell et al. 2015). The latter is mainly explained by industrialization and urbanization dynamics, armed conflicts, and environmental disasters. According to the International Organization for Migration (IOM), in 2018, the share of the population living in mid-urban areas reached 55% compared to 30% in 1950. In 2019, there were 8.5 million forced[2] internal migrations due to conflict, mainly in Syria and the Democratic Republic of Congo, as well as 24.9 million due to natural disasters, mainly in India, the Philippines, Bangladesh, and China.

---

1 For example, the Cambridge Dictionary states, "the process of people travelling to a new place to live, usually in large numbers". The Larousse French dictionary states that it is "the voluntary movement of individuals or populations from one country to another or from one region to another, for economic, political, or cultural reasons".

2 According to the IOM, "a migratory movement which, although the drivers can be diverse, involves force, compulsion, or coercion" (IOM Glossary on Migration 2019).

Migration dynamics are also linked to changes in the territory's economic structures, which reconfigure the employment pools and the residential offer. They are part of individual and family life projects, formulated from different levels of constraint. As early as 1955, the sociologist Peter Rossi showed that there is a relationship between the family life cycle and household migration. Subsequently, models to explain migration have been refined, taking into account the extended environment and the diversity of life courses (Kulu and Milewski 2007).

Although data are lacking for assessing internal migration trends around the world more finely, authors have recently proposed "migration intensity" indicators[3] to characterize interregional movements (Bell et al. 2015). North America, Australia, and New Zealand emerge as hubs of high internal migration, while Asia experiences lower intensity movements (with the exception of South Korea and Japan). Some regions of the world, however, are characterized by significant internal disparities:

– in Africa, mobility hubs are identified in the east, west, and south of the continent;

– in Europe, the intensity of migration declines from north and west to south and east;

– in South America, it decreases from the Andes to Central America.

At the European level, a closer look at the geography of regional migration also shows that the model, according to which population flows are directed primarily toward the major metropolises, must be put into perspective, since an "urban rebalancing" can be observed in many states (Rowe and Patias 2020).

7.2.2. *More diversified and feminized international migration?*

According to the United Nations, the number of migrants[4] crossing national borders decreased from 250 million in 2000 to 214 million in 2018. However, only 3% of the world's population is involved, a figure that has been stable for the past 50 years or so (Haas et al. 2019)[5]. International migration, on the other hand, has

---

3 These indicators are constructed from the set of permanent address changes identified or projected in each country at 1- and 5-year intervals.
4 In this chapter, we will use the terms "migrants" and "immigrants" alternately, depending on the type of work and authors used. The importance of differentiating between these two terminologies is discussed in more detail below.
5 The increase in numbers can further be related to the increasing accuracy with which international movements are recorded, particularly with regard to asylum claims (Haas et al. 2019).

diversified since 1945, involving an increasing number of states (Haas et al. 2020). During the second half of the 20th century, Europe became the main region of arrival for migrants, but from the 1973 oil crisis onward, the Gulf countries and Libya, and then Asian countries such as the Philippines, Indonesia, Pakistan, and India, also emerged as major destinations, followed by East African states, mainly Eritrea and Ethiopia (Haas et al. 2019). However, the overall figures do not indicate a net increase in the distances traveled by migrants and show that in some regions of the world, flows have not so much diversified as reconfigured, particularly in South America and Sub-Saharan Africa. The prism of diversification would thus be primarily a Western-centric perspective to be put into perspective (Haas et al. 2019).

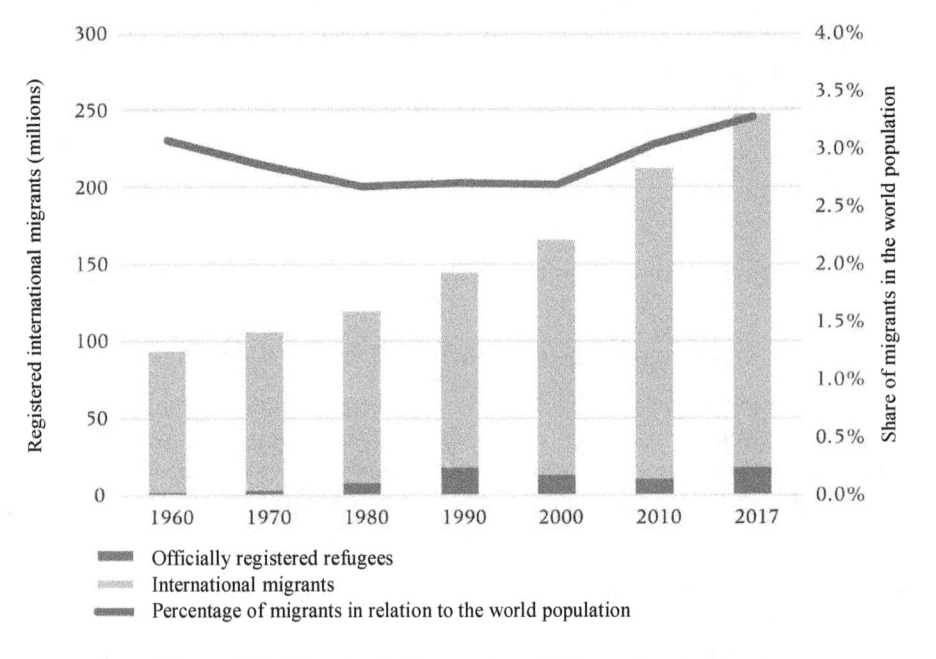

Figure 7.1. *Changes in the number of international migrants and refugees globally (source: Haas et al. (2019))*

This diversification corresponds rather to a European reality, insofar as the successive enlargements of the European Union have given rise to new migration patterns. Whereas it was mainly seasonal migration, movements from Eastern to Western European countries have given way to longer-term labor migration (Sert 2018). At the same time, research has paid attention to the migration of the most stigmatized and precarious populations in the European space, particularly the Roma (Potot 2016) and sex workers (Agustín 2006).

The theory of the "feminization" of migration, put forward in many publications, also deserves some qualification. Far from being a novelty, the participation of women in the migration phenomenon has been highlighted by statistics covering the entire 20th century (Gabaccia 2016). While the number of female migrants increased more rapidly than male migrants between 1960 and 2000, the trend was reversed thereafter, keeping women's share of total movement stable (at around 47%) and lower than that of men (Dumitru and Marfouk 2015).

However, another structural change in migration, in which women are significantly overrepresented, is the increase in educated migrant populations. While the demand for low-skilled workers has continued in the agricultural, construction, and personal service sectors, the social sciences have described the growing importance of movements of people designated as "highly skilled migrants" (Findlay and Gould 1989; Beaverstock 2005). Dumitru and Marfouk (2015) show that in 2010, "more than one out of every two migrants with higher education is a woman". While their influence is greater, women remain more often exposed to employment discrimination in the country of arrival. As the authors summarize: "In a way, the more a woman is born in a poor country, the more invisible her diploma is on the labor market". This work shows that a new approach to migration, marked by the intersectional paradigm (Amelina and Lutz 2020), is developing, attentive to the intersections of class, gender, and race in the analysis of migrations.

7.2.3. Deconstructing the European "migration crisis"

Finally, we turn to one last persistent belief about migrations, that the increase in arrivals has plunged Europe into a "migration crisis" in recent years. For Héran (2018), the crisis cannot describe a real imbalance in the European migratory balance, a situation that only occurred between 2015 and 2016, when the war in Syria began. This term sheds light on the inadequacy of reception arrangements in the various countries of the continent.

Let us look more precisely at the case of France, the oldest European country of immigration (Noiriel 1988). From the end of the 19th century, when border countries such as Belgium and Italy were experiencing strong emigration, France attracted their inhabitants in search of work. France's fertility rate was low at the time, but the demand for workers was growing due to the industrial boom and agricultural development. During the 20th century, particularly after the two world wars and during periods of economic growth, France confirmed its status as the leading country of immigration in Europe, organizing the arrival of thousands of workers with the establishment of national agencies such as the *Société générale d'immigration* and the *Office français d'immigration*. These public bodies implemented the recruitment of a foreign workforce. They recruited foreign workers according to the needs expressed by French business leaders in various sectors.

At the same time, immigrants increasingly came from countries colonized by France, both before and after their decolonization, to supply workers to sectors in need of them (Phan 2017). Since Algeria was a French department until 1962, mobility from that country was easier and developed rapidly (Temime 1999). After its independence, specific agreements were signed between the two countries to maintain this flexibility of movement (Laurens 2008). But these periods of great openness to immigration were followed by times when borders were closed and the conditions for entering and staying in the territory were hardened. This is the cyclical dimension highlighted by Noiriel (1988), which clearly shows the link between economic conditions, public management, and migratory flows. In this case, since the mid-1970s and the so-called economic crisis at the end of the *Trente Glorieuses* (30 years following the end of World War Two), France, like most European countries, has implemented a restrictive and increasingly secure migration policy.

In this context, current migratory flows to France do not appear to be quantitatively much greater than those observed throughout the 20th century. The proportion of immigrants in the French population has remained between 5% and 10%. If we now look at the migratory balance, that is, the difference between entries and exits from the territory over the past 30 years, we see that it has been fluctuating between 0.1% and 0.2% of the population (INSEE 2018). Other European countries have experienced the same cyclical movements of immigration of workers. This is the case, for example, for Belgium, which in the post-war period set up massive recruitment arrangements through bilateral agreements with other countries, and then sought to reduce immigration dramatically during the recession, particularly in the 1970s (Rea and Tripier 2008).

The history of immigration in Germany is also marked by the same processes, with a particular openness to refugees after the First World War and a public approach of having contracts with emigration countries (Turkey, Morocco, Portugal, Tunisia, Yugoslavia) after the Second World War, always with the aim of recruiting labor. Here, again, the economic crisis linked to the price of oil led Germany to put a stop to its migration policies. It was in 1992, after the fall of the Wall, that the number of immigrants in Germany peaked at nearly 1.2 million (Geddes and Scholten 2016). In 2015, thanks to a proactive policy of welcoming refugees, particularly Syrians, this figure reached 2.1 million, only to fall back to 1.6 million in 2019.

Italy is somewhat different from these countries in that it was initially a nation of emigration. However, since the end of the Second World War, its territory has been marked by the appearance of camps for displaced persons fleeing the repercussions of conflict, but also, from the 1950s onward, of refugees from the former Yugoslavia. At the same time, economic growth led Italy to recruit workers, whose settlement was only temporary. From the 1960s onward, the emigration of Italians decreased as internal movements, especially from the south to central and northern Italy, increased. Although the economic crisis of the 1970s also led to a decrease in arrivals, the flow of so-called economic immigration increased in the 1990s. After a decrease in immigration due to the crisis of 2008, the arrival of people wishing to seek asylum in Europe via the Mediterranean is once again making Italy a major immigration country (Colucci 2019).

In general, the increase in the flow of asylum seekers in 2015 and 2016 has subsided at the European level. This movement is largely the consequence of border control policies and arrangements implemented from European Union directives, particularly through Frontex, the European Coast Guard, and Border Agency (Tassin 2014, 2016).

In distinguishing between interregional and international migration, this chapter has started from a strong presupposition, that of determining the influence of state borders and the central role of the nation-state. In doing so, we have considered that movement from one country to another is a specific phenomenon, both in terms of the material conditions under which it is undertaken and its effects on social position. In section 7.3, we take up the criticisms of this statocentric approach and propose alternative ways of understanding migration.

7.3. "Transnationalism", "privilege" and "bordering": taking into account other scales of migration

Two types of work dominated the field of migration studies in the second half of the 20th century. On the one hand, the neoclassical approach led to the formulation of numerous microeconomic models, which aimed to identify the push and pull factors that explain the movement of individuals from one place to another, thereby imputing decision-making power and excessive rationality to actors (Piché 2013). On the other hand, an abundant literature has seized on the processes by which foreigners find themselves "integrated" into an arriving society, this time adopting an ethnocentric, even neocolonial, perspective on migration (Schinkel 2018). In this section, we outline three ways in which these approaches have been challenged.

7.3.1. From "immigrants" to "migrants"

In the United States, in 1919, a founding survey by William Thomas and Florian Znaniecki on the migration of Poles to the United States (Thomas and Znaniecki 2005) laid the foundations for an analysis of migration that took into account both the societies of departure and arrival by describing the cyclical phenomena of disorganization of traditional societies in Poland and reorganization of Polish immigrants in the United States. In France, it was not until the 1960s and the work of Abdelmalek Sayad that a type of sociology was developed to consider the processes of emigration and immigration together. From the in-depth study of several generations of emigrants–immigrants from Algeria living in France, the sociologist deconstructs the traditional approaches of migration, and in particular the economic literature that tends to homogenize the migrations. This approach allows Sayad (1999) to emphasize the influence of "state thinking", which "radically separates 'nationals' and 'non-nationals'". The sociology of immigration, which exists only because such a distinction is made, is, according to him, inseparably a sociology of the State, of its raison d'être, and of its limits. Although Sayad's work had a strong echo in France, particularly within the multidisciplinary laboratory Migrinter, founded in 1985 by Gildas Simon[6], it is above all with the development of the transnational paradigm that this concern became central (Martiniello and Lafleur 2008).

In the 1990s, the globalization of the economy and the emergence of new communication technologies led some authors to announce the decline of nation-states and the advent of a borderless world, a world where national borders would become obsolete (Appadurai 1999). The rise in the level of education and the diversification of migratory trajectories also challenged the classic approach in which the notion "immigrant" is used to designate the proletariat (Terrazzoni and Peraldi 2016). The sociological focus on immigrants' integration in the destination country was challenged by a sociological perspective looking at migrants as autonomous actors, able to make strategic migration projects (Ma Mung 2009).

This migrant-centered perspective and the development of new perspectives on borders are part of a general critique of the "methodological nationalism" prevailing in social sciences. For Dumitru (2014), this approach refers to "a cognitive bias" that consists in "understanding the social world by taking the nation-state as the unit of analysis". Focusing on the networks and movements of migrants rather than their settlement allows us to go beyond the statocentric perspective that Sayad already denounced. This critique is developed particularly through the concept of

---

6 For an overview of the work and transformations of this laboratory, see in particular the dossier "Migrinter a 30 ans : analyses et portraits" published in 2017, www.journals.openedition.org/e-migrinter/802.

"transnationalism", a term coined in the United States mainly by anthropologists Bash et al. (1992). According to these authors, transnationalism refers to "the processes by which immigrants build social fields that link together their country of origin and their country of settlement" (p. 1).

For Glick-Schiller (1992), the transnational links established by migrants are of a different nature and intensity than those built by economic immigrants whose flows have marked the industrialized countries since the 1950s. Understanding the migrant as an autonomous actor then requires a new theoretical paradigm. In fact, "transmigrants" do not simply rebuild an immigrant community in the country of arrival, but maintain relations with the country they have left by various means that depend on their origins and their degree of politicization. They maintain not only family but also economic, political, religious, and organizational ties that bring several societies together into a single "transnational social field". In connection with transnationalism, the concept of migratory "circulation" (Tarrius 1992) seeks to capture the displacements that are characterized by the absence of a single, fixed place of residence. It invites us to focus on "the practices and initiatives of people, on the routes and spaces they travel" (Berthomière and Hily 2006).

This new interpretation of migration coincides with the mobility turn that marked the social sciences in the 2000s. This scientific paradigm, which is notably supported by Sheller and Urry (2006), maintains that society can only be thought of in terms of a system of circulations: migrations, daily mobilities, tourism, but also flows of goods, capital, and ideas. However, many studies have criticized and qualified the idea of a shift to a regime of "generalized mobility" (Bourdin 2004). On the one hand, increased mobility brings into play a set of unevenly distributed skills and dispositions (Kaufmann 2002). On the other hand, the setting in motion of the world responds to a set of injunctions carried by a neoliberal ideology, translated particularly in professional circles in the form of individual projects (Boltanski and Chiapello 2002; Colombi 2016). The "mobile elites" or "highly skilled migrants" (Beaverstock 2005) embody, from this point of view, a population valued for its open-mindedness, its dynamism, and its entrepreneurial motivation (Favell 2008). Sedentary life, on the other hand, is negatively connoted and associated with the deprivation of economic, cultural, and social resources (Orfeuil and Ripoll 2015).

7.3.2. *The notion of migratory privilege*

In her survey of foreign executives in Paris, Wagner (1998, p. 23) had already shown that the "silence of the sources" on immigrants from rich countries can be explained by the fact that this is generally a population that "does not pose a problem" from the point of view of the public authorities and the media and political discourse of the host society. Guided by a critique of neoliberalism, a lot of research have developed at the intersection of the sociology of elites and the sociology of migration. In describing the emergence of what he calls the transnational capitalist class, Sklair (2012), for example, posits the existence of a globalized elite united by the same economic interests. Croucher (2012), on the other hand, proposes the notion of "migratory privilege", which is more appropriate to the heterogeneity of the migrant class[7].

This notion refers to the resources that allow individuals from rich countries to move internationally and to carry out a migration project without their physical or moral integrity being threatened. They have the advantage of their nationality, have easier access to visas, and benefit from the structural inequalities between their country of origin and the country they are moving to. Their purchasing power is increased tenfold and they can access much better employment and housing conditions compared to the populations they live with in the host society. Privileged migrants are thus endowed with "international capital" (Wagner 2007), i.e., professional, linguistic, economic, administrative, and legal resources that ensure a "nonchalant" migration (Croucher 2012) across the globe. Again, attention to these categories, as well as to expatriates (Adly 2013), highlights the role of international experience in professional trajectories (Colombi 2016) and the growing inequalities in mobility (Croucher 2012). In the same vein, the literature on lifestyle migration describes the social and economic logics that see "relatively affluent migrants" leave their country of origin to seek better living conditions in poorer countries (Benson and O'Reily 2009). These middle-class migrations can take place in medium-sized metropolises, such as Seoul (Gellereau 2017), but also on the margins of metropolises, in rural or seaside spaces. Most authors using this framework refer to places of immigration identified for their landscape quality or the authentic character of village life (Torkington 2012). These social groups may encounter remote processes from host societies and experience forms of ethnicization through which they "discover themselves as immigrants" (Clément 2018), but they remain privileged groups nonetheless.

The notion of migratory privilege also echoes work that highlights the prevalence of "white privilege" (Lundström 2014) and "Western privilege" (Le Renard 2019) in the international migration field. These two expressions point to the way in which migration transforms the experience of "whiteness" for individuals who did not experience white racialization in their country of origin due to their belonging to the dominant group (Cosquer 2018). These concepts emerge in the

---

[7] On this subject, see the dossier "Les migrations des privilégiés" in the journal *Métropolitiques*, coordinated by Garance Clément, Camille François and Claire Gellereau, published in 2021.

broader context of invitations to decolonize migration studies and the social sciences (Rodriguez et al. 2016), i.e., to move away from a northern-state-centric interpretation of migration, both in epistemological and empirical terms.

Looking at pre-colonial migration between Mexico and the southern United States, Ramirez (2020) shows how the conceptual frameworks, traditionally used to study migration, are marked by colonial thinking and fall into the "time trap" that makes migration a recent phenomenon linked to the construction of the nation-state.

On the contrary, *Chicanx studies* break with an imperialist and universalist sociology of migration, and restructure a critical thinking of colonialism inscribed in "indigenous knowledge". In contrast to the dominant explanations of neoclassical economics, Ramirez shows, with the support of the writings of the academic and activist Gloria Anzaldúa, that the migratory practices that precede the creation of national borders are akin to "long walks" ontologically linking individuals to their traditions. The decolonization of migration studies thus involves challenging the European monopoly on migration studies and opening up to "migrant epistemologies" (Ramirez 2020).

7.3.3. *The contributions of border studies*

In reaction to the mobility turn and transnational approaches to migration, several authors have been keen to point out the permanent barriers put in place by states to limit human movement, through border surveillance, migration policies, but also police control of urban and residential space (Balibar 2005; Babels 2019a). The structural inequalities that force certain social groups into immobility or, on the contrary, into nomadism have then been placed at the center of the sociology of migration (Tarrius 1992; Waldinger 2006; Potot 2016), while the field of border studies has developed widely (Wilson and Donnan 2012).

Since the 1970s, under the influence of sociology, the renewal of geography has made it possible to break with a strictly geopolitical or naturalistic approach to borders in order to emphasize that borders are an ambivalent social and political construction. Although they constitute a concrete obstacle to mobility, they also represent an interface that generates exchanges (Grasland 1997). As a discontinuity, the border separates two systems of institutions and norms. It creates economic, political, demographic, and cultural differentials that become an incentive for mobility (Grasland 1997).

These differentials have been understood by some authors as "resources" that can be exploited by different actors (Morokvasic-Muller 1999; Sohn 2014).

Moreover, as a barrier, the border filters passages and limits the possibilities of transgression. This function refers to the control devices put in place on a territory and the security issues associated with it (Casella 2013). The most recent works show that the border materializes in the form of devices for sorting populations (Fassin 2011). The walls that are multiplying around the world are the most obvious manifestation of this and are part of a general policy of hardening and reinforcing national borders for a set of populations that do not have a set of migratory privileges (Rosière and Jones 2012). The barrier functions of borders are turned on or off depending on the audience, through new technologies geared toward the "electronic management of 'people at risk'" (Ceyhan 2010). "Smart borders" at airports, train stations, and various ticket offices, which mobilize an increasing amount of individual data such as biometric data, are part of this growing selectivity of national borders (Ceyhan 2010).

Finally, legal tools in themselves form "paper borders" (Aprile 2018) that assign individuals to certain positions within the migratory field and national spaces, determining who has a permanent place or who is condemned to exile (Ticktin 2016). They intervene in society's representations of foreigners by forging categories that are taken up by the media and more or less valued. In Europe, for example, the term "dublined", which refers to the European "Dublin III" regulation (according to which the country responsible for an asylum application is the first country in the Schengen area through which the person entered or was checked for the first time, or the one that granted a visa or an established residence permit), is an administrative category that has also entered everyday language, labeling people who are the subject of particularly repressive measures (Bassi and Souiha 2019). The category "descendants of immigrants", constructed by the French social sciences and public policy, perpetuates "a status that is supposed to be transitional between the foreign and the 'natural'" (Guénif-Souilamas 2005, p. 392) and maintains a symbolic and social border between a national "us" and a "them" forged by the experience of migration. This dichotomy is particularly reinforced through "integration contracts", which can be found in France as well as in the Netherlands and Austria, or in the specific programs developed by Spain and Poland, which are based on the demonstration by immigrants of their desire to integrate by mastering the language and elements of history and culture considered to be the foundation of the country of immigration (Jacobs and Rea 2007).

7.4. Cities in migration studies

The critique of statocentric readings of migration through the analysis of transnational movements and networks has revived interest for the role of cities in the understanding of migration. At the end of the 19th century, the Chicago School proposed to make the city a laboratory of social change by promoting direct observation as a method of investigation. This was followed by the sociology of immigration, which was attentive to the way in which immigrants were considered and integrated in the country of arrival (Wihtol de Wenden 1982). In France, as in other national contexts, these surveys revealed dynamics of domination based on forms of systemic racism (Guillaumin 1972; De Rudder et al. 2000), ethnicization of social issues (Fassin and Fassin 2006; Jounin et al. 2006), and urban segregation (Dureau and Giroud 2007). In the early 2000s, the development of a transnational approach to migration went hand in hand with a growing interest in metropolization phenomena (Katz and Bradley 2013). Metropolises appear both as key actors in the production of wealth and as the site of increasing social polarization (Sassen 2001). Gradually, however, interest is shifting to so-called "average" or "ordinary" cities (Robinson 2013). The city no longer appears as an integrative totality but as a topos at the heart of the circulatory territories that migrants create along their journey (Missaoui and Tarrius 2006).

More recently, urban space was also put at the center of a renewed and pluralistic conceptualization of hospitality (Agier 2018; Stavo-Debauge 2017). In Europe, this new agenda of urban research can be explained by the "local turn" taken by migration governing strategies. Before returning to urban hospitality, we will briefly outline these transformations.

7.4.1. *Spatial dispersion policies and practices*

While migration policies are establishing a growing selectivity of borders, we can identify a complementary approach through which migrations are governed: the institutionalization of dispersion logics, which can be observed at several levels. For several years, European countries have agreed to organize the dispersal of immigrant populations wishing to apply for asylum throughout the Union. This process involves multilateral discussions between the different member states on the number of asylum seekers that each should receive. It has led to the creation of the Frontex agency, and of control centers, called hotspots, which are sorting points found in border areas of the Schengen zone, in Italy and Greece. In addition, controls have been outsourced to countries bordering Europe (Pian 2009).

Indeed, the logic of dispersion is linked to the logic of categorization and selection of people (Agier 2008), distinguishing between those whom the public authorities recognize as legitimate to try to immigrate to Europe, those who can apply for asylum, and those who are considered not able to enter. The latter are immediately turned back at the borders, while asylum seekers are dispersed within

Europe. In legal terms, this policy is embodied in the European Dublin III regulation, which gives rise to practices of expulsion and deportation to the first country of entry into Europe. Migrants are thus prevented from deciding, as they move along their journey, where they wish to live.

Dispersal policies and practices can also be found at the national level. In France, for example, they are visible through various public action mechanisms for access to accommodation or housing for migrants. For example, after the dismantling of the large street camps in Paris and the Calais Jungle at the end of 2016, the people who were staying there were arbitrarily distributed to reception and orientation centers (*centres d'accueil et d'orientation*, CAO), set up throughout France and, in particular, in small- and medium-sized, non-metropolitan and non-border towns. The public authorities want to deconcentrate the populations by moving them away from the points of fixation, particularly arguing that the Île-de-France region is saturated in terms of accommodation facilities but also in terms of access to housing. A national rehousing platform has been set up to enable "geographical mobility" of refugee status holders to territories outside the Paris region. The idea is to match local configurations with an available housing supply with the migration policy of dispersing immigrants (Gardesse and Lelevrier 2020).

The same logic can be found in countries that have reacted somewhat differently to the large influx of asylum seekers in Europe. Germany developed an open reception policy and practices in 2015 and 2016, but also organized a quantitative and spatial distribution at the level of the Länder. Italy, whose national policy is, on the contrary, extremely harsh toward these immigrants, especially since the arrival of Matteo Salvini, has also developed a set of devices throughout its territory to disperse those arriving via the Mediterranean.

7.4.2. *A local turn in migration governance?*

While migration policies are defined at centralized national or even supranational levels, leading to forms of Europeanization (Guiraudon 2010), there is talk of a local turn in migration studies that focus on governance (Scholten and Penninx 2016; Zapata-Barrero et al. 2017). Indeed, local governments are increasingly involved when immigrants arrive, whether in metropolitan territories, small- and medium-sized cities, or even rural[8] areas. Even in highly centralized countries such as France, some authors

---

8 Thus, the Babels program codirected by Michel Agier and Stefan Le Courant studied the so-called "migration crisis" in Europe by asking what migrants "do to cities" and, conversely, what the latter offer to immigrants, through forms of hostility or, on the contrary, rejection, organized by the public authorities but also by civil society. Three types of cities were

mention forms of informal decentralization, even though cities have few legislative possibilities to intervene in migration policy (Pauvros 2014). The local level intervenes in the reception of immigrant populations, responding to decisions imposed by the central level, but in some cases also developing specific policies in opposition to state trends. The constitution of networks of cities (Flamand 2017; Lacroix 2020), which call themselves "refugee cities", like Paris or Barcelona, or "welcoming territories", as is the case within Anvita (*association des villes et territoires accueillants*, association of welcoming cities and territories), can be analyzed as forms of neomunicipalism (Furri 2017), i.e., a takeover by municipalities of areas where the state appears to be failing.

The local turn in migration governance is also visible in the localized emergence of new actors to ensure the reception of migrants, particularly from the civil society (Bassi 2015). However, these unofficial decentralization processes and localist policies on immigration run the risk of reinforcing the segregative and unequal effects of reception, depending on the means and wishes of local authorities. Indeed, at the intramunicipal level, the strong reference to social diversity as an essential element of settlement policies can lead different urban actors to scatter people according to their nationality in different neighborhoods or even in different shared housing (Gardesse and Lelevrier 2020; Gardesse 2021).

7.4.3. *Thinking about reception and hospitality*

Beyond the issues of governance, the city can also be thought of through the various forms of hospitality it offers (Gotman 2004; Agier 2018). Some cities distinguish themselves by setting up support systems to help recently arrived people integrate into the local community, while others, on the contrary, are very clearly hostile to their arrival and logically do not organize any reception process. Between the two, a range of positions can be observed (Babels 2018). But those involved in reception are not only institutional, far from it: indeed, one of the major facets of hospitality toward immigrants is the development of social movements of support and help among the inhabitants of the cities concerned. For example, in the face of the structural absence of accommodation for people living on the streets, numerous initiatives of so-called citizen or solidarity accommodation have developed in a more or less formal way (Babels 2019b).

---

studied: crossroads cities such as Istanbul, refugee cities such as Paris or Berlin, and border cities such as Calais or Lampedusa. The ANR Camigri, coordinated by David Lessault, is interested in the settlement of immigrants in different local contexts, such as small rural towns and the French countryside.

Beyond the crucial question of housing, a myriad of activities and assistance are put in place, from administrative and medical support to cultural outings, French courses, and material donations enabling people to dress and furnish their homes. Thus, while the migration phenomena are regularly presented as a threat to European societies, leading to the development of security policies to control it rather than social policies to accompany it (Schmoll et al. 2015), there are positive reactions within civil society that allow urban hospitality to unfold in the context of restrictive migration policies.

At the same time, the control of immigrants is also delegated to the protagonist of civil society, for example, transporters risking sanctions if they allow irregular entry, which leads them to position themselves as controllers of their vehicles and the transported people (Guenebeaud 2017). In this context, the functions of places are sometimes troubled and can evolve: when public hospitality is provided by so-called reception places that can turn into spaces of confinement or seclusion (Kobelinsky 2010) or, conversely, when street encampments stabilize and give rise to relatively livable and structuring urban and social forms (Agier 2008, 2015; Hanappe 2018).

In the same way, the arrival locations for privileged migrants are not as established as they appear. In his investigation of "International Geneva", Hossam Adly (2013) explains how the urban and cultural development of Geneva, based on a cosmopolitan myth, has favored the reception of a "privileged urban minority", that of expatriates. But it also shows how the urban insertion of these elites varies greatly, far from being reduced to expatriate neighborhoods. Claire Cosquer's work highlights how the city of Abu Dhabi, where about 80% of the population is foreign, is marked by strong urban segregation: there is a "bubble space" reserved for expatriates from northern countries. But here again, the urban boundaries between these elites and migrants from the South are recomposed and transgressed in practice (Cosquer 2020).

7.5. Investigating migration

Working on migration requires a critical approach to border and governmental classification processes that distinguish between individuals according to their origins and migration paths. As far as quantitative surveys are concerned, these usually separate interregional and international migration. They provide an objective basis of what contemporary migrations represent and, as such, allow the deconstruction of the rhetoric of the migration crisis (Héran 2018). The United Nations High Commissioner for Refugees (UNHCR) is a leading institution in the production of these data. Each state may also conduct a census of inward and outward migration on its territory, which always raises the question of the definition of migration, both in terms of the legal status, duration, and geography considered (Richard 2017).

Designing quantitative surveys on migrations requires the construction of categories, but this work must be accompanied by a reflection on the emancipatory or, on the contrary, reductive effects of these tools. In this case, the categories by which migration is studied vary considerably from one state to another, as shown by the very different relationship between France and the United States to statistics on "race" or "ethnicity". While many authors denounce the French color blindness and defend the idea that statistics on ethnicity would make it possible to objectify the discrimination encountered by nonwhite immigrants in Western societies (Fassin and Fassin 2006), others fear that the introduction of ethnoracial variables into the French public statistical system constitutes an "ethnicity trap"[9] that could fuel racist thinking. The dispute between "anti" and "pro" ethnicity statistics crystallized in the 1990s around the debate between Michèle Tribalat, who introduced ethnicity categories into a survey on the integration model of French immigrants, and Hervé Le Bras, who was firmly opposed to this approach[10].

Another difficulty with quantitative surveys is the time frame studied. Some *ad hoc* surveys, such as the "Trajectoires et origines en France" survey, coauthored by Cris Beauchemin, Christelle Hamel, and Patrick Simon, make it possible to identify in greater detail the reasons for entering a territory from a retrospective perspective (Beauchemin et al. 2016). Other surveys conducted on cohorts aim to avoid the approximations of retrospective methods (Windzio et al. 2011).

Different types of qualitative surveys invite us to approach migratory phenomena without locking them into classifications of minority immigrant groups constructed by the majority group. We will highlight three of them:

– spatialized methods;

---

9 www.lemonde.fr/idees/article/2007/11/09/la-statistique-piege-ethnique-par-alain-blum-france-guerin-pace-et-herve-le-bras_976492_3232.html.
10 The geographic mobility and social integration survey (Mobilité géographique et insertion sociale, MGIS) directed by Michèle Tribalat and financed by the HCI aimed to quantitatively measure the efficiency of the French integration model and proposed for the first time categories that the demographer herself presents as ethnicity categories. Criticism of the survey focused in particular on the creation of a "native French" category opposed to "other origins", as well as on the normative dimension of the survey, which assumes that migrants should integrate by attenuating their differences (for example, endogamous marriage is presented as an indicator of the group's self-segregation). For more details, see especially Pfefferkorn (2019).

– observations through migration "windows";

– interview and observation surveys that analyze the migration trajectories of individuals.

Research whose field of study is a specific geographical entity, such as a city, a camp, a neighborhood, or even a residence, develops spatialized methodological approaches. Thus, at these different scales, the surveys are partly based on the collection of discourses through semistructured interviews, but they are often accompanied by techniques that make it possible to identify the different places that are used or, on the contrary, avoided by the immigrant populations.

The cartographic tool then makes visible the perceived elements in an ethnographic approach, which can also be based on *in situ* observation (Guenebeaud 2017; Le Bars 2017). At the crossroads of these issues, methods such as mental maps or commented routes are implemented, but also experiments such as time-use studies – that is, the people surveyed themselves fill in their actions on a daily basis, specifying their temporalities and locations, and then relate them in the form of notes and narratives to the researchers (Runet 2019). Maps can then illustrate large territories such as urban areas or very specific places such as buildings.

Another approach is to study how migrant individuals interact with the various actors who help shape, support, or control their journeys and living conditions. Ethnographic surveys shed light on the role of state officials, and the "discretionary power" of certain agents (Spire 2008) in the concrete implementation of migration policies. Through their more or less strong allegiance to the State's doctrine, but also through their subordinate position in certain highly hierarchical services, they participate in a "policy of numbers" in which the aim is to limit the possibilities of settling permanently on a national territory (Spire 2016). This type of investigation "through the window" of migration can also take the allocation of housing (Bourgeois 2015) or social aid as its object. They involve long periods of immersion or even work with the agents being observed as well as interviews in which they are asked to describe their professional practices. Another type of investigation consists of reconstructing the transnational social networks of migrants in order to show that migration does not break the links between "here" and "there" but, on the contrary, organizes new forms of solidarity and exchange. This approach is different from the "community" prism through which migrants' social relations are often approached and focuses on observing and describing the concrete practices that bring individuals together (Vertovec 2009).

Finally, other research endeavors to reconstruct the migration trajectories of individuals in detail, based on life stories or interviews that are regularly repeated in order to get a closer look at the stages of the life course. This approach makes it possible to highlight the individual adjustments and family negotiations that take place during migration. It provides explanations for the entry into a "migratory career" (Martiniello and Réa 2011) by pointing out the resources and dispositions that are activated in the realization of a migratory project (Roulleau Berger 2010; Clément 2018). It also offers a better understanding of postmigration social mobility processes by taking into account previous and secondary socializations in the host country. Finally, it makes it possible to correlate migratory and residential trajectories by revealing the links between places and living conditions for immigrants (Bully 2019).

While these approaches to migration are described here separately, it is possible to combine several scales of analysis by crossing statistical data (macroscale) with attention to social interactions (mesoscale) and individual dispositions (microscale) to reveal the different social forces that construct migration phenomena. In this respect, the ethnographic method developed by Douglas Massey (called an ethnosurvey) is distinguished both by the combination of approaches and the emphasis on investigation from the point of departure, when most works continue to favor the point of view of the society of arrival (Massey 1987).

7.6. Conclusion

This chapter has proposed a reflection on spatial and temporal scales within migration studies, with a particular focus on the debates surrounding the national scale, which is contested on several grounds. Firstly, it leads to thinking about migration through a "temporal trap" that starts the phenomenon with the advent of nation-states, and consequently subjects it to a reading dominated by the former colonial powers. Because it tends to confine migration to an irreversible movement between countries of departure and arrival, this scale also prevents a detailed reading of the movements and relationships that continue beyond migration, which the paradigm of transnationalism, by restoring greater agentivity to migrants, makes possible.

However, it is clear that States remain central actors in the definition of migration policies and that the national level continues to be a structuring factor in the formation and reproduction of social inequalities (Hugrée et al. 2017). Faced with the risk that transnational critique might blind us to the state dimension of restricting or facilitating migration, border studies allow us to update a reading of national borders, no longer as fixed lines but as thick, filtering devices, continually worked by the practice of different public and private agents. More recently, the urban scale has reappeared as essential to the understanding of migratory logics, no longer with the aim of understanding the processes of integration of immigrants, but to grasp their potential for reception, both in terms of local public institutions and through the solidarity of the inhabitants.

7.7. References

Adly, H. (2013). Fonctionnaires internationaux à Genève : le poids du privilège. *Espaces et sociétés*, 154(3), 71–85.

Agier, M. (2008). *Gérer les indésirables. Des camps de réfugiés au gouvernement humanitaire*. Flammarion, Paris.

Agier, M. (2018). *L'étranger qui vient. Repenser l'hospitalité*. Le Seuil, Paris.

Agustín, L. (2006). The disappearing of a migration category: Migrants who sell sex. *Journal of Ethnic and Migration Studies*, 32(1), 29–47.

Amelina, A. and Horvath, K. (2017). Sociology of migration. *The Cambridge Handbook of Sociology: Core Areas in Sociology and the Development of the Discipline*, Volume 1, Korgen, K.O. (ed.). Cambridge University Press, Cambridge.

Amelina, A. and Lutz, H. (2020). *Gender and Migration: Transnational and Intersectional Prospects*. Routledge, London.

Appadurai, A. (1999). *Modernity at Large: Cultural Dimensions of Globalization*. University of Minnesota Press, Minneapolis.

Aprile, S. (2018). Expériences et représentations de la frontière. Proscrits et exilés au milieu du XIXe siècle. *Hommes & Migrations*, 1321(2), 75–82.

Babels, Bontemps, V., Makaremi, C., Mazouz, S. (2018). *Entre accueil et rejet : ce que les villes font aux migrants*. Le passager Clandestin – Bibliothèque des frontières, Lyon.

Babels, Barnier, S., Casella, S., Gardesse, C., Guenebeaud, C., Le Courant, S. (2019a). *La police des migrants : filtrer, disperser, harceler*. Le passager Clandestin – Bibliothèque des frontières, Lyon.

Babels, Agier, M., Gerbier Aublanc, M., Masson Diez, E. (2019b). *Hospitalité en France : mobilisations intimes et politiques*. Le passager Clandestin – Bibliothèque des frontières, Paris.

Balibar, É. (2005). *Europe, constitution, frontière*. Éditions du Passant, Bègles.

Bash, L., Glick-Schiller, N., Szanton-Blanc, C. (1992). *Toward a Transnational Perspective on Migration. Race, Class, Ethnicity, and Nationalism Reconsidered*. NG Schiller, New York.

Bassand, M. and Brulhardt, M.-C. (1983). La mobilité spatiale : un processus social fondamental. *Espace Populations Sociétés*, 1(1), 49–54.

Bassi, M. (2015). Mobilisations collectives et recomposition de l'action publique autour de l'enjeu migratoire en Sicile (1986–2012). PhD thesis, Institut d'études politiques de Paris, Paris.

Bassi, M. and Souiah, F. (2019). La violence du régime des frontières et ses conséquences létales : récits et pratiques autour des morts et disparus par migration. *Critique internationale*, 83(2), 9–19.

Beauchemin, C., Hamel, C., Simon, P. (2016). *Trajectoires et origines : enquête sur la diversité des populations en France.* INED, Paris.

Beaverstock, J.V. (2005). Transnational elites in the city: British highly-skilled inter-company transferees in New York City's financial district. *Journal of Ethnic and Migration Studies*, 31(2), 245–268.

Bell, M., Charles-Edwards, E., Ueffing, P., Stillwell, J., Kupiszewski, M., Kupiszewska, D. (2015). Internal migration and development: Comparing migration intensities around the world. *Population and Development Review*, 41(1), 33–58.

Benson, M. and O'Reilly, O. (2009). Migration and the search for a better way of life: A critical exploration of lifestyle migration. *The Sociological Review*, 57(4), 608–625.

Berthomière, W. and Hily, M.A. (2006). Décrire les migrations internationales. *Revue européenne des migrations internationales*, 22(2), 67–82.

Boltanski, L. and Chiapello, È. (2002). Inégaux face à la mobilité. *Projet*, 271(3), 97.

Bourdin, A. (2004). L'individualisme à l'heure de la mobilité généralisée, In *Les sens du mouvement*, Allemand, S., Ascher, F., Lévy, J. (eds). Belin, Cerisy.

Bourgeois, M. (2015). Catégorisations et discriminations au guichet du logement social. Une comparaison de deux configurations territoriales. In *L'État des droits. Politique des droits et pratiques des institutions*, Baudot, P.-Y., Revillard, A. (eds). Presses de Sciences Po, Paris.

Bully, E. (2019). Between militantism and academic research: Rethinking hospitality and solidarity in the context of the EU's political crisis. *IRIS UniPA*.

Casella, S. (2013). Surveiller les personnes, garder les frontières, définir le territoire : la Police Aux Frontières après la création de l'espace Schengen (1953–2004). PhD thesis, IEP Paris, Paris.

Ceyhan, A. (2010). Les technologies européennes de contrôle de l'immigration : vers une gestion électronique des "personnes à risque". *Réseaux*, 159(1), 131–150.

Clément, G. (2018). Migrer près de chez soi. Trajectoires résidentielles et migratoires de membres des "classes moyennes" dans l'agglomération lilloise. PhD thesis, Université Paris-Est, Paris.

Colombi, D. (2016). Les usages de la mondialisation : mobilité internationale et marchés du travail en France. PhD thesis, Institut d'études politiques, Paris.

Colucci, M. (2019). Foreign immigration to Italy: Crisis and the transformation of flows. *Journal of Modern Italian Studies*, 24, 427–440.

Cosquer, C. (2018). Expat' à Abu Dhabi : blanchité et construction du groupe national chez les migrants français(es). PhD thesis, Institut d'Études Politiques de Paris, Paris.

Cosquer, C. (2020). La production d'un entre-soi expatrié à Abu Dhabi. *Métropolitiques* [Online]. Available at: https://metropolitiques.eu/La-production-d-un-entre-soi-expatrie-a-Abu-Dhabi.html.

Croucher, S. (2012). Privileged mobility in an age of globality. *Societies*, 2, 1–13.

Donnan, H. and Wilson, T. (1999). *Borders: Frontiers of Identity, Nation and State*. Berg, Oxford.

Dumitru, S. (2014). Qu'est-ce que le nationalisme méthodologique ? *Raisons politiques*, 54(2), 9–22.

Dumitru, S. and Marfouk, A. (2015). Existe-til une féminisation de la migration internationale ? Féminisation de la migration qualifiée et invisibilité des diplômes. *Hommes & migrations. Revue française de référence sur les dynamiques migratoires*, 1311, 31–41.

Dureau, F. and Giroud, M. (2007). Ségrégation et discrimination en milieu urbain : introduction. In *Les nouveaux territoires migratoires : entre logiques globales et dynamiques locales*, Audebert, C., Ma Mung, E. (eds.). Humanitarian Net, Bilbao.

Fassin, D. and Fassin, E. (eds) (2006). *De la question sociale à la question raciale ? Représenter la société française*. La Découverte, Paris.

Favell, A. (2008). *Eurostars and Eurocities: Free Movement and Mobility in an Integrating Europe*. Blackwell, Oxford.

Findlay, A. and Gould, W.T.S. (1989). Skilled international migration: A research agenda. *Area*, 21(1), 3–11.

Flamand, A. (2017). Les cadres de l'action publique locale en charge des politiques d'intégration des étrangers : entre réseaux de villes et spécificités nationales des politiques publiques. *Politique européenne*, 57, 84–115.

Furri, F. (2017). Villes-refuge, villes rebelles et néo-municipalisme. *Plein droit*, 115, 3–6.

Gabaccia, D.R. (2016). Feminization of migration. In *The Wiley Blackwell Encyclopedia of Gender and Sexuality Studies*, Wong, A., Wickramasinghe, M., Hoogland, R., Naples, N.A. (eds). John Wiley & Sons, New York.

Gardesse, C. (2021). Dispersion et invisibilisation de personnes exilées dans des villes petites et moyennes : ce que la spatialisation des CAO révèle des politiques migratoires et urbaines en France. *Revue Européenne des Migrations Internationales*.

Gardesse, C. and Lelevrier, C. (2020). Refugees and asylum seekers dispersed in non-metropolitan French cities: Do housing opportunities mean housing access? *Urban Planning*, 5, 3.

Geddes, A. and Scholten, P. (2016). *The Politics of Migration and Immigration in Europe*. Second, London [Online]. Available at: https://doi.org/10.4135/9781473982703.

Gellereau, C. (2017). "Life is easy here" : Migrer, travailler, se loger, s'éduquer, pratiques et privilèges des Nord-Américains, Britanniques et Français à Séoul. PhD thesis, Université de Lille 1, Lille.

Glick-Schiller, N. (1992). Transnationalism: A new analytic framework for understanding migration. *Annals of the New York Academy of Science*, 1–24.

Gotman, A. (2004). *Villes et Hospitalité. Les municipalités et leurs "étrangers"*. Éditions de la MSH, Paris.

Grasland, C. (1997). L'analyse des discontinuités territoriales. *L'Espace géographique*, 26, 309–326 [Online]. Available at: https://doi.org/10.3406/spgeo.1997.1097.

Guenebeaud, C. (2017). Dans la frontière : migrants et lutte des places dans la ville de Calais. PhD thesis, Université Lille 1, Lille.

Guénif-Souilamas, N. (2005). Femmes, immigration, ségrégation. In *Femmes, genre et sociétés. L'état des savoirs*, Maruani, M. (ed.). La Découverte, Paris.

Guillaumin, C. (1972). *L'idéologie raciste, genèse et langage actuel*. La Haye/Moutin, Paris.

Guiraudon, V. (2010). Les effets de l'européanisation des politiques d'immigration et d'asile. *Politique européenne*, 31, 7–32

de Haas, H., Czaika, M., Flahaux, M.-L., Mahendra, E., Natter, K., Vezzoli, S., Villares-Varela, M. (2019). International migration: Trends, determinants, and policy effects. *Population and Development Review*, 45(4), 885–922 [Online]. Available at: https://doi.org/10.1111/padr.12291.

de Haas, H., Castles, S., Miller, M.J. (2020). *The Age of Migration: International Population Movements in the Modern World*. Red Globe Press, London.

Hanappe, C. (2018). *La Ville accueillante : accueillir à Grande Synthe : questions théoriques et pratiques sur les exilés, l'architecture et la ville*. PUCA, Huddersfield.

Héran, F. (2018). *Migrations et sociétés*. Fayard/Collège de France, Paris.

Hugrée, C., Penissat, É., Spire, A. (2017). *Les classes sociales en Europe : tableau des nouvelles inégalités sur le vieux continent*. Agone, Marseille.

Jacobs, D. and Rea, A. (2007). The end of national models? Integration courses and citizenship trajectories in Europe. *International Journal on Multicultural Societies*, 9(2), 264–283.

Jounin, N., Palomares, E., Rabaud, A. (2008). Ethnicisations ordinaires, voix minoritaires. *Sociétés contemporaines*, 70(2), 7–23.

Katz, B. and Bradley, J. (2013). *The Metropolitan Revolution: How Cities and Metros Are Fixing Our Broken Politics and Fragile Economy*. Brookings Institution Press, Washington [Online]. Available at: https://www.jstor.org/stable/10.7864/j.ctt4cg7km.

Kaufmann, V. (2002). *Re-Thinking Mobility: Contemporary Sociology*. Ashgate Publishing Limited, Farnham.

Keely, C.B. (2000). Demography and international migration. In *Migration Theory: Talking Across Disciplines*, Brettell, C., Hollifield, J.F. (eds.). Routledge, London.

Kobelinsky, C. (2010). *L'accueil des demandeurs d'asile. Une ethnographie de l'attente*. Éditions du Cygne, Paris.

Kulu, H. and Milewski, N. (2007). Family change and migration in the life course: An introduction. *Demographic Research*, 17, 567–590.

Lacroix, T. (2020). Réseaux des villes hospitalières : un panorama global. *Emigrinter*, 20.

Laurens, S. (2008). L'immigration : une affaire d'États. Conversion des regards sur les migrations algériennes (1961–1973). *Cultures & Conflits*, 33–53 [Online]. Available at: https://doi.org/10.4000/conflits.10503.

Le Bars, J. (2017). Conquérir la galère. Géographie féministe de femmes sans-papiers venues d'Afrique subsaharienne et du Maghreb en région parisienne. PhD thesis, Paris.

Le Courant, S. (2015). Vivre sous la menace : ethnographie de la vie quotidienne des étrangers en situation irrégulière en France. PhD thesis, Paris.

Le Renard, A. (2019). *Le Privilège occidental. Travail, intimité et hiérarchies postcoloniales à Dubaï.* Presses de Sciences Po, Paris.

Lundström, C. (2014). *White Migrations. Gender, Whiteness and Privilege in Transnational Migration.* Palgrave Macmillan, London.

Ma Mung, E. (2009). Le point de vue de l'autonomie dans l'étude des migrations internationales : "penser de l'intérieur" les phénomènes de mobilité. In *Les mondes de la mobilité*, Dureau, F., Hily, M.A. (eds.). Presses de l'Université de Rennes, Rennes.

Martiniello, M. and Lafleur, J.-M. (2008). Towards a transatlantic dialogue in the study of immigrant political transnationalism. *Ethnic and Racial Studies*, 31(4), 645–663.

Martiniello, M. and Rea, A. (2011). Des flux migratoires aux carrières migratoires. *Sociologies* [Online]. Available at: https://doi.org/10.4000/sociologies.3694/.

Massey, D. (1987). The ethnosurvey in theory and practice. *The International Migration Review*, 21(4).

Missaoui, L. and Tarrius, A. (2006). Villes et migrants, du lieu-monde au lieu-passage. *Revue européenne des migrations internationales*, 22(2), 43–65.

Morokvasic-Muller, M. (1999). La mobilité transnationale comme ressource : le cas des migrants de l'Europe de l'Est. *Cultures & Conflits*, 33–34.

Noiriel, G. (1988). *Le creuset français, histoire de l'immigration, XIXe–XXe siècles.* Le Seuil, Paris.

Orfeuil, J.P. and Ripoll, F. (2015). *Accès et mobilités. Les nouvelles inégalités.* Infolio, Gollion.

Pauvros, M. (2014). Les politiques locales d'immigration : un redéploiement des frontières de l'État. PhD thesis, Paris.

Pfefferkorn, R. (2019). Retour sur la controverse française autour des "statistiques ethniques". *Raison présente*, 211(3).

Phan, B. (2017). *Colonisation et décolonisation : XVIe–XXe siècles.* PUF, Paris.

Pian, A. (2009). *Aux nouvelles frontières de l'Europe. L'aventure incertaine des Sénégalais au Maroc.* La Dispute, Paris.

Piché, V. (2013). Les théories migratoires contemporaines au prisme des textes fondateurs. *Population*, 68(1), 153–178.

Potot, S. (2016). Mobilités intra-européennes : quel accueil pour les indigents? *Savoir/Agir*, 36(2), 53–58.

Ramirez, C. (2020). Decolonizing migration studies: A Chicanx Studies perspective and critique of colonial sociological origins. *Río Bravo: A Journal of the Borderlands*, 24.

Rea, A. and Tripier, M. (2008). *Sociologie de l'immigration*. La Découverte, Paris.

Richard, J.-L. (2017). Les enquêtes quantitatives sur les migrations : Spécificités et en-jeux. *Migrations Société*, 167(1), 121–132.

Robinson, J. (2013). *Ordinary Cities: Between Modernity and Development*. Routledge, London.

Rodriguez, E.G., Boatcă, M., Costa, S. (2016). *Decolonizing European Sociology : Transdisciplinary Approaches*. Routledge, London.

Rossi, P. (1955). *Why Families Move: A Study in the Social Psychology of Urban Mobility*. Macmillan Publishers, New York.

Roulleau-Berger, L. (2010). *Migrer au féminin*. Presses universitaires de France, Paris.

Rowe, F. and Patias, N. (2020). Mapping the spatial patterns of internal migration in Europe. *Regional Studies, Regional Science*, 7(1), 390–393 [Online]. Available at: https://doi.org/10.1080/21681376.2020.1811139.

de Rudder-Paurd, V., Poiret, C., Vourc'h, F. (2000). *L'inégalité raciste, l'universalité républicaine à l'épreuve*. Presses Universitaires de France, Paris.

Runet, P. (2019). Habiter Paris aux marges de l'Aide Sociale à l'Enfance. Conditions individuelles et structurelles d'accès à la ville des mineurs isolés étrangers déboutés. Master's thesis, EHESS.

Sassen, S. (ed.) (2001). *Global Networks, Linked Cities*. Routledge, New York.

Sayad, A. (1999). Immigration et "pensée d'État". *Actes de la Recherche en Sciences Sociales*, 129(1), 5–14.

Schinkel, W. (2018). Against "immigrant integration": For an end to neocolonial knowledge production. *Comparative Migration Studies*, 6(1), 31.

Schmoll, C., Thiollet, H., Whitol de Wenden, C. (2015). *Migrations en Méditerranée. Permanence et mutations à l'heure de révolutions et des crises*. CNRS, Paris.

Scholten, P. and Penninx, R. (2016). The multilevel governance of migration and integration. In *Integration Processes and Policies in Europe: Contexts, Levels and Actors*, Garces-Mascarenas, B., Penninx, R. (eds). IMISCOE, Berlin.

Sert, D. (2018). The diversification of intra-European movement. In *Between Mobility and Migration*, Scholten, P., van Ostaijen, M. (eds). Springer International Publishing, Berlin [Online]. Available at: https://doi.org/10.1007/978-3-319-77991-1_2.

Sheller, M. and Urry, J. (2006). The new mobilities paradigm. *Environment and Planning A: Economy and Space*, 38(2), 207–226.

Simmel, G. (2019). *L'étranger : et autres textes*. Payot, Paris.

Sklair, L. (2012). Transnational capitalist class. In *The Wiley-Blackwell Encyclopedia of Globalization*. American Cancer Society [Online]. Available at: https://doi.org/10.1002/9780470670590.wbeog585.

Sohn, C. (2014). Modelling cross-border integration: The role of borders as a resource. *Geopolitics*, 19(3), 587–608.

Spire, A. (2008). *Accueillir ou reconduire : enquête sur les guichets de l'immigration*. Raisons d'agir, Paris.

Spire, A. (2016). La politique des guichets au service de la police des étrangers. *Savoir/Agir*, 36(2), 27–31.

Stavo-Debauge, J. (2017). *Qu'est-ce que l'hospitalité ? Recevoir l'étranger à la communauté*. Éditions Liber, Montreal.

Tarrius, A. (1992). Circulation des élites professionnelles et intégration européenne. *Revue européenne des migrations internationales*, 8(2), 27–56.

Tassin, L. (2014). Accueillir les indésirables : les habitants de Lampedusa à l'épreuve de l'enfermement des étrangers. *Genèses*, 96(3), 110–131.

Tassin, L. (2016). Le mirage des *hotspots* : nouveaux concepts et vieilles recettes à Lesbos et Lampedusa. *Savoir/Agir*, 36(2), 39–45.

Temime, E. (1999). *France, terre d'immigration*. Gallimard, Paris.

Terrazzoni, L. and Peraldi, M. (2016). Migrations, États-nations et frontières. Interview de Roger Waldinger. *Emulations*, 17.

Thomas, W. and Znaniecki, F. (2005). *Le Paysan polonais en Europe et en Amérique, récit de vie d'un migrant*. Armand Colin, Paris.

Ticktin, M. (2016). Thinking beyond humanitarian borders. *Social Research: An International Quarterly*, 83(2), 255–271.

Torkington, K. (2012). Place and lifestyle migration: The discursive construction of "glocal" place-identity. *Mobilities*, 1, 71–92.

Vertovec, S. (2009). *Transnationalism*. Routledge, New York.

Wagner, A.-C. (1998). *Les nouvelles élites de la mondialisation : une immigration dorée en France*. Presses Universitaires de France, Paris.

Wagner, A.-C. (2017). *Les classes sociales dans la mondialisation*. La Découverte, Paris.

Waldinger, R. (2006). Transnationalisme des immigrants et présence du passé. *Revue européenne des migrations internationales*, 22(2).

Wihtol de Wenden, C. (1982). Droits politiques des immigrés. *Études*, 1, 33–44.

Wihtol de Wenden, C. (2001). Un essai de typologie des nouvelles mobilités. *Hommes et migrations*, 1233(1), 5–12.

Windzio, M., Valk, H., de Wingens, M., Aybek, C. (2011). *A Life-Course Perspective on Migration and Integration*. Springer Nature, Berlin.

Zapata-Barrero, R., Caponio, T., Scholten, P. (2017). Theorizing the "local turn" in a multi-level governance framework of analysis: A case study in immigrant policies. *International Review of Administrative Sciences*, 83(2), 241–246.

8

Work and High Mobility in Europe

Emmanuel RAVALET

Mobil'homme, Laboratoire de sociologie urbaine (LaSUR), École polytechnique fédérale de Lausanne, Switzerland

8.1. Introduction

Understanding spatial mobility behaviors of people is a prerequisite for the formulation of informed policy objectives for transportation (infrastructure and services) and land-use planning. However, the spatial fragmentation of sociabilities and activities in the era of facilitated mobility produces forms of mobility that remain largely unobserved by analysts' observation tools. Among these hybrid spatial mobilities, the high work-related mobilities concern a significant proportion of the active population and condition novel lifestyles. They are in fact part of a context of changes in the world of work and profound transformation of private and family life, and are deployed all the more widely as transport networks expand and become more efficient. This chapter aims to describe the practices and discourses of the people concerned by these high mobilities, challenge a number of preconceptions and fantasies, and paint a protean picture that highlights the largely unknown financial, social, human and environmental costs.

In this chapter, we describe the nature of high work-related mobilities and what makes them hybrid. We then describe the populations involved, in socioeconomic, demographic and geographic terms. Our approach is therefore to "enter" through specific forms of mobility in order to account for the populations and territories concerned. Contrary to a widely held view, the populations concerned by these forms of large-scale mobility are very diverse, particularly in social terms.

Mobility and Geographical Scales,
coordinated by Guillaume DREVON and Vincent KAUFMANN. © ISTE Ltd 2023.

Faced with the demands for flexibility imposed by the labor market, the propensity of workers to move over a wide area is an undeniable quality for access to employment. But the injunction to be mobile to remain in employment excludes people who cannot or do not want to be highly mobile and forces those who have decided to do so to continue along a path they do not wish to follow.

This chapter also examines the consequences that high mobility practices may have on sociability, health or the balance of life as a couple. Highlighting these costs, which are not well known, makes it possible to put the merits of widespread mobility in the working population into perspective.

In order to understand the phenomenon of work-related high mobility, we must consider the role played by digital technologies, which is widely used by the populations concerned. Contrary to what is claimed as its virtue, telework goes hand in hand with high mobility practices. In particular, it provides a permanent home base far from the workplace.

All of these elements are presented and discussed on the basis of international scientific knowledge. We will conclude by outlining a few avenues for reflection.

8.2. High work-related mobility

The propensity of people to travel tends to increase. Thus, in most Western countries, there has been a global increase in travel distances per day and per person since the 1980s. This increase was strong until the beginning of the 2000s (Hubert 2009; Department for Transport 2010; Sandow 2011; OFS 2012). It has tended to be more limited in recent years (OFS 2017) and average times are almost stable, especially in Switzerland (Drevon et al. 2019).

In parallel with the average trends mentioned so far, new forms of temporally and spatially intensive mobility are appearing, which can be referred to as "large-scale mobilities" (Schneider and Meil 2008). However they are approached, these are far from marginal, whether they are work-related (Schneider et al. 2002; Ravalet et al. 2015), leisure-related (Pierre 2006; Vincent-Geslin and Kaufmann 2012), or family-related, such as long-distance relationships (Levin 2004), shared custody, or, more generally, children with separated parents (Widmer et al. 2008).

In this chapter, we will discuss several forms of large-scale mobility, but we will focus on forms that are related to employment. These are intensive daily commuting (long duration or long distance), weekly commuting (with dual residences that involve going back and forth between the two places of life), fluctuating commuting (with job locations or jobs that vary over days, weeks, or seasons), and finally frequent travel for work. This last category covers a wide variety of situations (tram or train drivers, delivery drivers, home care workers, salespeople, etc.), ranging from those who travel for work to those whose very job is linked to mobility. In recent years, a number of research studies have attempted to describe these forms of mobility and to understand the reasons for them. Although links exist between these four types of practices, most scientific works study one or the other of them without trying to articulate them.

High mobility is only one part of the intensive spatial and temporal mobility practices. A large part of the European population is characterized by multiple spatial anchors, or to use Stock's (2006) terms, a "polytopic dwelling". One of the manifestations of these multiple anchorings refers to the great mobility. But it is not the only one, or even the main one. The fact remains that by working on the great mobilities linked to work, we are dealing with a practice that constitutes a social revelation of the major trends that characterize the relationship with space in contemporary lifestyles (Duchêne-Lacroix 2014).

Before reporting on these forms of mobility, it is necessary to point out that there is a lack of data sources for analyzing these mobility behaviors, since these are hybrid mobilities that conventional data sources do not describe or do not describe well (Vincent-Geslin and Kaufmann 2012; Viry and Kaufmann 2015).

8.2.1. Intensive daily commuting

In order to address the issue of intensive commuting, it is necessary to account for commuting distances and what determines them. In section 8.4 of this chapter, we will have the opportunity to present several of the intrinsic logics that explain the development of intensive forms of commuting. But it is quite clear that they result from an absence of relationships (or its weakness) between what determines residential choices and what determines occupational choices, whether this is the result of a choice assumed by certain workers or whether the individual's professional, private, and territorial context makes it de facto impossible to achieve a better spatiotemporal reconciliation of residence and work.

In terms of magnitude, it is difficult to provide comparable figures across countries and historical periods, as studies and research on this issue are often based on ad hoc data constructed with different assumptions. Nevertheless, these studies show that in the late 2010s, 7% of the European population made long commutes, i.e., commutes for more than two hours each way (Lück and Ruppenthal 2010). Similarly, the Swiss Federal Statistical Office estimates that 10.2% of the employed population spent more than one hour commuting to and from work in 2010, but that this proportion declined to 9.1% in 2017[1].

Most studies use distance rather than time thresholds. In France, the share of trips of more than 80 km (work and personal reasons) is 1.3%, but represents 40% of the total distances traveled. Long-distance mobility increased by nearly 10% between 1994 and 2006, with fewer round trips in a day and more frequent use of the train (Grimal 2010). On the Swiss side, the share of working people traveling more than 50 km to work (one-way trip) increased from 4% in 2010 to 4.6% in 2017[2].

International comparison is difficult in that thresholds are almost always different from each other, and data collection methods and dates are often different. Ravalet et al. (2015) published a book in which they present international differences between four countries (Germany, Spain, France, and Switzerland) evaluated from the same database. Switzerland emerges as a territory that is particularly conducive to long-distance and long-term commuting, and the proportion of the working population involved in long-distance commuting even increased between 2007 and 2011 for a sample of the same population, who had therefore aged four years over the period. In the Tables[3] of the book in question (Ravalet et al. 2015), 7% of Swiss workers surveyed in 2007 were long-distance commuters, and 9% of these same workers were long-distance commuters in 2011. In the three other countries considered, the share of commuters decreased by 1% in Germany, 1% in France and 5% in Spain over the same period. Several elements can be mentioned to explain this Swiss specificity in terms of commuting:

– the Swiss urban system, with its medium-sized cities relatively close to each other;

– the transport infrastructure, particularly the railways, is very efficient in terms of supply (frequency, service, timetables, etc.) and pricing (for example, there is a season ticket that allows travel on all Swiss urban and interurban public transport networks);

– the housing market is extremely strained in several large cities;

– the administrative functioning at the level of the Swiss canton imposes on people who move by changing their canton of residence to change their school and tax system;

---

[1] Data is available on the OFS website: www.bfs.admin.ch/bfs/fr/home/statistiques /mobilite-transports/transport-personnes/pendularite.assetdetail.7226470.html.
[2] Data is available on the OFS website: www.bfs.admin.ch/bfs/fr/home/statistiques /mobilite-transports/transport-personnes/pendularite.assetdetail.7226470.html.
[3] See Ravalet et al. (2015, p. 31).

– the ease of daily commuting and the difficulty of moving would thus result in an increasing recourse to long-term commuting.

Beyond these elements, it is the determinants of so-called intensive daily commuting whose logics concern the private, professional and territorial dimensions (Vincent-Geslin and Ravalet 2016). Territorial dynamics also play a major role, with a significant recourse to intensive daily commuting for people who live or work in the largest European urban areas (Eurostat 2018).

In this analysis, Eurostat also highlights the importance of cross-border interregional commuting, in the sense that wage and cost-of-living differentials between the regions of departure and arrival justify daily trips that can sometimes be very long (Schmitz et al. 2012; Eurostat 2018).

It is also important to mention that the use of these forms of intensive commuting is largely via the train (Orfeuil 2010; Moss et al. 2012). For example, Jones et al. (2008) show that train users dominate the longest commutes in terms of travel time. While the car dominates for trips of less than 50 km, between 50 and 75 km, the car (49%) and train (51%) are equal, while the train (67%) dominates for longer trips (OFS 2017). Beyond one hour, people prioritize comfort and are willing to concede a slight time loss by choosing the train over the car. Indeed, during the train journey, it is possible to work, relax, sleep, or talk with friends or family members.

Finally, this question of the dynamics of intensive daily commuting is described in monographic studies that focus on train users. For example, the French studies by Meissonnier (2001), Lanéelle (2006), and Beauvais et al. (2007) focus, respectively, on commuters between Rouen, Le Mans and Tours for their origin (place of residence), and Paris for their destination (place of work).

8.2.2. Weekly commuting

Weekly commuting can be considered as bi-residence for professional reasons. These practices are linked, in concrete terms, to the existence of a pied-à-terre (second home, sleeping quarters with family or friends, rented room, etc.) near the workplace. In France and Spain, practices of moving away from work leading to bi-residence have been observed respectively between Paris, Lyon and the south of France, Madrid and the coastal regions at the opening of high-speed train lines (Viard 2011; Vincent-Geslin and Kaufmann 2012).

It is very difficult to have reliable figures on the magnitude of this phenomenon, which, moreover, tends to increase in times of economic crisis (Ravalet et al. 2017). Based on 1995 census data, Green et al. (1999) put weekly long-distance commuting at about 1% of the employed population. Ravalet et al. (2015), on the other hand, point to 1–3% of long-distance couple relationships due to work among 29–58 year olds in 2011 depending on the countries they surveyed. Since the phenomenon is not well developed, quantifications are few and unreliable, and it is therefore not possible to report on trends.

This form of arbitration can be seen as an alternative to long-distance commuting practices (Kaufmann 2010). When distances are too great, it becomes difficult to commute every day and the option of using a pied-à-terre close to the workplace becomes more relevant. Beyond the distance between home and work, this choice can also result from a lesser attachment to the territory of residence and the ability of people to be "mobile" (Kaufmann 2010).

These forms of weekly commuting can also be linked to lifestyles organized over several countries, and this topic is more specifically addressed in the literature related to migration (Espinoza-Herold and Contini 2017).

8.2.3. *Fluctuating commuting patterns*

The distance or time difference between home and work can change dramatically depending on the nature of the jobs held. Ojala and Pyöriä (2018) emphasize that what may be called "traditional" jobs generate fluctuating commuting patterns. For example, they refer to construction workers (who must move from site to site throughout the year), agricultural workers and military personnel. The trends measured thus show that there is a clear link between the nature of the job and the mobility achieved in order to get to places where the job is performed, which are different during the week or the seasons.

In their survey conducted in France, Pearce et al. (2020) show that holding a job in several locations generates very significant commuting times and distances. People in these situations spend nearly 17 hours commuting each week, of which more than 10 hours are for work.

Although only partially covering the situation of fluctuating commuting, Ojala and Pyöriä (2018) show the great variability in the location of employment in European[4]

---

4 See Ojala and Pyöriä (2018, Table, p. 412).

countries. The Nordic countries (particularly Sweden, Denmark, Norway, the Netherlands, and Finland) are characterized by a very high propensity of the working population living there to work in several different locations (conventional workplace, clients' premises, vehicles, outdoor locations, public spaces or housing). Thus, more than 60% of the respondents in these countries work in several of these locations. This result is partly linked to a more frequent practice of teleworking (especially at home). The number of respondents who telework is between 17% and 23%, which is higher than in other European countries (e.g. 14% in Switzerland according to these data).

8.2.4. Frequent travel for work

The third form of high mobility that we wish to address here is that of frequent travel for work purposes. Demel and Mayrhofer (2010) describe the people concerned as "flexpatriates". Here, again, there is a lack of data to properly address this phenomenon.

Ravalet et al. (2015) cover these forms of mobility by defining them on the basis of the number of nights when the concerned professionals are absent from their main residence. It is clear that the boundary between this practice and the one mentioned above concerning work-related bi-residence is porous. But for want of a better term, we present here the figures obtained to illustrate the extent of this practice. Transport sector employees fall into this category in the sense that they travel a lot in the course of their work.

The analysis by Ravalet et al. (2015)[5] shows that this phenomenon is far from trivial and affected 2% to 6% of the workforce depending on the territory in 2007 and 2011. Demel and Mayrhofer (2010) also mention, without quantifying, that this phenomenon affects a significant proportion of European professionals. Recourse to this practice will be linked to the sector of activity in which people work. The commercial sector and the commercial profession are particularly concerned (Aguiléra 2008), but we must also consider the mobile workers (train drivers or airplane pilots, for example) who have to deal with daily returns home that are often impossible.

While numbers are scarce, several research studies attest to the daily lives of the professionals involved (Aguiléra 2008; Demel and Mayrhofer 2010; Unger et al. 2016; Sandoz 2019).

---

5 See Ravalet et al. (2015, Table, p. 31).

8.3. The profile of the highly mobile population

Characterizing the highly mobile population allows us to discuss the sociodemographic and economic specialization of the population concerned.

The high work-related mobilities in all their forms affect men more than women. These findings are consistent with most work on the topic (Sermons and Koppelman 2001; Clark et al. 2003; Dargay and Hanly 2003; Gimenez-Nadal and Molina 2016). Several explanations can be given for this phenomenon. The first is that female-dominated occupations are more evenly distributed geographically than male-dominated ones (Hanson and Johnston 1985). The second element relates to the private sphere and touches on shares of domestic tasks and household responsibilities (Hanson and Pratt 1990; Sermons and Koppelman 2001; Clark et al. 2003; Gimenez-Nadal and Molina 2016; Moen 2018). In dual-earner couples, women's work locations are more directly related to the residential location of the household than men's (Sermons and Koppelman 2001; Clark et al. 2003; Gimenez-Nadal and Molina 2016).

Thus, men's commuting distances are generally higher than women's, except when the woman's salary is higher than her spouse's (Sermons and Koppelman 2001). In France, Germany, Spain and Switzerland, 13% of men aged 30–59 were highly mobile in 2011, compared with 7% of women. At the same time, 6% of men were affected by frequent absences from home compared to only 2% of women (Ravalet et al. 2015).

The second sociodemographic element concerns family structure: single-parent families stand out the most, with more than 15% of those living in this situation either commuting for long periods of time or being absent from home (Ravalet et al. 2015). Other observations in the New York City area support this and tend to show that single women with children are increasingly moving away from dense urban centers and allocating more and more time to commuting (Maciejewska et al. 2019).

The third point concerns income and education levels. The literature is somewhat contradictory on this topic. Groot et al. (2012) show that commuting increases in distance and time with education level in the Netherlands. The destination areas are also located in dense urban centers for workers with the highest levels of education, allowing for a higher use of public transport. This same result is found in other work on commuting (Crane 2007; Lyons and Chatterjee 2008; Sandow 2011) and on frequent work trips in France (Grimal 2010). In the same vein, the results obtained by Ravalet et al. (2015) show that high incomes and high levels of education were associated with more likely use of high mobility in 2007.

In contrast, in 2011–2012, in a context of recovery from the economic crisis, all socioeconomic profiles were equally affected by long-term commuting. At the same time, Marion and Horner (2007) showed that belonging to a racial minority, having a low income, or not having a high school diploma would increase the probability of resorting to intensive commuting in the United States. This is explained by the spatial dissociation between the places of residence of the most disadvantaged workers and the job opportunities that might interest them (Van Ommeren and Van der Straaten 2008).

Spatially, it appears firstly that peri-urbanization is contributing to the increase in distance between home and work (Maoh and Tang 2012). However, the gradual increase in the distance traveled has been partially offset by an increase in the speed of travel (Crozet and Joly 2006). Three factors seem to emerge in the literature regarding the role of space on commuting times and distances: city size, density, and structure (Vincent-Geslin and Ravalet 2016).

Ravalet et al. (2015) show that highly mobile people do not reside solely in central urban centers. Thus, the degree of urbanization does not play a significant role in the propensity to develop long-term mobility. In other words, highly mobile people can live in dense urban centers, as well as in smaller cities, peri-urban areas, or even rural areas. This was true both in 2007 and in 2011. However, the choices in terms of transport modes, and therefore the conditions under which these intensive mobility activities take place, will not be the same at all depending on the area in which people live and the quality of public transport services in that area.

We can conclude by recalling that these people are more often men than women, single people with children, and that although the most affluent and the best educated may be particularly concerned, the most vulnerable are also affected, and even more so in certain contexts or periods such as crises. Spatially, the spread of location systems (for people and jobs), particularly through peri-urbanization, increases the distance between home and work and the use of intensive commuting.

8.4. Reasons for the use of large-scale work-related mobility

As we saw in section 8.3, the description of profiles of the people most concerned by major work-related mobility already provides some elements of explanation as to why working people are led to resort to these forms of mobility.

The literature on the subject highlights three major clusters of explanations that are articulated and combined. These three elements are related to the professional sphere, the private sphere and the mobility sphere.

The work context obviously plays a decisive role in the use of intensive forms of work-related mobility for several reasons. Firstly, and perhaps most obviously, several occupations involve, by their very nature, frequent travel that results in frequent absence from home. For example, railway workers, airline flight crews, sales representatives who have to cover customers spread over large areas, or highly specialized technicians who work in a series of very distant jobs all find themselves in a situation that requires them to travel a lot and sometimes be away from their families for long periods.

But, beyond these professions, it is the whole society that has become particularly mobile and within which an injunction to be mobile and flexible has developed over time (Boltanski and Chiappello 1999; Sheller and Urry 2006; Bacqué and Fol 2007). This injunction affects the labor market rather directly. The increase in the number and proportion of short-term and precarious contracts (fixed-term contracts, temporary work, part-time work) makes the labor market less stable (Wenglenski 2006; Ng et al. 2007), especially for the least qualified (Bihr and Pfefferkorn 1999). Thus, an employer expects their employees to be willing to travel for work purposes, whether for short trips or longer stays abroad (Kaufmann 2008).

Local housing and labor market conditions also affect the ability of workers to limit their distance to work (Schwanen et al. 2004). Decisions to move closer to work depend on the location of employment opportunities, which are not uniformly distributed across space (Pierrard 2008). In a highly constrained social context of high unemployment, the geographic perimeter within which job seekers accept job offers tends to expand. In most European societies, job seekers must be prepared to move to find work (Ravalet et al. 2017). Migration and intensive commuting are more frequent in the case of unemployment (Ahn et al. 1999; Eliasson et al. 2003).

This geographic expansion of employment conditions is even encouraged by the institutions. For example, in Switzerland, the unemployed must accept any job offer that is deemed suitable by the unemployment insurance, with suitability particularly referring to commuting times of no more than four hours per day. Finally, migration is strongly encouraged by the European Commission at the continental level to optimize the functioning of individual national labor markets and the European economy in general (Van Houtum and Van der Velde 2004). This is in line with the view that unemployment is a result of the lack of flexibility of the labor force (Van Ham et al. 2001).

In addition to these elements related to the professional sphere, travelling a lot for work can also be explained by elements that are part of the family or private sphere. These elements can be considered as part of people's life choices. They are clearly reflected in household structure and residential location. The presence of children in the household, for example, plays a limiting role in the propensity of parents (or at least of both parents) to engage in a professional activity associated with frequent travel. Very often, it is women who will adapt their career requirements, choosing (or reselecting) part-time work, less professional responsibility, or proximity between home and work to manage the needs of young children (Chidambaram and Scheiner 2019). There is also a preference for families to live in single-family homes.

More generally, it is useful to unpack the logic of residential choice. Residential choice is influenced by the preferences of each member of the household, the place(s) of current or future employment, the schooling of children, etc. The literature highlights factors such as location, housing characteristics, or the social and physical environment of the place of living to explain residential choices; the importance given to each factor varies across individuals and households (Thomas 2013). The location of housing near a range of services (shops, banks, schools, etc.), and the physical and social environment of housing are also important criteria. It is understood that the resulting difficult trade-offs do not necessarily place the distance between home and work at the forefront of the criteria that will be considered, especially when both members of the couple work. This difficulty in arbitrating is at least accentuated by the high prices of real estate and land, which limit the range of possibilities in terms of location.

While the choice of residence results in a difficult equation, it is even more important to consider that mobility is a very involved event and that it cannot be repeated on a regular basis at important stages of life: leaving the family home, forming a couple, the arrival of a child, but also separation, getting back together, children leaving the family home, interruption or change of job, etc. In this changing context, which we have mentioned particularly from the point of view of the professional sphere, moving is sometimes not the chosen solution, knowing that the anchors and the social network around the home do not favor it (Fischer and Malmberg 2001; Vincent-Geslin and Kaufmann 2012). Thus, intensive forms of commuting are related to housing affordability and the means households have to choose where to live (Cuff 2011).

The third set of explanations that we feel is important to mention is that of mobility. In recent decades, space–time has been transformed and compressed. Political, economic, social, and cultural dynamics have contributed to a questioning of regional and national institutional barriers, and the professional or friendly ties that unite people today can be woven and maintained, even when the people concerned are very distant from each other. The mobility potentials that these improvements have offered and continue to offer make it possible to combine and connect what was once socially and spatially inconcilable (Urry 2005). While information and communication technologies are obviously not unrelated to this state of affairs, we will return to the role they can play in relation to spatial mobility in section 8.6.

Transport services (road, rail, and air) have expanded, allowing more people to be transported faster, more often and at lower costs. At the same time, the deregulation of air travel between countries is continuing and is enabling the development of a range of services that is no longer limited to intercapital connections.

For several decades, it has been possible to observe a certain constancy in the amount of time spent by each of us on daily transport (Zahavi and Talvitie 1980; Joly et al. 2006). This constancy of "time budgets" suggested the idea of a reinvestment in distance, of the time savings made possible by the increase in average speeds of the means of communication. In recent years, probably for all the reasons discussed in section 8.3, it seems that the average time spent traveling is now increasing (van Wee et al. 2006; Lyons and Chatterjee 2008; Hubert 2009; Department for Transport 2010; Sandow 2011; Vincent-Geslin and Joly 2012; OFS 2017). Yet, improvements in transportation supply and average speeds across all modes continue to increase.

In order to better understand what motivates workers to resort to intensive forms of work-related mobility, it is possible to conclude that the employment context is increasingly inviting them to do so, that preferences in terms of location only include the criterion of proximity to the workplace(s) in a secondary manner, that it is often not possible to move as often as changes (of a professional or private nature) occur, and that, finally, these trips are also made because they can be made, with infrastructures and services that facilitate mobility.

8.5. The experience of high work-related mobility

In general, highly mobile people who practice reversible forms of mobility see their mobility as a way of reconciling private and professional life. Indeed, long-term commuting, frequent absence from home and living as long-distance couples make it possible to combine a stable place of residence while working in one or more distant places (Vincent-Geslin and Kaufmann 2012).

In Ravalet et al.'s (2015) book, a Table[6] shows some of the discourses and perceptions of high work-related mobility. Even before the economic crisis of 2008, a relatively large number of Spaniards were already worried about their professional future (48% were afraid of losing their job), and many considered high mobility as negative (33%) or coercive (24%). After the economic crisis in 2011, half of the country's high-mobility workers (54%) said that high mobility had helped them escape a period of unemployment. On the other hand, it was less often perceived as a way to keep their homes, and 39% of Spanish high-mobility individuals did not feel at home anywhere. More generally, we note that the people surveyed in all four countries said they were more tired in 2011 than they were in 2007.

---

6 See Ravalet et al. (2015, Table, p. 50).

The rhetoric of long-term commuters is less positive than that of working people who resort to weekly commuting or frequent travel for work (Ravalet et al. 2017). The former report feeling more tired and having to deal with significant expenses. Moreover, they do not tend to see their careers enhanced by the concessions they make on a daily basis.

Finally, various costs can be identified. Thus, the literature shows that long journeys, and particularly commuting, have negative effects on well-being, including stress and fatigue (Lyons and Chatterjee 2008; Stutzer and Frey 2008; Gottholmseder et al. 2009; Koslovski et al. 2013; Aybeck et al. 2014), and these affect commuters whether they travel by car (Wener and Evans 2011) or by train (Aybeck et al. 2014). Of course, these elements are quite largely dependent on the distances traveled on a daily basis, and for Ingenfeld et al. (2019), stress increases sharply above 50 miles traveled per day per direction. Beyond the stress experienced on a daily basis, effects on obesity and difficulty in walking can be demonstrated (Mattisson et al. 2018).

It also seems that the use of intensive forms of mobility plays a role in the fragility of couples, even more so when it is women who are highly mobile (Ravalet et al. 2015). This obviously refers to the way in which domestic and parental tasks are distributed between them (Drevon 2019). The effect of intensive mobilities on separations in couples is confirmed in several scientific works (Brömmelhaus et al. 2019; Sandow 2019).

High mobility is perceived very differently by highly mobile people across Europe (Viry et al. 2015). For some of them, high mobility is a necessity and is imposed for economic reasons, while for others, it is more of a free choice in response to professional opportunities. For others still, high mobility will enable them to combine a job in a far away location with a local attachment to their place of residence. Finally, it should be noted that a significant proportion of highly mobile people are in a professional situation that is in fact accompanied by large-scale mobility (military, train drivers, sales representatives, etc.). The analysis of perceptions of high mobility thus highlights the importance of individuals' skills to cope with situations of mobility. These skills are constructed over time, as high mobility is practiced (Ravalet et al. 2015).

8.6. High mobility linked to work and digital technology, what prospects?

The development of telecommunication technologies has helped reconfigure the relationship that each of us has with the near and far. These technologies contribute to the acceleration of lifestyles and the development of large-scale mobility (Jemelin et al. 2004). Digital technology as a whole and the tools linked to it promote instantaneous exchanges, at any time of day and in any place. They imply permeability in the spheres of life and allow us to be together, connected, without necessarily being in proximity (Ravalet et al. 2015).

Vincent-Geslin et al. (2015) show that communication tools serve two purposes for the highly mobile. Firstly, they allow people to be connected remotely with family members when away from home, and with work colleagues during working hours, but also outside. Thus, these tools contribute to the permeability of the family, personal and professional spheres (Belton-Chevallier 2010). The communication tools then allow the highly mobile to withdraw into a bubble of familiarity or intimacy when they are in places that they are unfamiliar with or in which they are not comfortable. Finally, while they allow a certain appropriation of spaces and times of high mobility, it is partly to escape them and thus connect to people and places that are close and familiar to them (Vincent-Geslin et al. 2015).

Beyond this important role of Internet technology on the daily experience of the highly mobile, it seems interesting to us to discuss the way in which spatial and virtual mobilities can substitute each other or accumulate.

From a general point of view, we can note that the development of informal telework is often associated with work flexibility (Taskin and Schots 2005; Ernst 2007; Ravalet and Rérat 2019). It is important to consider that telework very often concerns only a (more or less significant) part of the worker's working time concerned. In most cases, it will involve one or two days per week (Sullivan 2003; Parent-Thirion et al. 2007; De Vos et al. 2019; Ravalet and Rérat 2019). Parent-Thirion et al. (2007) estimate that 20% of European employees work at least a quarter of their working time at home. In 2015, in Switzerland, the proportion of regular teleworkers (more than 50% of their working hours) was estimated at 1.3%, while the proportion of occasional teleworkers (less than 50% of their working time) was estimated at 19.7% (Confédération suisse 2016).

In a context where teleworking would be a simple substitution of a commute, it could limit the number of round trips to work in a week. However, according to Gubins et al. (2019), remote working has no measurable impact on the structuring of the labor market or on commuting, which would mean that commuting is not reduced by the new technologies. Beyond this, it has been hypothesized that longer commutes would be made acceptable by the possibility of teleworking from home or near home (Janelle 1986; Nilles 1991). This hypothesis has not been proven, but there is strong evidence that telecommuters live farther from their principle workplace than others (Mokhtarian et al. 2004; Peters et al. 2004; Ory and Mokhtarian 2006; Helminen and Ristimaki 2007; Zhu 2013; Ravalet and Rérat 2019). De Vos et al. (2019) even estimate a 16% growth in commuting distances for those who telework one day per week.

Teleworking could be a decision made after the residential choice, but to date, we do not have research to assess the greater tolerance for distance or commuting time induced by the possibility of telework. To date, it can be considered that teleworking may be an incentive (1) to choose a home away from the workplace, (2) not to move, or (3) to accept or keep a job away from home. However, for the time being, we can only observe that teleworking and long-distance commuting go hand in hand.

8.7. Conclusion

Our relationship with distance and time is in a state of perpetual change, and this is reflected in our work by intensive travel. This takes different forms, between daily, weekly and fluctuating commutes and frequent job-related travel. All of these forms of mobility are articulated together and are part of lifestyles that are less and less sedentary. In this context, the relationship between working people and the transport they use, the territories they travel through and the places in which they settle needs to be better understood so that all are adapted to this new mobile situation (Vendemmia 2020).

We have shown that major work-related mobility tends to involve men more often than women, and people living alone with their children, and that although the most affluent and the best trained may be particularly affected, the most vulnerable are also affected, and even more so in certain contexts or periods such as crises. Spatially, the spread of localization systems (of people and jobs), particularly through peri-urbanization, accentuates the distance between home and work and the need for intensive commuting.

In order to better understand what ultimately motivates workers to resort to intensive forms of work-related mobility, it is possible to conclude that the employment context is increasingly inviting them to do so, that preferences in terms of location only incorporate the criterion of proximity to the workplace(s) in a secondary manner, that it is often not possible to move as often as changes (of a professional or private nature) occur, and that, finally, these trips are also made because they can be, with infrastructures and services that facilitate mobility.

This chapter also takes stock of the consequences that high mobility practices can have on sociability, health and the balance of married life. The highlighting of these costs, which are very poorly known, makes it possible to put the merits of widespread mobility of the working population into perspective.

We have shown that teleworkers live further from their workplace than those who do not (by choice or not). But the causal link between these two parameters is difficult to assess. Residential location choices are the result of complex compromises involving all persons in the household. The multiplicity of criteria taken into account means that residential location is never optimized solely on the basis of its proximity to the workplace, especially in the case of dual-career couples (Deding et al. 2009). There is also a structural inertia to residential mobility, especially as various anchors are built around housing (Rérat and Lees 2011; Vincent-Geslin and Kaufmann 2012; Rérat 2014). These structuring choices and their temporality are therefore of great importance. At the same time, the place of work is a decisive factor in the spatialization of people's activities and mobility, but this choice is only weakly influenced by its location (Bunel 2009). These elements argue for an analysis of the logic of residential location through biographical or life-course approaches. This could allow a better appreciation of the role of telework on employees' tolerance of distance from work or on what could be considered as a support to residential inertia.

8.8. References

Aguilera, A. (2008). Business travel and mobile workers. *Transportation Research Part A*, 42, 1109–1116.

Ahn, N., de la Rica, S., Ugidos, A. (1999). Willingness to move for work and unemployment duration in Spain. *Economica*, 66(263), 335–357.

Aybek, C.M., Huinink, J., Muttarak, R. (2014). *Spatial Mobility, Migration, and Living Arrangements*. Springer, Berlin.

Bacqué, M.-H. and Fol, S. (2007). L'inégalité face à la mobilité : du constat à l'injonction. *Revue Suisse de Sociologie*, 33(1), 89–104.

Beauvais, J.-M., Fouquet, J.-P., Assegond, C. (2007). Recherche sur le développement de la grande vitesse et de la birésidentialité. Rentrer chez soi chaque soir ou une fois par semaine ? Report, DRAST, Paris.

Belton-Chevallier, L. (2010). Mobile ICTs as tools of intensification of travel time use? Results of qualitative study based on French workers. *12th World Conference on Transport Research*, Lisbon.

Bihr, A. and Pfefferkorn, R. (1999). *Déchiffrer les inégalités*. Syros, Paris.

Boltanski, L. and Chiapello, E. (2005). *The New Spirit of Capitalism*. Verso, London.

Brömmelhaus, A., Feldhaus, M., Schlegel, M. (2019). Family, work, and spatial mobility: The influence of commuting on the subjective well-being of couples. *Applied Research in Quality of Life*, 1–27.

Bunel, M. (2009). Concilier travail et vie familiale : que cachent les déclarations des hommes et des femmes. In *Entre famille et travail, des arrangements de couples aux pratiques des employeurs*, Pailhé, A., Solaz, A. (eds). La Découverte, Paris.

Chidambaram, B. and Scheiner, J. (2019). Understanding commuting behavior between partners. *Transportation Research Procedia*, 41, 376–379.

Clark, W.A., Huang, Y., Withers, S. (2003). Does commuting distance matter? Commuting tolerance and residential change. *Regional Science and Urban Economics*, 33(2), 199–221.

Confédération suisse (2016). Conséquences juridiques du télétravail. Report, Conseil fédéral en réponse au postulat 12.3166 Meier-Schatz, November 16th [Online]. Available at: https://www.bj.admin.ch/dam/data/bj/aktuell/news/2016/2016-11-16/ber-br-f.pdf.

Crane, R. (2007). Is there a quiet revolution in women's travel? Revisiting the gender gap in commuting. *Journal of the American Planning Association*, 73, 298–316.

Crozet, Y. and Joly, I. (2004). Budgets temps de transport: les sociétés tertiaires confrontées à la gestion paradoxale du bien le plus rare. *Les cahiers scientifiques du transport*, 45, 27–48.

Cuff, D. (2011). Los Angeles: Urban development in the postsuburban megacity. In *Megacities*, Sorenson, A., Okata, J. (eds). Springer, Tokyo.

Dargay, J. and Hanly, M. (2003). Travel to work: An investigation based on the British Household Panel Survey. *NECTAR Conference*, 13–17.

Deding, M., Filges, T., Van Ommeren, J. (2009). Spatial mobility and commuting: The case of two-earner households. *Journal of Regional Science*, 49(1), 113–147.

Demel, B. and Mayrhofer, W. (2010). Frequent business travelers across Europe: Career aspirations and implications. *Thunderbird International Business Review*, 52(4), 301–311.

Department for Transport (2010). Transport Trends. Transport Statistics. Report, DfT, London.

Drevon, G. (2019). *Proposition pour une rythmologie de la mobilité et des sociétés contemporaines. Espaces, mobilités et sociétés*. Alphil/Presses universitaires suisses, Neuchâtel.

Drevon, G., Dubois, Y., Ravalet, E., Kaufmann, V. (2019). L'importance croissante de la qualité des temps de déplacements. *Metis Presses*, 7, 159–170.

Duchêne-Lacroix, C. (2014). Habiter plusieurs logements habituels: éléments conceptuels et typologiques d'une pratique plurielle. In *Questionner les mobilités résidentielles à l'aune de la multilocalité*, Hamman, P., Blanc, M., Duchêne-Lacroix, C., Freytag, T., Kramer, C. (eds). Néothèque, Strasbourg.

Eliason, K., Lindgren, U., Westerlund, O. (2003). Geographical labour mobility: Migration or commuting? *Regional Studies*, 37(8), 827–837.

Ernst, M. (2007). La flexibilité du temps de travail : entre autonomie et contraintes. Une étude de cas en Suisse. PhD Thesis, Université de Marne-La-Vallée, Champs-sur-Marne.

Espinoza-Herold, M. and Contini, R.M. (eds) (2017). *Living in Two Homes*. Emerald Publishing, Bradford.

Eurostat (2018). Statistics on commuting patterns at regional level [Online]. Available at: https://ec.europa.eu/eurostat/statistics-explained/pdfscache/50943.pdf.

Fischer, P.A. and Malmberg, G. (2001). Settled people don't move: On life course and (im-) mobility in Sweden. *International Journal of Population Geography*, 7(5), 357–371.

Gimenez-Nadal, J.I. and Molina, J.A. (2016). Commuting time and household responsibilities: Evidence using propensity score matching. *Journal of Regional Science*, 56(2), 332–359.

Gottholmseder, G., Nowotny, K., Pruckner, G.J., Theurl, E. (2009). Stress perception and commuting. *Health Economics*, 18(5), 559–576.

Green, A., Hogarth, T., Shackleton, R. (1999). Longer distance commuting as a substitute for migration in Britain: A review of trends, issues and implications. *International Journal of Population Geography*, 5, 49–67.

Grimal, R. (2010). Mobilité à longue distance : plus de voyages s'effectuent en train, mais les seniors restent adeptes de la voiture. *La Revue du CGDD*, December.

Groot, S., De Groot, H.L., Veneri, P. (2012). The educational bias in commuting patterns: Micro-evidence for the Netherlands. Tinbergen Institute Discussion Paper, Amsterdam.

Gubins, S., van Ommeren, J., de Graaff, T. (2019). Does new information technology change commuting behavior? *The Annals of Regional Science*, 62(1), 187–210.

van Ham, M., Mulder, C., Hooimeijer, P. (2001). Spatial flexibility in job mobility: Macrolevel opportunities and microlevel restrictions. *Environment and Planning A*, 33, 921–940.

Hanson, S. and Johnston, I. (1985). Gender differences in work-trip length: Explanations and implications. *Urban Geography*, 6(3), 193–219.

Hanson, S. and Pratt, G. (1990). Geographic perspectives on the occupational segregation of women. *National Geographic Research*, 6, 376–399.

Helminen, V. and Ristimaki, M. (2007). Relationships between commuting distance, frequency and telework in Finland. *Journal of Transport Geography*, 15, 331–342.

van Houtum, H. and van der Velde, M. (2004). The power of cross-border labour and market immobility. *Tijdschrift voor Economische en Sociale Geografi*, 95(1), 100–107.

Hubert, J.-P. (2009). Dans les grandes agglomérations, la mobilité quotidienne des habitants diminue, et elle augmente ailleurs. *Insee Premiere*, 1252.

Ingenfeld, J., Wolbring, T., Bless, H. (2019). Commuting and life satisfaction revisited: Evidence on a non-linear relationship. *Journal of Happiness Studies*, 20(8), 2677–2709.

Janelle, D.G. (1986). Metropolitan expansion and the communications – Transportation trade-off. In *The Geography of Urban Transportation*, Hanson, S. (ed.). The Guilford Press, New York.

Jemelin, C., Vodoz, L., Pfister, B. (2004). Entre accélération et rupture d'équilibre : une société à deux vitesses. In *Les Territoires de la mobilité. L'aire du temps*, Vodoz, L., Pfister, B., Jemelin, C. (eds). Presses polytechniques et universitaires romandes, Lausanne.

Joly, I., Littlejohn, K., Kaufmann, V. (2006). La croissance des budgets-temps de transport en question : nouvelles approches. Final research report, PREDIT.

Jones, M.H., Massot, J.P., Orfeuil, L.P., Proulhac, L. (2008). Links between daily travel times and lifestyles of families. Report, La Fédération Internationale Automobile (FIA Foundation), Paris/London.

Kaufmann, V. (2010). Pendulaires ou bi-résidentiels en suisse : un choix de vie ? In *Élire domicile : la construction sociale des choix résidentiels*, Authier, J.-Y., Bonvalet, C., Lévy, J.-P. (eds). Presses universitaires de Lyon, Lyon.

Koslowsky, M., Kluger, A.N., Reich, M. (2013). *Commuting Stress: Causes, Effects, and Methods of Coping*. Springer, Berlin.

Lanéelle, X. (2006). Navette domicile-travail à grande vitesse : situation d'exception, arrangement traditionnel. *Cahiers du Genre*, 41(2), 159–180.

Lück, D. and Ruppenthal, S. (2010). Mobile living: Spread, appearances and characteristics. In *Mobile Living Across Europe II: Causes and Consequences of Job-Related Spatial Mobility in Cross-National Comparison*, Collet, B., Schneider, N. (eds). Barbara Budrich, Leverkusen/Opladen.

Lyons, G. and Chatterjee, K. (2008). A human perspective on the daily commute: Costs, benefits and trade-offs. *Transport Reviews*, 28(2), 181–198.

Maciejewska, M., McLafferty, S., Preston, V. (2019). Women's changing commutes: The work trips of single mothers in the New York region, 2000–2010. *Built Environment*, 45(4), 544–562.

Maoh, H. and Tang, Z. (2012). Determinants of normal and extreme commute distance in a sprawled midsize Canadian city: Evidence from Windsor. *Journal of Transport Geography*, 25, 50–57.

Marion, B. and Horner, M.W. (2007). A comparison of the socioeconomic and demographic profiles of "extreme" commuters in several US metropolitan statistical areas. *Transp. Res. Rec.*, 38–45.

Mattisson, K., Idris, A.O., Cromley, E., Håkansson, C., Östergren, P.O., Jakobsson, K. (2018). Modelling the association between health indicators and commute mode choice: A cross-sectional study in southern Sweden. *Journal of Transport and Health*, 11, 110–121.

Meissonnier, J. (2001). *Provinciliens : les voyageurs du quotidien*. L'Harmattan, Paris.

Moen, P. (ed.) (2018). *It's About Time: Couples and Careers*. Cornell University Press, New York.

Mokhtarian, P.L., Collantes, G.O., Gertz, C. (2004). Telecommuting, residential locations, and commute distance traveled: Evidence from state of California employees. *Environment and Planning A*, 36(10), 1877–1897.

Moss, M.L., Qing, C.Y., Kaufman, S. (2012). Commuting to Manhattan. A study of residence location trends for Manhattan workers from 2002 to 2009. Report, Rudin Center for Transportation Policy/New York University, New York.

Ng, T., Sorensen, K., Eby, L., Feldman, D. (2007). Determinants of job mobility: A theoretical integration and extension. *The Journal of Occupational and Organizational Psychology*, 80, 363–386.

Nilles, J.M. (1991). Telecommuting and urban sprawl: Mitigator or inciter? *Transportation*, 18, 411–432.

OFS (2012). La mobilité en Suisse. Résultats du microrecensement mobilité et transports 2010. Report, Office fédéral de la statistique, OFS 841-1000, Neuchâtel.

OFS (2017). Comportement de la population en matière de transports. Résultats du microrecensement mobilité et transports 2015. Report, Office fédéral de la statistique, OFS 841-1500, Neuchâtel.

Ojala, S. and Pyöriä, P. (2018). Mobile knowledge workers and traditional mobile workers: Assessing the prevalence of multi-locational work in Europe. *Acta Sociologica*, 61(4), 402–418.

van Ommeren, J.N. and van der Straaten, W. (2008). The effects of search imperfections on commuting behavior: Evidence from employed and self-employed workers. *Regional Science and Urban Economics*, 38(2), 27–147.

Orfeuil, J.-P. (2010). Les grands migrants au quotidien. In *Mobilités et modes de vie Métropolitains : les intelligences du quotidien*, Massot, M.-H. (ed.). L'Œil d'Or, Paris.

Ory, D.T. and Mokhtarian, P. (2006). Which came first, the telecommuting or the residential relocation? An empirical analysis of causality. *Urban Geography*, 27(7), 590–609.

Parent-Thirion, A., Fernandez Macias, E., Hurley, J., Vermeylen, G. (2007). Fourth European working conditions survey, European foundation for the improvement of living and working conditions. Report, Office for Official Publications of the European Communities, Luxembourg.

Pearce, M., Landriève, S., Gay, C., Dubois, T. (2020). Enquête Nationale Mobilité et modes de vie 2020. Report, Forum Vies Mobiles.

Peters, P., Tijdens, K.G., Wetzels, C. (2004). Employees' opportunities, preferences and practices in telecommuting adoption. *Information and Management*, 41, 469–482.

Pierrard, O. (2008). Commuters, residents and job competition. *Regional Science and Urban Economics*, 38(6), 565–577.

Ravalet, E. and Rérat, P. (2019). Teleworking: Decreasing mobility or increasing tolerance of commuting distances? *Built Environment*, 45(4), 582–602.

Ravalet, E., Vincent, S., Kaufmann, V., Viry, G., Dubois, Y. (2015). *Grandes mobilités liées au travail, perspective européenne*. Economica, New York.

Ravalet, E., Vincent-Geslin, S., Dubois, Y. (2017). Job-related "high mobility". Times of economic crisis: Analysis from four European countries. *Journal of Urban Affairs*, 39(4), 563–580.

Rérat, P. (2014). Highly qualified rural youth: Why do young graduates return to their home region? *Children's Geographies*, 12(1), 70–86.

Rérat, P. and Lees, L. (2011). Spatial capital, gentrification and mobility: Evidence from Swiss core cities. *Transactions of the Institute of British Geographers*, 36(1), 126–142.

Sandow, E. (2011). On the road: Social aspects of commuting long distances to work. PhD Thesis, Umeå University, Umeå.

Sandow, E. (2019). Til work do us part: The social fallacy of long-distance commuting. In *Integrating Gender into Transport Planning*, Scholten, C.L., Joelsson, T. (eds). Palgrave Macmillan, London.

Schmitz, F., Drevon, G., Gerber, P. (2012). La mobilité des frontaliers du Luxembourg : dynamiques et perspectives. Report, Les cahiers du CEPS/INSTEAD, Luxembourg.

Schneider, N.F. and Meil, G. (eds) (2008). *Mobile Living Across Europe I: Relevance and Diversity of Job-Related Spatial Mobility in Six European Countries*. Barbara Budrich, Leverkusen Opladen.

Schneider, N.F., Limmer, R., Ruckdeschel, K. (2002). *Mobil, flexible, gebunden – Familie und Beruf in der mobilen Gesellschaft*. Campus, Frankfurt/New York.

Schwanen, T., Dieleman, F.M., Dijst, M. (2004). The impact of metropolitan structure on commute behavior in the Netherlands: A multilevel approach. *Growth and Change*, 35(3), 304–333.

Sheller, M. and Urry, J. (2006). The new mobilities paradigm. *Environment and Planning A*, 38(2), 207–226.

Stock, M. (2006). L'hypothèse de l'habiter poly-topique. *Espacestemps*.

Stutzer, A. and Frey, B. (2008). Stress that doesn't pay: The commuting paradox. *The Scandinavian Journal of Economics*, 110(2), 339–366.

Sullivan, C. (2003). What's in a name? Definitions and conceptualisations of teleworking and homeworking. *New Technology, Work and Employment*, 18(3), 158–165.

Taskin, L. and Schots, M. (2005). Flexibilité du temps de travail et relation d'emploi. *Économies et Sociétés/Série Socio-Économie du Travail/Presses de l'ISMEA*, 26, 1471–1501.

Thomas, M.-P. (2013). *Urbanisme et modes de vie. Enquête sur les choix résidentiels des familles en Suisse*. Alphil/Presses universitaires suisses, Neuchâtel.

Unger, O., Uriely, N., Fuchs, G. (2016). The business travel experience. *Annals of Tourism Research*, 61, 142–156.

Urry, J. (2005). *Sociologie des mobilités : une nouvelle frontière pour la sociologie ?* Armand Colin, Paris.

Vendemmia, B. (2020). *Spaces for Highly Mobile People: Emerging Practices of Mobility in Italy*. Routledge, London.

Viard, J. (2011). *Nouveau portrait de la France : la société des modes de vie*. Éditions de l'Aube, La Tour d'Aigues.

Vincent-Geslin, S. and Joly, I. (2012). Raisons et pratiques de la pendularité intensive. Le temps de trajet, entre temps subi et temps choisi. *Cahiers scientifiques des transports*, 61, 159–186.

Vincent-Geslin, S. and Kaufmann, V. (2012). *Mobilité sans racines. Plus loin, plus vite... plus mobiles*. Descartes, Paris.

Vincent-Geslin, S. and Ravalet, E. (2016). Determinants of extreme commuting. Evidence from Brussels, Geneva and Lyon. *Journal of Transport Geography*, 54, 240–247.

Vincent-Geslin, S., Ravalet, E., Kaufmann, V. (2015). L'appropriation des temps et des espaces de la grande mobilité à l'ère du numérique. *Géo-regards : revue neuchâteloise de géographie*, 7, 17–36.

Viry, G. and Kaufmann, V. (eds) (2015). *High Mobility in Europe: Work and Personal Life*. Springer, Berlin.

Viry, G., Ravalet, E., Kaufmann, V. (2015). High mobility in Europe: An overview. In *High Mobility in Europe*, Viry, G., Kaufmann, V. (eds). Palgrave Macmillan, London.

de Vos, D., van Ham, M., Meijers, E.J. (2019). Working from home and commuting: Heterogeneity over time, space, and occupations. Working document, IZA.

van Wee, B., Rietveld, P., Meurs, H. (2006). Is average daily travel time expenditure constant? Search of explanations for an increase in average travel time. *Journal of Transport Geography*, 14(2), 109–122.

Wener, R.E. and Evans, G.W. (2011). Comparing stress of car and train commuters. Transportation Research Part F: Traffic. *Psychology and Behaviour*, 14(2), 111–116.

Wenglenski, S. (2006). Regards sur la mobilité au travail des classes populaires. Une exploration du cas parisien. *Cahiers scientifiques du transport*, 49, 103–127.

Zahavi, Y. and Talvitie, A. (1980). Regularities in travel time and money expenditure. *Transportation Research Record*, 750, 13–19.

9

Event-Driven Mobility: From a Theoretical Approach to Practical Management

Pascal VIOT

Laboratoire de sociologie urbaine (LaSUR), École polytechnique fédérale de Lausanne, Switzerland

9.1. Introduction: the challenges of contemporary event-driven mobility

Defined as a change of place by one or more persons, but also as the crossing of geographical space associated with a transformation of the self, regarding the actors concerned, mobility opens up a space for theoretical reflection with significant practical implications in terms of planning, land use, and infrastructure choices. The significance of daily travel in social practices has increased exponentially over the past 50 years, fuelled by the development of public transport and the democratization of access to an individual vehicle. This trend has had significant effects in terms of residential and professional choices and in terms of lifestyles more generally.

As soon as it becomes possible to move more quickly and therefore to cover greater distances by optimizing travel time, all the logics of the use of time and space in society are modified to the point that the analysis of mobility practices is at the heart of the object of the knowledge of sociologists, geographers, and urban planners. In this sense, we are now witnessing a relatively broad acceptance within the scientific community of the idea of a mobility turn (Sheller and Urry 2006), which led Éric Le Breton, for example, to say:

> Mobility is not a sectoral and autonomous dimension of social life; on the contrary, it is a dimension that cuts across all social practices without exception. (Le Breton 2006).

This correspondence of a theoretical moment and a practical moment, starting from questioning daily mobilities, is now being deployed in the field of leisure mobility. For although mobility is often understood primarily as daily, its definition as "all the travel practices of a population within its usual framework" (Segaud et al. 2001) also covers more exceptional travel, or at least travel outside the professional routine. Among all the leisure activities, the supply and demand of which are constantly increasing, participation in major cultural, sporting, or commercial events is of particular interest in the analysis of mobility. By their very nature, these events bring together large numbers of participants and generate large inflows and outflows that often push existing transport networks to the limit in terms of their capacity to absorb exceptional use, which is often in addition to daily travel.

The first part of the analysis proposed in this chapter will be the issues at stake when a territory is put to the test by the organization of a major event. How can we think about the impact of event-driven mobilities on a territory that will have to transform and adapt itself to make room for the organization of a major event? Through various examples and case studies drawn from our surveys at the local and regional levels in French-speaking Switzerland, and more broadly by taking into account the evolution of event management practices at the international level, we will discuss the problems faced by managers (organizers, public authorities) in terms of mobility and accessibility when holding a large event. We will also present the tools used in this form of management by the actors, oriented toward the management of what we will call "the maintenance of road order".

In a second step, starting from the difficulties and limits faced by the actors in charge of the systems, we will broaden the reflection by approaching the planning of the offer with regard to an anticipation of the demand based on calculation and forecasting. This will allow us to propose a vision of event mobility that takes more into account the factors that influence the mobility behaviors and modal choices made by event participants. Based on the current theories of "motility", which denotes "the capacity of a person or a group to be mobile" (Kaufmann 2000), we will try to combine in the analysis a reflection on the social conditions of access (to which it is possible to use the offer in the broad sense), the knowledge and skills that the use of this offer requires, and the mobility projects that the effective use of the offer allows to materialize.

Indeed, travel, understood as "the movement of a person from an origin to a destination" (Merlin and Choay 2005), while representing the basic unit of mobility, is rarely an end in itself; it is the product of an intention and a goal related to the intended destination. This goal, which constitutes the reason for travel, is part of a logic of individual or collective planning that is much more complex than the current approaches, which are based in particular on transport engineering. Understanding these issues in terms of analysis will allow us to pave the way for the presentation of alternative approaches emerging today on an international scale around event mobility management. As a practical counterpart (applied to events) to mobility turn theories, these new approaches advocate taking into account event mobility issues not as constraints or undesirable effects but as a component to be integrated into an organizational process. In this sense, it is necessary to take into account the expectations and the logic of the mobile behaviors of the participants and to integrate them into an experienced path by proposing an organized accessibility concept with an adapted service offer. In conclusion, we will lay the programmatic foundations of a "sociology of event mobility", which, from a theoretical point of view, aims to consider major events as concentrates of urbanity that allow us to see the issues at work that are present but diluted on the scale of everyday mobility. From a practical point of view, we will finally show how these reflexive tools can contribute to improving the quality of the experience for event managers and organizers as well as participants.

9.2. Mobility and major events: testing the host territory

Leisure can be defined as time spent away from work and domestic activities and encompasses activities such as relaxation, cultural or sporting events, visits, etc. (Ettema and Schwanen 2012). An important part of leisure time is part of the daily routine in the broad sense and concerns activities that people do once or several times a week (often sport, cultural, or society activities). Others take place at a slightly lower frequency but on a recurring basis during the year (trips to the movies, restaurants, etc.). These two elements can be grouped under the term daily leisure mobility (Munafo 2016). Traditional surveys such as the Household Travel Surveys (HTS) or even the microcensus in Switzerland allow for a fairly good analysis of such leisure activities, although their frequencies are variable. Other leisure activities are more exceptional. Their very low frequency means that their study using conventional databases is not relevant.

It is precisely these exceptional trips that will interest us in this chapter. Indeed, while the mobility inherent in "regular" leisure activities is generally integrated into the framework of usual and routine travel, the travel of participants to a major event, which takes place over an exceptional period of time and volume, will put a strain on the mobility infrastructures of the area concerned and pose specific management problems.

9.3. A qualitative and quantitative test

The influx of participants during a major event will constitute a test of the city in both qualitative and quantitative terms (Viot et al. 2010), which is particularly important when it comes to mobility. Indeed, the territory affected by the event sees its daily organization disrupted by a supernumerary influx of individuals who come to participate in the event. From a quantitative point of view, it is then a question of managing these people who will be present, in addition to the population residing in the territory. With 40,000 visitors per day and located near a highway junction that constitutes an obvious access point to the site, the Paléo Festival de Nyon constitutes a typical case of collusion of regular flows of commuters on the Geneva–Lausanne highway and festival-goers whose peak arrival time corresponds with the average "leaving the office" times. This addition of flows obviously generates a risk of congestion that the actors in charge of the road regulation system try to manage as best as they can by setting up relief routes and diversionary routes or by promoting carpooling (Ravalet and Viot 2017).

Qualitatively, too, these participants in major events will have mobility behaviors that differ from the daily norm and that will create difficulties. Indeed, as habits do necessarily play a different role in the movements to participate in an event rather than in the usual local mobility, participants will find themselves in a logic of defining *ad hoc* routes and thus choosing means of transport in order to plan their journey. Of course, those who go to an event such as a festival will prefer to use their car because they are used to using it on a daily basis, or public transport because they already use it regularly, but in this case, the route concerned will not be a usual route, which is well known and full of landmarks, and this will generate a specific need for information. This form of loss of autonomy of participants in their mobility behavior is all the more pronounced when the management of urban fluidity is accompanied by exceptional traffic management measures (detours, street closures, changes in traffic direction). The two typical figures of the "event tourist" who is trying to find their way and the "local participant" whose spatial reference points for orientation and finding their way are disrupted, are then combined.

The Geneva International Motor Show is an interesting case study in this respect. In 10 days, the event attracts between 670,000 and 720,000 visitors each year, with peaks of 80,000 people per day on weekends. The entire city is affected by this event, particularly because of the overloaded road network, since between 55% and 60% of visitors come to the show by car, causing numerous traffic jams. In order to mitigate the situation as much as possible, the event organizers and the authorities have defined a modular management concept for the situation, allowing access flows to be switched according to the expected or observed number of visitors, the opening or closing of parking lots according to their occupancy rate, or any particular problem disrupting traffic (accidents). However, this agility in operational management has its limits in the blurring of information available to motorists, whose distribution can be disrupted by material contingencies (unsuitable signage, competition from GPS, etc.)[1].

This testing of the event's territory reconfigures the issues and requires management measures to be put in place to guarantee the continuity of "normal" activities. The fluidity of the networks is indeed an essential condition for the current territories to function. The risk of congestion leads to blockages in the networks (overloading of public transport, traffic jams on the roads). What is lost here is the ability for individuals to move around and thus to articulate mobility in the space and the time resources available.

If mobile individuals become immobile, then the entire organization of social life can see its working routines being threatened. The test generated by the organization of the event is therefore of this order. It is necessary to maintain the fluidity of the networks at a satisfactory level both from the point of view of "normal" social activities and from the exceptional activity that participation in the event represents. This exercise is increasingly common in city development [2]. The payoff is as great as the challenge: cities need to demonstrate plasticity as an indicator of urban quality, that is, they need to be able to adapt to changes in flows in order to demonstrate that they are cities with every desirable quality.

In order to understand how the territories concerned rise to this challenge, we must now enter into the details of the strategies and tools for managing event mobility.

9.4. Road policing strategy

This approach is the most routinized and corresponds to a state of grappling with the issues where the problem of mobility and accessibility to major events is defined in terms of difficulty and public safety. In view of the potentially large flows generated by the event, the public authority mobilizes its resources and capacities in terms of public safety management to regulate the flows. The logic at work is reminiscent of that caricature of the police officer at a crossroads equipped with a signaling baton who successively directs the flows of vehicles in order to limit blockages (and the mood swings of motorists!). In a way, it is an extension of this vision that is still largely found today in the mobilization of police forces to manage measures to adapt traffic lanes on the outskirts of an event. Whether it is a question of closing lanes or setting up alternative routes, it is logically the police in charge of security on the public highway who are at the forefront of management.

---

1 See on this subject Viot et al. (2017).
2 This is reflected in the notion of *eventful cities*, according to Richards and Palmer (2010).

This classic road policing strategy is also reflected in the vision of the organizers. The *Health and Safety Guide*, an international reference in terms of good practices for organizers, makes the following recommendation:

> Traffic management proposals need to be planned to ensure safe and convenient site access and to minimize off-site traffic disruption. Set your traffic management proposals out in a transport management plan and agree the plan with the police and local highway authority.

The main issue related to mobility management for events is the management of an overload of traffic on constant infrastructure. This is a complex approach where the organizers and their partners will have to play with the provisional arrangement of access or relief roads in order to guarantee the best possible combination between regular traffic and event mobility. All this must be anticipated and planned well in advance. According to the *Health and Safety Guide*, the following recommendations can be made for the operational management of road traffic generated by a major event:

> Identify the need for temporary traffic signs before the event. If temporary traffic signs are needed, prepare and agree detailed traffic signs plans and schedules with the police and local highway authorities before the event. It may be necessary for people living in the area to be consulted over route changes and to be advised of the impact, once agreement has been reached. Consider using a traffic sign contractor for events where the majority of people will be arriving by cars or coaches.

This relatively effective historical approach is nevertheless reaching its limits for a number of reasons. The number of events is increasing and the ability of police forces to provide a presence and service at each event is problematic. This is in addition to other public safety needs, such as managing the behavior of participants outside of the mobility route (arrival of fans/hooligans in the vicinity of the stadium) or the risks inherent to safety issues (malicious acts, crime, terrorism). Finally, by concentrating on a "road" approach to the problem of mobility, it struggles to integrate other complementary or alternative modes of travel into a general and integrated concept in terms of management.

The organization of the Euro 2008 soccer tournament in Geneva required the implementation of supporting measures in terms of mobility combining the three domains of automobile traffic (or motorized traffic in general), soft, namely nonmotorized, mobility, and in this case essentially pedestrian, and urban, rail, and even international public transport. In order to avoid problems with congestion, the canton of Geneva took significant measures in terms of traffic, based on a concept that had already been tested on the occasion of other major past events. Thus, the city had a system and experience prior to the event (Frankauser et al. 2008).

Nevertheless, while there was a basic concept of traffic regulation for major events in Geneva, Euro 2008 required some adaptations linked to the particular context of these festivities. On the one hand, there were multiple sites of entertainment, and the event was not concentrated in one single place. On the other hand, the simultaneous management of several activity sites was combined with the long duration of the event, which took place over 3 weeks. Finally, it was necessary to take into consideration the importance of the usual daily activities of the permanent residents, as well as the mobility of the "ephemeral" residents, i.e. the supporters.

The pedestrian course, for example, was deployed only on the sidewalks of the streets that ran along the route, illustrated by markings on the ground. The desire to offer a protected route for soft mobility therefore came up against a higher objective, that of not obstructing the traffic lanes and not having to confront any cars. Two points are in contradiction here: on the one hand, the separation of modes of transport, which was a recurrent concern of the organizers, particularly for safety reasons, and on the other, the refusal to prioritize modes of transport despite the prevailing and much publicized discourse promoting public transport.

This tension between the desire to promote soft mobility as a mode of transport suitable for the event and the fear of hindering motorists accompanied the entire preparation and planning phase of the event. In the end, the implementation of specific collaborations at the canton level, integrating different modes of transport in the reflection, contributed to a rather balanced distribution of modal shares on match days. The overall result was positive in terms of traffic flow management and alternative public transport supply, at least from a quantitative point of view (Viot 2013).

This result reveals the interest of an approach to mobility in general, moving away from an approach based on traffic problems *stricto sensu*. It is the product of specific collaborations set up by a working group led by a delegate of the State of Geneva and integrating a transport engineering office commissioned alongside representatives of the cantonal police and Geneva public transport.

9.5. Toward a mobility turn of event-driven management practices

The case of Euro 2008 in Geneva allows us to address a management strategy that is constantly developing today in the management of event-driven mobility: that of planning supported by the engineering sciences in the field of transportation. This approach, which is complementary to road policing, has become an important field of expertise over the last 20 years with the development of engineering and consulting firms in mobility planning that propose analyses and models upstream of the event in order to plan exceptional flows and anticipate them in order to better manage them.

9.5.1. *The engineer's planning strategy*

For a long time underestimated in relation to the management of road safety and traffic flows, expertise in mobility planning in the broad sense of the term for major events is now a sector of activity in its own right, based on established knowledge forged by a growing number of specialists. These specialists, often from the engineering sciences, rely for example on modeling to anticipate the arrival and departure of vehicles and to identify the risks of congestion according to the characteristics of the road network. The same logic also applies to public transport and pedestrian flows. Simulations can be used to visualize flows and assess the impact of traffic regulation measures to help optimize participants' waiting time.

Thanks to these information and visualization tools, managers are able to benefit from more precise information on the flows to be expected: number of people per time slot, impact study on infrastructure capacities, waiting times, or congestion to be expected. With this knowledge, they are in a better position to make choices about facilities or improvements to match the capacity of the service to the demand of users.

This approach to transport engineering also makes it possible to work on the modal split in relation to event mobility by calibrating the offer according to the objective of optimizing the networks or by thinking about the intermodality of participants' journeys, i.e., the use of several means of transport in a chain for the same trip. Indeed, it is not only a question of adapting services quantitatively but also of thinking qualitatively about the connections between the different modes of travel used in order to provide credible incentives for the target audiences. In this sense, the organization of shuttles to transport participants to a large event from planned car parks takes on a crucial importance. Of equal importance is the management of connections from the railway stations to the event site. Two important dimensions of event mobility management are often underestimated: on the one hand, the need for a true multimodal vision to define a plan that guarantees the best possible accessibility to the event perimeter, and on the other hand, the interweaving of mobility and safety issues, in the sense that the last part of the participants' journey will require specific crowd flow management.

The *Fête des vignerons*, a traditional event organized every 20 years in Vevey, Switzerland, is an example of the complexity of managing this type of problem. With a budget of 100 million Swiss francs, the last event, which took place in 2019, brought together 375,000 spectators for the 20 official performances of the show designed by Daniele Finzi Pasca, designer of the ceremony for the Winter Olympics in Turin (2006) and Sochi (2014). Adding the audience present in the perimeter of the spectacular arena built to host the show, the organizers estimated that about 1 million spectators came to Vevey during the 25 days of festivities.

Confederation Day, on August 1, attracted 100,000 people, making it the busiest day of the festival. The conditions for arrival and accessibility were the major challenges for the organizers of the event, which had to be held in an urban area of 20,000 inhabitants over 239 hectares, i.e., a density of more than 8,300 inhabitants per kilometer (the densest in the canton of Vaud and the second densest in Switzerland). As the event took place in the heart of the city on the market square and its surrounding areas, the problems linked to the management of public flows in the cramped streets of the city center proved to be particularly difficult to manage. In an urban environment where traffic is a recurrent problem in normal times, it was quite unthinkable to welcome a mass of extra vehicles close to the festival. The promotion of public transport was therefore deployed on a large scale in order to reach a target of 75% of visitors "without a car".

The mobility planning consultancy firm commissioned (late) by the organizers produced and coordinated a management concept in collaboration with the partners in charge of public transport (buses, trains) and public safety, which provided for, in addition to limiting traffic in the city center, a reinforcement of the offer to promote accessibility to public transport. The point of disruption was the Vevey railway station, where visitors from the carparks and users of local, regional, and national public transport converged.

The fact that the Vevey train station (partially redeveloped to accommodate this exceptional flow) is located about 300 m from the central location of the event was a particular asset in promoting a choice of alternative means of transportation to the car. On the other hand, the concentration of pedestrian flows in the "last kilometer" of the visitors' route (in this case, concentrated in the 500 m around the arena) was a permanent headache for the organizers. The arrival and departure routes from the station to the arena and back, as well as the management of the queues in front of the station during the mass departures at the end of the shows, focused the attention of the managers throughout the preparation and operation, for fear that an overcrowding of pedestrians could lead to a safety problem (jostling, crowd movement, malicious acts).

This consideration of the wider perimeter of the event is therefore one of the major lessons learned from this example. In a logic of event mobility management, traffic calculations and forecasts in order to influence participants' choice of transport or to calibrate the transport offer must take into account the entire visitor experience, and in particular what happens in the so-called last mile between the drop-off point and the access to the event site itself.

The characteristic of this interstitial space is that it is largely underestimated today, both in terms of the design of the use of space and the planning of flow management measures (following the example of Vevey, which has just been developed), and that it does not belong to any of the actors in the organization in terms of management and responsibility. In addition, there is a lack of skills in the ability to think about the challenges of this last part of the organization, between specialists in mobility planning and public safety specialists who are more attentive to crowd behavior than to the risks associated with density. It is on this basis that a new space for reflection and practice is opening up around a global vision of event mobility in relation to the experience of participants as a whole and the multiple issues that run through it, between flow and safety management.

9.5.2. *The user-spectator's experience pathway*

"People don't follow signs!" This comment, often heard in the control rooms of major events, sums up the difficulties encountered by mobility managers at major events, who are confronted with constantly changing mobility behaviors. Until recently, mobile individuals lived their travel experience on the model of the travelling tourist, who opens themself up to the unknown of the new territory to be explored and bases their choices of direction to find their way on the information made available in the course of their action (map, boards). Today, individuals have a different behavior, fueled by the multiplicity of sources of information on how to travel, real-time information, and by the compression of the perception of time that leads to a desire to optimize periods of travel[3]. This generates a stronger inclination to plan one's trips before the experience. Individuals equip themselves and organize themselves before the event to plan their travel to and from the event.

This leads us to a first observation: participants in an event are no longer lost tourists looking for their way; they have become experts in planning in order to optimize their trip, arbitrating between cost, time, and practicality. In doing so, they are looking for reliable information in order to complete their travel plans. They are also looking for up-to-date information, which is why they check, for example, whether their information matches that given by the traffic officer in charge of the traffic management system. The driver is also hybridized with the technological tools

---

3 On the uses of guidance apps and its effects on traffic control, see Courmont (2018).

at their disposal that provide them with continuous information: GPS, smartphone, applications, etc.

Whether by private vehicle or public transport, participants seek to make their journey as smoothly and as quickly as possible by making continuous adaptations according to the information made available to them. This immediacy in the search for up-to-date information requires an extreme reactivity in the updating of the information made available[4]. This behavior can also be explained by the fact that systems and networks that are just-in-time in normal times can become rapidly saturated during an event. In such an environment, the planning of trips for optimization purposes becomes a condition of survival in the organization of one's daily life.

A second observation: approaches in terms of managing flows and mobility of organizers are still largely fueled by a vision of the "stupid" crowd whose behavior must be constrained to avoid chaos. In the same way that current innovations in policing street demonstrations are beginning to integrate crowd psychology approaches (Fillieule et al. 2016), the management of participant flows applied to events must take into account the factors influencing behavior and consider that these are determined according to the raft of information available to them at the time of choosing their travel route. Indeed, individuals who gather to participate in a leisure event will see their choice of travel behavior influenced by the information distributed or accessible before and during their experience (special transportation schedules, site maps, numbering of car parks, signage along the route). This distribution of information creates a global experience path where travel choices are updated in real time according to the information available (traffic jams on the road, transport disruptions, etc.).

Taking these elements into account, the role of event managers will be to take into consideration the experience of participants in their journey to the event site and to support them in this process, so that they gain autonomy and the ability to move around. The aim here is to implement the theoretical paradigm shift proposed by Kaufmann (2002) when he suggests moving from mobility to "motility" in order to think about the way in which an actor makes the possibilities of movement provided by remote transport and communication systems their own. Motility is thus understood as the way in which a person or a group makes the field of possible travel their own and makes use of it: it is a matter of intentionality and projects.

---

4 For an analysis of the impact of social network information on the behaviors of event participants, see Cottrill et al. (2017).

9.5.3. *The development of event mobility management practices*

At the crossroads of theory and practice, a new field of professional activity has emerged in recent years – particularly in the English-speaking world – around event mobility management. This approach was first developed in the context of major events with a global reach such as the Olympic Games, which has acted as a prototype for event mobility management, with the particularly successful experience of the Sydney Olympics in 2000, which resulted in 90% of spectators using public transport (Bovy 2003). In this sense, the Olympic Games are a benchmark for mobility policies applied to major urban events. Since they take place on multiple sites that are necessarily interconnected within the city perimeter, they have a strong impact on mobility balances over a long period.

This is why specialists in this field recommend the creation of special units dealing specifically with transport and mobility management very early on the preparation process events:

> Every major event organization must have a transport unit or cell in charge of planning, designing operations, traffic management, parking and special transport to support the event. This transport unit is also responsible for close coordination with the public authorities in charge of transport, road management, parking and public transport, and security (Bovy et al. 2004).

The link with the theme of safety – which we have already mentioned in section 9.4 – goes hand in hand with taking into account all of the stages that make up the experience of the participants. It is therefore necessary to reverse the logic based on "professional skills" (that of the transport engineer, the public order specialist, or the event manager) and adopt a planning and management mode that is at the level of the participant's experience. It will also be necessary to articulate time and space in this process, and also to understand the participants' logic of action according to their social characteristics and their behavioral dynamics. This reasoning will have to be deployed over the entire journey, i.e., from the starting point of the experiment and integrating all the modes of travel available, up to walking the last part of the journey.

Still (2014), in his book *Introduction to Crowd Science*, makes an interesting contribution to this approach by developing the RAMP (Routes, Areas, Movement, People) model. Initially a specialist in the modeling of pedestrian flows, the author extends his theory by integrating factors that influence the movement of individuals in a crowd context, whether sociological (who are the participants, where do they come from, when will they arrive at the event site?) or architectural and urbanistic (analysis of the spatial configuration of the site, anticipation of congestion, positioning of barriers or elements to direct the flows, signage)[5].

Fueled by this feedback on mega-events and by applied research approaches similar to the one presented, a sector of activity is currently being established to meet the growing need to integrate mobility management into the general process of organizing an event. It should be noted that this new know-how is deployed at the interface between mobility issues (accessibility to the periphery of the event site) and safety issues (management of pedestrian crowds in the immediate vicinity in the last mile). We can therefore see that there is a strong link between event mobility management and crowd safety management (Kemp et al. 2007) in order to match the reality of the experience lived by the participants. A traffic jam on the highway will cause delays in arrivals or departures. An overcrowded public transport system will result in longer waiting times to get on the bus and a longer journey time. Overcrowding in a pedestrian area can lead to discomfort and even serious accidents. In all cases, it is a matter of matching demand and capacity to adjust supply, make travel more fluid, and manage crowds in an appropriate manner. Otherwise, the event itself is threatened in its sustainability, as in the case of the "T in the Park" festival in Scotland, which after more than 20 years of existence, did not recover from the chaos in terms of accessibility during the 2015 event, due to a poorly anticipated[6] change of site.

9.6. Conclusion: toward a sociology of event-driven mobility

Current specialists in crowd psychology, breaking with earlier visions of the instinctive and irrational crowd (Le Bon 2013), consider, on the contrary, that a crowd, gathered for example during a political demonstration, reacts to the messages that are addressed to it (prior information on the routes, direct communication by megaphone, police posture). They even base their theory on the idea of a social process of constitution of a common identity that explains the feeling of collective belonging and the alignments of norms, practices, and behaviors (Drury and Stott 2013). In the field of mobility, Kaufmann (2008) defines mobility as "the intention and then the realization of a crossing of geography involving social change". The originality of the analysis lies in the fact that, based on this general definition, the investigations focus on mobility intentions and the act of moving, rather than on the movements themselves (Kaufmann 2014).

Inspired by these two approaches, the aim is to see, within the framework of an analysis of event mobility, how individuals transport themselves and move around in

---

5 See also Still (2019).
6 www.bbc.co.uk/newsbeat/article/36742993/t-in-the-park-boss-says-hes-learnt-massive-lessons-from-last-years-festival and https://www.bbc.com/news/newsbeat-48961495.

space, but also how this mobility transforms them and makes them members of the community of participants in the event. The fan dressed to support his team (make-up, jersey, scarf, foghorn, flag) lives this experience in an ideal-typical way when he makes the journey between his home and the stadium. At the beginning, he is the only one to wear this outfit (which will not fail to attract the amused looks of the other travelers on the subway), but his identity as a supporter will be validated as he travels along the route, by joining the flow of his fellow travelers until the climax of the arrival in the stands, where an ephemeral, but intense community will vibrate together for 90 minutes. The same process can be seen in the movements of activists on their way to a political demonstration, fans of a band on their way to a concert, or festival-goers on their way to set up their tent at the campsite.

The theoretical and practical approaches that we have discussed in this chapter open up a new space for investigation into the analysis of modes of "being in a crowd" that begins well before the experience of physical proximity in front of a stage or in a stadium. An entry through mobility associated with attention to questions of flow and security management allows the research project to be deployed over the entire process, from the remote constitution of a logic of gathering – based on the planning of aggregated trips – to the moment of convergence that constitutes the crowd around the event site. This process is a continuum of experience for the participants and must be taken into account in its entirety in order to understand, from a theoretical point of view, the social and behavioral dynamics at work and, from a practical point of view, to support, supervise, and manage the phenomenon that is generated.

9.7. References

Bovy, P.H. (1999). Les grandes manifestations : des laboratoires en vraie grandeur de gestion des déplacements. Des tests de gestion du trafic pour les jeux olympiques Sydney 2000. *Revue Transports*, 397.

Bovy, P.H., Potier, F., Liaudat, C. (2004). *Les grandes manifestations ; planification, gestion des mobilités et impacts*. Éditions de l'Aube, La Tour d'Aigues.

Cottrill, C., Gault, P., Yeboah, G., Nelson, J.D., Anable, J., Budd, T. (2017). Tweeting Transit: An examination of social media strategies for transport information management during a large event. *Transportation Research Part C: Emerging Technologies*, 77, 421–432.

Courmont, A. (2018). Les effets de Waze sur les politiques de régulation du trafic. *Revue française de sociologie*, 59, 423–449.

Drury, J. and Stott, C. (2013). *Crowds in the 21st century: Perspectives from Contemporary Social Science*. Routledge, London.

Ettema, D. and Schwanen, T. (2012). A relational approach to analysing leisure travel. *Journal of Transport Geography*, 24, 173–181.

Fillieule, O., Viot, P., Descloux, G. (2016). Vers un modèle européen de gestion policière des foules protestataires ? *Revue française de science politique*, 66(2), 295–310.

Frankhauser, E. (2008). Un Euro 2008 riche en enseignements sur la mobilité événementielle. *Route et trafic*, 12.

Frankhauser, E., Tufo, F., Wittwer, F. (2008). Genève pose les bases d'une mobilité conviviale à l'EURO 2008. *Route et trafic*, 1–2.

HSE (1999). *The Event Safety Guide*, 2nd edition. HM Stationary Office, London.

Kaufmann, V. (2000). De la mobilité à la motilité. In *Enjeux de la sociologie urbaine*, Bassand, M., Kaufmann, V., Joye, D. (eds). Presses polytechniques et universitaires romandes, Lausanne.

Kaufmann, V. (2008). *Les paradoxes de la mobilité*. Presses polytechniques et universitaires romandes, Lausanne.

Kaufmann, V. (2014). *Retour sur la ville – Motilité et transformations urbaines*. Presses polytechniques et universitaires romandes, Lausanne.

Kemp, C., Hill, I., Upton, M., Hamilton, M. (2007). *Case Studies in Crowd Management*. Entertainment Technology Press, Cambridge.

Le Bon, G. (2013). *Psychologie des foules*. PUF, Paris.

Le Breton, E. (2006). Homo mobilis. In *La ville aux limites de la mobilité*, Bonnet, M. and Aubertel, P. (eds). PUF, Paris.

Merlin, P. and Choay, F. (eds) (2005). *Dictionnaire de l'urbanisme et de l'aménagement*. PUF, Paris.

Munafo, S. (2016). *La ville compacte remise en cause ? Formes urbaines et mobilités de loisirs*. Alphil, Neuchâtel.

Ravalet, E. and Viot, P. (2017). Choix modaux et covoiturage dans la mobilité de loisirs liée à l'événementiel. Enseignements tirés du Paléo Festival Nyon en Suisse. *Cahiers Scientifiques du Transport*, 17.

Richards, G. and Palmer, R. (2010). *Eventful Cities: Cultural Management and Urban Revitalisation*. Routledge, London.

Segaud, M., Brun, J., Driant, J.C. (2001). *Dictionnaire critique de l'habitat et du logement*. Armand Colin, Paris.

Sheller, M. and Urry, J. (2006). The new mobilities paradigm. *Environment and Planning A, Economy and Space*, 38(2), 207–226.

Still, G.K. (2014). *Introduction to Crowd Sciences*. CRC Press, Boca Raton.

Still, G.K. (2019). Crowd science and crowd counting. *Impact*, 1, 19–23.

Viot, P. (2013). Le territoire sécurisé des grandes manifestations contemporaines. PhD thesis, École Polytechnique de Lausanne, Lausanne.

Viot, P., Pattaroni, L., Berthoud, J. (2010). Voir et analyser le gouvernement de la foule en liesse. Eléments pour l'étude des rassemblements festifs à l'aide de matériaux sonores et visuels. *Ethnographiques*, 21(November).

Viot, P., Kaufmann, V., Ravalet, E. (2017). Diagnostic et propositions pour l'optimisation du dispositif de gestion des mobilités au Salon international de l'automobile de Genève. Report, police cantonale genevoise/Direction générale des transports du canton de Genève, Geneva.

10

Inland Navigation: Rethinking Mobility from an Aquatic Perspective

Laurie DAFFE

Laboratoire de sociologie urbaine (LaSUR), École polytechnique fédérale de Lausanne, Switzerland

10.1. Introduction

In Europe, inland navigation represents only 6% of the modal share of freight transport. However, this low rate may well change, since, in the age of energy transition, waterborne freight is returning to the political and economic forefront as a profitable means of transport. At the same time, in recent decades, the waterways have acquired a cultural, recreational, and residential value in their own right. It thus appears that, by offering narratives, practices, and motives for mobilities previously relegated to spatial and mental sidelines, navigations respond to current needs not only to move differently but also to inhabit differently (Anderson and Peters 2014; Hastrup and Rubow 2014; Daffe 2019). Yet, boats and waterborne pathways still occupy a secondary place in mobility studies, in contrast to trains, automobiles, or airplanes (Anim-Addo et al. 2014).

The study of aquatic mobility was long limited to the economics of maritime and river transport and to the modeling of "origin–destination" routes. In the meantime, research in the humanities and social sciences has highlighted the relevance of considering the rhythms and perceptions of speed, as well as the movement of goods, ideas, and people, and the policies associated with this (Hannam et al. 2006; Sheller and Urry 2006). Over the past decade, the multiplication of works adopting this approach to the study of aquatic environments and mobilities testifies both to a paradigm shift in human geography and social anthropology, as well as to a growing interest in these themes within these disciplines. This watery turn (Hasty and Peters 2012, p. 660; Anim-Addo et al. 2014, p. 340; Vallerani and Visentin 2018), advocating for research from the water and involving those who live in it, seeks to build analytical and methodological baggage that can illuminate some of the blind spots in land-based studies, in favor of redefining the boundaries of water/land, nature/culture, and mobile/immobile (Helmreich 2011; Bowles et al. 2019).

In this chapter, we will see how these "aquatic" approaches allow us to rethink these notions, by studying constantly changing realities. The European inland waterways will serve as a starting point and a common thread for our purpose. Firstly, we will examine the contemporary issues related to these navigations, whether commercial, recreational, or touristic. We will see how their current development induces new relationships with local and global territories, to the potential of speed, as well as to the traces of (im)mobilities. Then, we will review the current state of knowledge in order to account for the evolution of scientific thinking on this subject, from the study of domestic units to the trajectories of boats and inhabitants, as well as the present shortcomings in this area. In the last section, we will take stock of the epistemological and methodological tools that are being consolidated, "from and with the water," in favor of a renewed knowledge of boats, of aquatic and amphibious environments, of the populations that live there, and of mobilities in general.

10.2. Societal and environmental issues of inland navigation

Faced with the imperatives of the decarbonization of transport, the inland navigation boat seems to stand out not only as a profitable and less energy-consuming mode of transport but also as a way of living and moving differently, according to more deferred rhythms in particular. The redevelopment of infrastructures, legal frameworks, and technologies supports this renewed interest and redefines fluvial landscapes as much as the possibilities of interaction between the general public and water.

10.2.1. *Modal share of inland waterways in the European Union*

The European Union has 52,332 km of waterways, half of which are located in France, Germany, the Netherlands, and Belgium (Wiegmans and Konings 2017, p. 4). This network of rivers and canals open to the circulation of tourist, leisure, and commercial vessels allows the transport of 250 to 400 t on small-gauge canals and up to 18,000 t on waterways of "international importance". By way of comparison (and to use a popular image), the total permissible laden weight of a vehicle or road convoy used to transport goods does not exceed 44 t. In Europe, half of the population lives close to an inland waterway (coast or inland course), and most industrial centers are accessible by this means (Cour des comptes européenne 2015). Still, inland navigation accounts for only 6% of the EU's modal share of freight transport, thirteen times less than road and three times less than rail (Eurostat 2017). The Netherlands, Germany, Romania, Belgium, and France alone account for 92% of transport performance on inland waterways (Wiegmans and Konings 2017, p. 6).

However, these figures belie significant disparities between countries. These reflect historical and political choices, generating contrasts in terms of the size and quality of the infrastructure, rather than a proportional correlation with the size of the national waterway networks. Thus, in the European Union, the Netherlands has the highest share of freight carried by inland waterways, at 45%, compared with 50% by road. The country has 5,000 km of waterways. Most of them are of large gauge (over 1,000 tonnes). In contrast, in France, the modal share of commercial barge transport falls to 2% (Eurostat 2017), even though it has more than 8,000 km of navigable waterways, but a significant part of which (75%, according to Wiegmans and Konings (2017, p. 7)) does not allow the transport of more than 400 t. Infrastructure that is hardly competitive with road transport and limits its market (Konings 2017).

In terms of the goods transported by ship, building materials and minerals have the largest market share, followed by metal and refined oil products, fertilizers, and agricultural products. These are all bulk commodities that can cope with the slower speed of ship transport, as they do not require rapid delivery (Cour des comptes européenne 2015, p. 12). Moreover, as economists Wiegmans and Konings (2017, p. 9) point out, while coal and oil products are transported over long distances in large convoys from and to a limited number of transport nodes (seaports, steel plants, power plants), sand and gravel are transported over shorter distances, even domestically, with smaller volumes and more disparate loading and unloading points.

10.2.2. Prospects for the development of river activities and the shift from road to waterways

In the context of the environmental crisis and the decarbonization of travel, inland navigation is returning to the political and economic forefront as a cost-effective and "energy-efficient" means of transport, particularly over long distances (EU, Commission implementing decision 2019/1118 of 27 June 2019). In this context, improving the modal share of inland waterway transport is one of the European Union's priority actions to combat climate change. According to data from the European Court of

Auditors (2015, p. 12), with equivalent energy consumption, an IWT vessel travels 370 km for 1 t of goods, compared with 300 km by train and 100 km by truck. Given their carrying capacity, river vessels offer massification of tonnage per kilometer, jointly leading to lower costs. Consequently, as many observers note, a shift to waterways would also help to reduce road traffic and relieve congestion on land routes.

It is with this in mind that the European Union has allocated large budgets to improve navigability and increase the volume of traffic on inland waterways. The elimination of bottlenecks should be completed by 2030 (Cour des comptes européennes 2015, p. 50), in particular through the completion of missing links on core networks. Among these, the construction of the Seine-Northern Europe large-gauge canal (Vb gauge, up to 4,400 t of goods) will allow continuous navigation over 20,000 km between the Seine basin, the ports of Le Havre and Dunkirk, and the large-gauge waterways of the Benelux countries and northern Europe. This major project involves the construction or widening of more than 1,100 km of navigable waterways in 10 years. These developments are likely to change the face and dynamics of the territories crossed, through major land consolidation operations as well as the construction of engineering structures and river infrastructures (locks, harbor stops, bridges, transshipment quays, etc.).

The emerging markets targeted by these operations also have the potential to restructure local space (Parlette and Cowen 2011 (in Cresswell 2014, p. 717)). Indeed, urban logistics services within large urban areas are beginning to prove their worth. As long as suitable transshipment areas are provided, waterways can replace trucks for supplying construction sites or for transporting recyclable materials in the circular economy. River transport also benefits from the "explosion in the number of deliveries due to the development of e-commerce" (VNF 2019a, p. 33). In combination with other modes of transport such as cargo bikes, it takes advantage of the distance of sorting warehouses from urban centers and allows rounds to be made locally, replacing vans (VNF 2019a).

On a more global scale, according to Wiegmans and Konings (2017), container transport by inland waterways represents one of the most promising growth opportunities, both for long-distance and domestic traffic in the hinterlands. This sector, they explain, is particularly well suited to the needs of shippers, for example, by offering complete supply chain solutions (handling, labor, etc.) or additional services (warehousing, high value-added logistics services, etc.) (Wiegmans and Konings 2017, p. 11). These activities participate in the creation of global landscapes made of bulk and containers waiting to be conveyed. Geographer Julie Cidell (2012) has worked to demonstrate this by highlighting the importance of temporary immobilities in the transportation of goods, as much as their setting in motion. Indeed, many artifacts remind us of the extent to which the river world, often associated with constant travel, is in fact marked by fixed stops and landmarks. Paradoxically necessary to the flows, they circumscribe the routes and temporalities of navigations and generate specific socialities (Raimbault and Paul 2013; Daffe 2019).

While commercial boats contribute to the emergence of global landscapes made of temporary immobilities, for their part, pleasure and residential boats contribute to reintegrating the waterways into the motives and lifestyles of the general public.

Between the 1960s and the early 2000s, the industrial and commercial role of inland waterways considerably weakened. Gradually, new lifestyles and leisure activities focused on the water developed, marking an important shift in the socioeconomic function of urban waterscapes and their public spaces (Kinder 2015). Reappearing in collective mental maps, rivers and canals are becoming central actors in new narrative frameworks touting their recreational, environmental, cultural, and patriotic qualities (Romain 2010; Vallerani and Visentin 2018). This was an evolution produced and accompanied by the renewal of legal frameworks, as much as by technologies and practices redefining the possibilities of interaction between the public and water (Kinder 2015, p. 141).

The development of river tourism is typical of this transformation (rental of habitable boats without a license, hotel barges, river cruise ships, etc.). It is also the case of the transport of people by waterway and in particular of the intra-urban river shuttles such as bus-boats or tour boats. The river dwelling – i.e., living permanently on board a boat, often a former merchant barge that has been completely converted into a dwelling – is also part of these activities, which have contributed (for half a century in this case) to a change of perspective with regard to navigable waterways (Kinder 2015; Daffe 2019). As these practices are still considered as niche products and secondary activities vis-à-vis commercial freight, figures and data on them are scarce and incomplete. However, there are a few reports that quantify their growing popularity.

Thus, following a cruise and river tourism development operation, France has seen a steady increase in the number of passengers transported by hotel barges (+14% from 2017 to 2018) or river liners (+8.2% from 2017 to 2018) in recent years (VNF 2019b). Between 2015 and 2018 alone, the number of cruise ships calling on the Rhine in Strasbourg almost doubled (VNF 2019b). As another example of the success of waterways and boats for noncommercial purposes, in Belgium, the lists for obtaining a long-term berth for a houseboat are getting longer and longer involving a wait of several years (Daffe 2016). Finally, in London, Paris, Toulon, Rotterdam, Liege, etc., waterbuses and shuttles have become part of the public transport system as a sign of the normalization of daily passenger transport via inland waterways.

Similar to what geographers and historians Anim-Addo et al. (2014) point out about maritime environments, it is likely that rivers and inland waterways are central to the mobility transition. Boating and navigable waterways supposedly respond to a contemporary desire, indeed necessity in times of ecological transition, to move and inhabit differently, requiring: "When such a transition occurs it will necessitate new patterns of movement, new narratives of mobility and new configurations of mobile practice" (Cresswell 2014, p. 715). The development of waterborne transport leads to a restructuring of landscapes and public spaces, as we have seen, but also to a renewed relationship with speed and to the practice of territories, regardless of the sector considered (commercial, tourist, or residential).

Choosing to travel by river implies different conditions that profoundly modify the reference points in terms of sensations, range or efficiency criteria developed from road, and land references. The physical qualities of the water and weather conditions (freezing, flooding, drought, etc.), as well as the extent of the network (linear and rigid) and the technical specificities of the boats, condition and circumscribe the trajectories, potential distances, and experiences on board (Daffe 2019). To take just one example, the average travel speed rarely reaches more than 10 km per hour. The implications of developing these practices of "anchored temporary mobilities" are thus numerous, from a sensory, spatial, environmental, and social perspective.

10.2.3. *Faster, less far, more anchored: the scales of future navigation*

Thinking of inland waterways solely in terms of a boat's movement on the water as a flat surface obscures a significant part of the understanding of this mode of transport, which is also a place of habitation, and its issues. Indeed, a barge spends on average 45% of its commercial time at the quay (Denhez 2019), a river liner 65% (VNF 2019a), and approximately 95% for a houseboat (author's data). In other words, on the water, places and times of stopping (loading, sassing, resting, visiting, working, etc.) are not residual. They are the norm on board rather than an anomaly, where the moments of actual travel, from a point of origin to a destination, of varying lengths, are conditional and temporary (contracts, weather conditions, seasons, family or professional obligations, etc.).

Sailing is therefore made up of stops, whether mandatory or not, and generally revolves around ports of call, fixed social contacts, and familiar landmarks, often not far from the boat. For example, a study on the impact of houseboats rentals in France showed that, during their stopovers, only a quarter of boaters travelled more than 5 km from the place where their boat was moored and, in any case, did not travel more than 10 km (VNF 2013, p. 39). In our previous work, we explained that boaters generally made the same trips, in particular so that the rest stops would be located near their homes on land, family, or children's schools (Daffe 2012, p. 116). For their part, in their research, sociologist Charlotte Paul and geographer Nicolas Raimbault (2013) confirm these repetitive movements at the same rest stops, as well as a low frequentation of urban centers during stops, with daily organization centered on the home on board.

Although waterborne transport is more environmentally friendly than road transport, CO_2 and particle emissions during stops (which, as we have seen, represent a substantial amount of time during navigation) are nevertheless problematic. Indeed, during stoppage, the generators that guarantee the functioning of the electrical installations on board (water pumps, heating, stoves, etc.) cause nuisance and pollution. The switch to cleaner motorization is becoming all the more imperative as a growing number of cities aim to ban diesel and gasoline vehicles within 5 to 10 years (VNF 2019a). Electricity and hydrogen are among the options that have already been tested and are considered promising for inland waterways (Denhez 2019; VNF 2019a). However, these energies need to be stored and available for refueling, implying storage throughout the entire navigable infrastructure – and not just in the ports.

As we have illustrated in this section, river dwellers are transforming commonly accepted definitions of "sedentarity" and "nomadism." In the words of anthropologist Urbain (2003, p. 152), river dwellers embody the "countertype" of the traveler, the one who becomes immobile and "travels not to circulate but to find a place to stay, a 'drop-off', a 'corner of the earth', a shelter that he or she does not intend to leave afterwards, except out of social, professional or medical obligation". The environment of navigable waters reverses our terrestrial landmarks and reference points. In this sense, the study of river environments also requires a conceptual shift to approach and discuss them, a shift that has recently taken place in the field of so-called "aquatic" or "amphibious" studies.

10.3. Current state of knowledge

While in early socio-anthropological studies water was treated in an impressionistic way or as a geographical marker (Helmreich 2011), with the acceleration of urbanization and then in the face of climate change, the humanities and social sciences have taken a fresh look at the links between water and human societies. Currently, for the proponents of the "new anthropology of water" or "amphibious anthropology," aquatic materialities, temporalities, and movements are proving to be central to the understanding of navigations (Bowles et al. 2019). These approaches promote the study of the affordances of water as a substance, but also the changes and adaptations caused by the encounter between humans and nonhumans, as well as the (variable and evolving) modalities of this interaction (frictions, forms of knowledge, beliefs, etc.) (Daffe 2021). This is a paradigm shift that implies that aquatic mobilities are no longer viewed from the perspective of a consumption relationship alone, but as a co-production process from which a place emerges (Steinberg and Peters 2015; Krause 2017).

10.3.1. *Aquatic mobility, an emerging field of research*

Interest in this field of research is recent. At a time when water is proving to be both threatened and threatening, destructive, polluted, or scarce, it concurrently occupies a growing place in academic work (Krause and Strang 2016). On the side of the study of boats and navigation in general, the observation is the same: "[...] with the 'shrinking' of the world, the dominance of the ship has shrunk in our collective imagination" (Anim-Addo et al., p. 338, author's translation). Anim-Addo et al. (2014) raise this paradox: although the boat is among the oldest and most used means of human travel (by islanders, migrants, etc.), studies of this "mobile and mobilizing" object have been growing and diversifying for less than a decade. In their view, boats and waterways still occupy a secondary place in the study of mobilities, unlike trains, automobiles, and airplanes.

Moreover, the approach favored up to now struggled to focus on perspectives other than the legal aspects of shipping, the economics and logistics of transport, or the modeling of "origin–destination" routes. Although they contribute to drawing up a precise inventory of commercial transport on the basis of quantitative data, this work says nothing about the lifestyles and mobility practices of all kinds of sailors. Moreover, most of the work on these themes is to be found in geography, history, sociology, and anthropology. The questions then shift: who are the pilots and inhabitants of these inland navigation boats? For what reasons do they move (or not move)? What are their itineraries and how (speed, experience, friction, etc.) is the river space navigated? How is the activity of water transport structured, and how does it coexist with other uses of the river? How is life on board organized, how is the boat inhabited, and what are the effects of its mobile nature on the space?

In view of the close relationship between the evolution of inland navigation and the economic history of these regions, French-speaking Europe and the United Kingdom are judicious fields of study in this field. However, little by little, the waters of the Danube, the Nordic countries, or the Venetian canals are enriching the scientific literature devoted to inland navigation. At first, these works took for granted the nomadic nature of inland navigators, central objects of folkloristic and ethnographic approaches. Gradually, a jump in scale was made in favor of the study of the territories of these mobilities, their spatial and temporal dimensions, and their "fluid" character. Today, research currents advocating hydroperspectivism and the adoption of "wet ontologies" are asserting themselves in order to study these aquatic and amphibious lifestyles in their complexity, a decentering likely to shed new light on the study of mobilities.

10.3.2. Small-scale inland navigation and "people of the river," flurban lifestyles

The term "small-scale inland waterway transport" refers to all the activities of inland waterway transport of goods carried out by independent boatpeople who generally own their own boat. As a work tool, a production unit, and a residence unit, this type of boat was for a long time the central element of the reproduction of the profession and of the family. However, since the 1970s, the economic restructuring that the sector has had to face, particularly in France and Belgium, has contributed to the fragility of the profession, its organization, and its durability. Also, until the year 2000, many journalistic and photographic reports as well as novels highlighted the families of boatmen in narratives marked by nostalgia, facing the presumed disappearance of a secular activity. We will not mention these productions here. At the same time, the "water people," mainly in the north of France, benefitted from the interest of folklorists and ethnographers who documented the structures of kinship and alliances, as well as the systems of transmission of goods and names within the profession.

Among these, in a fundamental article, Wateau (1989) describes the way of life of these boatmen who, as she reminds us, only became itinerant with the motorization of boats at the end of the 19th century and the lengthening of routes made possible by the speed potential thus acquired. At first a seasonal activity linked to the harvest, the profession specialized in the permanent transport of raw and heavy materials. This allowed the family to live and work on board full time. The focus gradually shifted from the home to the way in which the boatmen constituted themselves as a social group through itinerant interactions. Manceron's (1996) work leads to the study of these particular mobilities and their places of anchorage, circumscribed by temporalities, events (birth, schooling, disembarkation, burial, etc.), as well as by travel habits defining borders and spaces of familiarity (Manceron 1996).

The introduction of much larger vessels, the appearance of electronic navigation instruments on board, and the globalized charter system have significantly changed the relationship with distance. In the literature, boatmen are no longer associated with unattached nomads and "showmen of a particular kind" (Merger 1985). The forms, conditions and rhythms, as well as the symbolic and physical attachments of their itinerancies, are taken seriously. Their study makes it possible to understand boatmens' lifestyles as well as their effects on the constitution of so-called "flurban" spaces[1].

---

[1] Neologism proposed by the historian Bernard Le Sueur. Echoing the "rurbanization" of the 1960s, the term applied to the river refers to the upgrading of urban waterways and the return of citizens to these spaces with now residential, recreational, and festive functions. It is also proposed by Paul and Raimbault to designate "the territoriality of boatmen between river and city" (2013, p. 19).

According to Paul and Raimbault (2013), who analyze the polytopic mobility practices of boaters, the way in which they inhabit the "professional flow" is similar to the way in which suburbanites inhabit their detached houses. A life centered on the home, a place of work on the scale of the metropolis, a community confined to an "in-between" on the fringes of urban centers that they rarely visit, only for domestic supplies. But "what characterizes them above all is that boatmen practice a mobile space to perform an activity in the service of the urban economy, without practicing that city" (Paul and Raimbault 2013, p. 8).

Finally, the diachronic analysis adopted by the historian Bernard Le Sueur in his work allows us to consider contemporary inland navigation within complex sociospatial processes and games of actors. This approach reminds us that the evolution of navigation units and canals over time, and the contemporary "heritage" redevelopments of waterfronts, echo broader technical, cultural, social, and economic developments (Le Sueur 2012). These reconfigurations explain the emergence of the river dwelling phenomenon in Europe in the 1970s, when many small commercial boats were abandoned by the trade because they were not very profitable in view of the enlargement of waterways and competition with the road sector. They then found a second life outside of the river transport circuit as permanent dwellings (Daffe 2016), giving way to other ways of living on and navigating the river, giving it meaning and dealing with its constraints, which were long considered anecdotal and consequently little-documented.

10.3.3. *Trajectories of houseboats and river dwellers*

The terms "houseboats" or "residential boats" are used to refer mainly to those boats whose transport holds have been converted for residential purposes, inhabited year-round by people who are not necessarily from the water transport sector, or indeed from outside of it. In France, Belgium, and the Netherlands, they are known to be lined up along the riverbanks, typically recognizable by their size (often Freycinet or Spits, commonly known as barges, 38.5 m by 5.05 m), their riveted steel hulls, and the overhanging superstructure. In Great Britain, because of the river network developed according to different standards than on the continent, narrowboats are the most common type of vessel. Built of steel, fiberglass, or wood, they are steered from the outside by a tiller and measure between 7 to (a maximum of) 20 m long and about 2 m wide. These boats were either converted into residences or used directly for housing, beginning in the 19th century (Bowles 2015:27). Depending on national contexts, populations, and legislation, these boats may be episodically or completely itinerant or completely stationary.

Once again, the observation that there is a lack of knowledge in this area is shared (Bowles 2015; Daffe 2016; Roberts 2019): in Great Britain, France, the Netherlands, or Belgium, where the phenomenon has been well established for several decades now, objective data and long-term fieldwork can be counted on the fingers of one hand. At the same time, the literature on maritime and oceanic mobilities or on the development of rivers as leisure environments is growing (Kaaristo and Rhoden 2017; Roberts 2019). Likewise, many "fine works" of architecture (see for example Gabor (1979) or Willemin (2008)) or press articles document the phenomenon by expressing surprise at the "alternative," "original" character of these "marginal" populations. The aesthetic "revolutionary" or "futuristic" qualities of these dwellings are praised, and the administrative, financial, and technical difficulties are generally listed. But these productions rarely question the heterogeneity of living patterns and internal hierarchies that nevertheless characterize these lifestyles (Roberts 2019, p. 57).

For example, Laura Roberts shows how, in England, among Continuous[2] Navigation Permit holders, the process of learning and acquiring the skills of life on the canals is constrained, accelerated, or shaped through the lens of gender:

> Situations that require certain practical knowledge such as plumbing, electrics, or engine work, create the realisation that these abilities were distributed unevenly growing up and continue to be distributed unevenly as adults (Roberts 2019, p. 64, author's translation).

In our French-speaking Belgian fieldwork, we have also shown how the choice to live aboard a residential boat was mostly made by men with a close and long-standing relationship with professions, hobbies, and interests that give rise to practices built around an ideal of autonomy and freedom (motor sports, caravanning, etc.) (Daffe 2019, p. 217). This results in different bodily performances, life courses on board, and sailing experiences. Added to these gendered learning barriers are tensions between newcomers and long-time residents (Bowles 2015). With expertise accumulated over time that is valuable to novices, seasoned river dwellers view the arrival of newcomers on already congested waterways with suspicion (Daffe 2019, p. 37; Roberts 2019, p. 63).

10.3.4. Toward "wet ontologies"

The attention paid to the trajectories, temporalities, and politics of hydraulic infrastructures resonates with the work that has been taking life around, on, and with

---

2 Continuous Cruising Licence: in the UK, a licence that exempts boat owners from buying or renting a mooring provided they travel every 2 weeks and travel a minimum of 32 km (20 miles) per year in the same direction (Roberts 2019, p. 60).

wetlands seriously in anthropology and human geography – deltas, marshes, rivers, oceans, etc. – for the past 10 years. By putting forward an approach refocused on the materialities, temporalities, and volume of hydrospheres, the shift intends to work toward deconstructing terrestrial ontologies in favor of "liquid" or "amphibious" ontologies. To inhabit aquatic environments, to live on water, to "navigate it," reverses landmarks and references. From the water, in the flow and the current, the borders of water/land, nature/culture, and mobile/immobile are drawn differently and are distinguished with difficulty, disturbing Euclidean conceptions of movement.

The study of aquatic mobilities thus follows the turn taken in mobility studies by placing an attention to the "forces" that drive travel, to the speeds that characterize it, to the frictions that stop or prevent it, to the rhythms that shape its movement, to the routes taken, and to the experiences of these movements at the center of its approach (Hannam et al. 2006; Sheller and Urry 2006; Cresswell 2010, p. 17). From this perspective, water is no longer the Other of land (Helmreich 2011), an empty space to be crossed as quickly as possible to reach meaningful places, but a mesh of movements, a place embedded in an entanglement of temporalities, a living space inscribed in the verticality and materiality of a multiple and changing water reality (Anim-Addo et al. 2014; Steinberg and Peters 2015; Krause and Strang 2016; Bowles et al. 2019).

This posture makes it possible to account for the complexity of mobilities such as those practiced by boatmen, for example, made up of numerous stops and repetitive journeys, or those of river dwellers moored at a long-term location. Indeed, from the land, it is tempting to conclude that they experience the movement by proxy and in a dreamlike way. Outside observers are often quick to lament the "false identity" of these boats moored to a chain, year-round, along the French and Belgian shores (sometimes dubbed "houseboats"), where they would like to see them (and thus, no longer see them) take their role as "nomads of rivers" more seriously (Daffe 2019). In reality, movement is indeed omnipresent, not horizontally in a forward movement, but within the volume of the river, vertically, laterally, caused by variations in the physical properties of the water (Daffe 2019). Like other territories of navigation (seas, oceans, etc.):

> […] its vertical depth, together and coalescing with its movement, its horizontal surface, its angled waves – is a space not moved on, but through [as Anim-Addo et al. (2014) note], and also under (Steinberg and Peters 2015, p. 253).

These works thus teach us to understand the river as a mobile space. Temporary and contingent, "its order is constantly called into question" (Retaillé 2014, p. 25). On the water, places "emerge at the intersection of itineraries provoking the reciprocal entry into correlation of elements that are at first dispersed" (Retaillé 2014). Thus, the river, like seas and oceans, is not simply "a space of discrete points between which objects move but rather as a dynamic environment of flows and continual recomposition where [...] 'place' can be understood only in the context of mobility" (Steinberg and Peters 2015, p. 257, author's translation). They emerge from the relationships between heterogeneous and independent elements that add to it (territorialize) and leave it (deterritorialize):

> Water presents itself simultaneously as a depth and as a surface, as a set of fixed points but also as an elusive space continuously reproduced by mobile molecules; water possesses a materiality taken as cash (liquidity or humidity), but which is only one of its three physical states that exist in a continuous exchange (the other two are ice and vapor). [...] in water, these properties are distinguished by the speed and rhythm of mobility, the persistent ease of transformation, and the encompassing materiality of depth (Steinberg and Peters 2015, pp. 252 and 255, author's translation).

We can see how terrestrocentric ontologies do not fit easily into these changing environments and aquatic ways of life. In this light, the watery turn, operating in anthropology and other social sciences, calls for the definition of a theoretical space and terrains redefining the boundaries between immobilities and anchorages, between staying and moving (Bowles et al. 2019, p. 6). More than a declaration of intent, this turn seeks to constitute, from the aquatic territories, analytical and methodological baggage likely to fit into the dead spots of terrestrial studies of the movements of goods, ideas, and people.

10.3.5. *The watery turn: grasping mobilities from an aquatic perspective*

As we have already shown, the humanities and social sciences are increasingly turning to the study of populations making their homes in aquatic environments (rivers, deltas, seas, oceans, etc.) and so-called "amphibious" environments (swampy, muddy, flooded, cyclically submerged, etc.) where the study of watercraft (motorized or nonmotorized boats, cargo ships or rafts, submarines, surfboards, etc.) is also taking on a central role. In line with the paradigmatic shift in mobility studies, this shift intends to put the politics of movement, the rhythms and movements of goods, ideas, and people under the microscope. It also serves as a reminder, in this way, of the role of the ship at the scale of individual sentient experience, right up to its central role in the functioning of capitalism as a global conveyor (Anim-Addo et al. 2014). Finally, this approach places at the center of its research the interactions between humans, nonhumans, and the "liquid" environments, near, on, and with which they settle (Krause and Strang 2016; Bowles et al. 2019).

In light of what has been developed throughout this chapter, how do studies of these phenomena challenge our sedentary, land-based assumptions?

First of all, we should note that, faced with the popularity of references to liquids in recent academic work ("flows," "waves," "liquid modernity," etc.), various authors warn against the essentialism of these terms, which, rather than renewing patterns of thought, continue to keep water at a distance as a metaphor, an object of thought (*theory machine*), and of otherness (Helmreich 2011; Steinberg and Peters 2015). However, since the "liquid" aspect of aquatic environments is only one of their multiple forms and physical states, for Steinberg and Peters (2015, p. 257), it is above all a matter of paying attention to the way in which this materiality intersects with global economic policies and with territories; how it facilitates or disrupts the circulations that constitute capitalism. Itself fluctuant, it is also the vessel for other materialities (Steinberg and Peters 2015).

Then, we evoked the fluctuating (sometimes liquid, sometimes dry, sometimes solid, etc.) and nonplanar character of these aquatic environments (rivers, deltas, oceans, etc.). Difficult to grasp as spaces of discrete points between which objects move, they are envisioned as co-constituent agents of multiple as well as dynamic experiences, relationships, and meanings (Krause and Strang 2016). With water, place emerges through the co-compositions of forces and materials and is thus only understood in motion (Steinberg and Peters 2015; Bowles et al. 2019; Daffe 2019). In this context, the different ways of living on, near, and with water challenge sedentary and land-centered logics (Bowles et al. 2019) insofar as this changing environment can appear as a welcoming and safe place to live, not least because of the multiple relationships that emerge (Bowles et al. 2019). In other words, the movement inherent in hydrospheres does not preclude feelings of belonging and anchors to place (Anim-Addo et al. 2014).

Taking this view, aquatic territories multiply both pro-deep and above ground into a series of fixed sites but also into elusive spaces constantly reproduced by mobile molecules (Steinberg and Peters 2015, p. 251). Thus rendered to their volume (understood as force, range, resistance, inclination, depth, and matter, rather than simply the opening of a vertical axis (Elden 2013)), aquatic territories question the political significance of the horizon, the boundary separating air from a surface:

> Thinking of the sea as a space of volume, through a wet ontology, enables us to recognise that the form of water opens new territories of control and conflict (Steinberg and Peters 2015, p. 252).[3]

---

3 To demonstrate this, the authors advance the example of the Malaysia Airlines flight search: "Whilst the vertical nature of the ocean has confounded both direct visual observation and

It is a space *with* which, *on* which, *through* which, and *under* which one moves, where time is expressed through matter in a nonlinear and fluctuating manner. A dynamic assembly that coproduces, suggests, and supports relationships, experiences, and meanings; that is, a new way of orienting oneself in the world (Anim-Addo et al. 2014; Steinberg and Peters 2015; Krause 2019).

These approaches have methodological implications. In his research on deltas, anthropologist Franz Krause (2017) suggests considering four dimensions (hydrosociabilities, volatility, wetness, rhythms) to study the dynamics of hydrospheres. Firstly, social relations and water flows should not be seen as external additions to predetermined contexts. It is about studying the ways in which people relate to each other, not only through "classical" forms of connection (kinship, friendship, etc.) but also, simultaneously, "[...], in hydrologic ways, quite literally through the water that flows – or does not flow – between them" (Krause 2017, p. 404, author's translation).

Secondly, in line with an approach widely developed by Ingold (2000), Krause suggests that volatility is essential and constitutive of the process of co-creation of places between landscapes and inhabitants. Instability and improvization are embodied in everyday practices that materialize particular social and semiotic configurations. Thirdly, Krause argues for the observation and consideration of specific social, economic, and political configurations emerging from the changing affordances of wet, dry, and in-between environments, extremes of a spectrum of possibilities (relative level of water saturation, physical states changing from liquid to frozen, etc.) (Krause 2017, p. 406). The author also emphasizes the importance of daily hydrosocial rhythms in understanding the emergence of conflicts, which he believes are more often related to rhythmic divergences than to divergences in use. They may be related to recurrent cycles (tides, seasons, political campaigns, etc.) or to nonrepetitive transformations (globalization, climate change, etc.) to which humans and nonhumans are constantly adapting (Krause 2017, p. 407).

In concrete terms, the long-term commitment of researchers to these amphibious sites is an advantageous means of understanding the rich diversity of places, lifestyles, and aquatic mobility. It is as close as possible to volumes, materialities, and aquatic temporalities that the temporary and contingent character of these environments, their materialities, and the relationships that are co-constructed there, can be seen and understood. It is an enterprise of knowledge through the sensitive

---

satellite surveillance, it has been the ocean's *volume* – that is its existence as a hydrodynamic arena in which waves (of water) restrict investigators' ability to observe the reflection of other waves (of light and sound) – that ultimately is making surveillance and, more generally, governance so challenging" (Steinberg and Peters 2015, p. 254).

where the immersive experience makes it possible to question new territories of life, control, and conflicts. In this sense, this research in motion, itinerant, multi-sited, includes imaginations, knowledge, and vernacular know-how, which they strive to bring into dialogue with academic knowledge. In this way, they offer new ways of "navigating the world"; to inhabit it, to explore it, to give it meaning, and to deal with its constraints.

10.4. Conclusion: meeting between water and land

Flows, waves, fluidity... In the media, in the scientific literature, the language of mobilities is impregnated with vocabulary linked to water and liquidity. A way of "rethinking the world in fluid terms and also in looking at those things – refugees, nomads, weapons, drugs, fish – that challenge borders because they are imagined to 'flow' across them" (Helmreich 2011, p. 137). While some see this "rising water" as a space of liberation and free movement, others more readily associate the idea of a "liquid" society with that of a social and ideological wreck. Either way, the properties of water that most capture our imagination are undoubtedly powerful metaphors (Bowles et al. 2019). Nonetheless, water remains material to think about for these forms of knowledge, which tend in this way to reinforce the idea of dry land as stable, hierarchically organized, in the face of a liminal watery element.

However, as this chapter has endeavored to show, water is not only a matter of thought. The environmental crisis, for example, makes the issues surrounding hydrospheres all the more tangible, and their reality permeates our daily lives, spaces, and lifestyles. On our rivers, the increase in the modal share of inland navigation, transshipment and supply infrastructures, and the artifacts transported is likely to change the face of the cities and the dynamics of the territories, but also our relationship with speed. Moreover, the rise in sea levels and the increase in the risk of flooding also have concrete effects, locally and globally, in the short and long term, on the presence of the aquatic element and its materialities.

Over the past decade, the humanities and social sciences have been working to reintegrate aquatic perspectives into the study of mobilities, focusing on habitats in motion, rhythms, movements of goods, ideas and people, and the politics associated with them. The role of the boat on the scale of individual sentient experience, to its central function in the functioning of capitalism as a global conveyor, is increasingly documented. Taking into account the volatility of these environments and the relationships that are co-constructed within them, their constantly changing materiality, and their contingent character opens up perspectives toward new territories of life, control, and conflict, where movements unfold not only on their horizontal surface but also through it and under it.

Ultimately, what happens if we comment on life on land from an aquatic perspective? How does being on board rather than on land contribute to shifting points of view, even if the cultural frame of reference remains the same, asks Krause (2019)?

We can, to conclude, retain some tracks. Firstly, thinking from the water necessarily implies a sensitive engagement of researchers with the forms of the aquatic element, which turn out to be manifold over time and space. Krause (2019) suggests that this multiscalar character, but also the discourses and practices of users, alternating between specificity and generality, can become the guiding principles of socioanthropological and geographical analyses. Thus, continues the anthropologist of amphibious worlds, this aquatic perspective can shed light on the temporalities of social and material processes by decentering the gaze on plasticities and instabilities rather than on fixed, stable, and solid forms. Finally, the aquatic perspective is an "in depth" thought which decompartmentalizes the movement of the plane surfaces by returning them to their verticality and their voluminosity.

But ultimately, it is at the intersection of land and water, where they meet in an amphibious spectrum, that these ways of traveling and understanding the world take shape. Many of them, as we have seen, remain to be explored.

10.5. References

Anderson, J. and Peters, K. (eds) (2014). *Water Worlds: Human Geographies of the Ocean*. Routledge, London/New York.

Anim-Addo, A., Peters, K., Hasty, W. (2014). The mobilities of ships and shipped mobilities. *Mobilities*, 9(3), 337–349.

Bowles, B. (2015). Water ways: Becoming an itinerant boat-dweller on the canals and rivers of South East England. PhD thesis, Brunel University, Uxbridge.

Bowles, B., Kaaristo, M., Rogelja Caf, N. (2019). Dwelling on and with water – Materialities, (im)mobilities and meanings: Introduction to the special issue. *Anthropological Notebooks*, 25(2), 5–12.

Cazaubon, J.-B. (2015). Mission de Jacques Maillot – Comment faire de la France l'une des premières destinations mondiales de croisières (maritimes et fluviales)? Report, Ministère des affaires étrangères et du développement international, Paris.

Cidell, J. (2012). Flows and pauses in the urban logistics landscape: The municipal regulation of shipping container mobilities. *Mobilities*, 7(2), 233–245.

Cour des comptes européenne (2015). Le transport fluvial en Europe : aucune amélioration significative de la part modale et des conditions de navigabilité depuis 2001. Report, European Union, Luxembourg.

Cresswell, T. (2010). Towards a politics of mobility. *Environment and Planning D: Socitey and Space*, 28(1), 17–31.

Cresswell, T. (2014). Mobilities III: Moving on. *Progress in Human Geography*, 38(5), 712–721.

Daffe, L. (2012). D'à-bord, d'à-terre : habiter entre deux eaux. Approche ethnographique des bateaux-logements namurois. Working document, Laboratoire d'Anthropologie Prospective, Louvain-la-Neuve.

Daffe, L. (2016). Trente-huit mètres sur cinq. Genèse du logement fluvial à Bruxelles et en Wallonie. *Uzance*, 5, 35–44.

Daffe, L. (2018). "Ce bateau, c'est l'argent de mon père" : la transaction monétaire comme condition de circulation et de transmission des bateaux. *La Revue du M.A.U.S.S.*, 52(2), 251–262.

Daffe, L. (2019). Amphibies. Une ethnographie des modes de vie des habitants de bateaux-logements en Wallonie et à Bruxelles. PhD thesis, Université catholique de Louvain, Louvain-la-Neuve.

Daffe, L. (2021). Sous la surface : une approche de la frontière aquatique lémanique par les navigations professionnelles et les apports de l'anthropologie amphibie. *Revue du Rhin Supérieur*, 3, 61–80.

Denhez, F. (2019). Le transport fluvial est-il enfin devenu un sujet politique ? [Online]. Available at: https://blogs.mediapart.fr/frederic-denhez/blog/201119/le-transport-fluvial-est-il-enfin-devenu-un-sujet-politique.

Elden, S. (2013). Secure the volume: Vertical geopolitics and the depth of power. *Political Geography*, 34, 35–51.

Eurostat (2017). Répartition modale du transport de fret [Online]. Available at: https://ec.europa.eu/eurostat/fr/web/products-datasets/product?code=t2020_rk320.

Gabor, M. (1979). *Maisons sur l'eau*. Éditions du Chêne/Hachette, Paris.

Hannam, K., Sheller, M., Urry, J. (2006). Mobilities, immobilities and moorings. *Mobilities*, 1(1), 1–22.

Hastrup, K. and Rubow, C. (2014). *Living with Environmental Change. Waterworlds*. Routledge, London/New York.

Hasty, W. and Peters, K. (2012). The ship in geography and the geographies of ships. *Geography Compass*, 6(11), 660–676.

Helmreich, S. (2011). Nature/culture/seawater. *American Anthropologist*, 113(1), 132–144.

Ingold, T. (2000). *The Perception of the Environment. Essays in Livehood, Dwelling and Skill.* Routledge, London/New York.

Kaaristo, M. and Rhoden, S. (2017). Everyday life and water tourism mobilities: Mundane aspects of canal travel. *Tourism Geographies*, 19(1), 78–95.

Kinder, K. (2015). *The Politics of Urban Water. Changing Waterscapes in Amsterdam.* The University of Georgia Press, Georgia.

Krause, F. (2017). Towards an amphibious anthropology of delta life. *Human Ecology*, 45(3), 403–408.

Krause, F. (2019). Hydro-perspectivism: Terrestrial life from a watery angle. *Anthropological Notebooks*, 25(2), 93–101.

Krause, F. and Strang, V. (2016). Thinking relationships through water. *Society & Natural Resources*, 29(6), 633–638.

Le Sueur, B. (2012). *Navigations intérieures. Histoire de la batellerie de la préhistoire à demain.* Glénat, Grenoble.

Manceron, V. (1996). "Être chez soi, être entre soi" : la question du territoire chez les mariniers berrichons. *Ethnologie française*, 26(3), 406–417.

Merger, M. (1985). Les mariniers au début du XXe siècle : "des forains d'une espèce particulière". *Le Mouvement social*, 132, 83–100.

Paul, C. and Raimbault, N. (2013). Habiter le fleuve : la "flurbanité" des bateliers du bassin de la Seine. *EspacesTemps* [Online]. Available at: https://www.espaces temps.net/articles/habiter-le-fleuve/.

Retaillé, D. (2014). De l'espace nomade à l'espace mobile en passant par l'espace du contrat : une expérience théorique. *Canadian Journal of African Studies*, 48(1), 13–28.

Roberts, L. (2019). Taking up space: Community, belonging and gender among itinerant boat dwellers on London's waterways. *Anthropological Notebooks*, 25(2), 57–69.

Romain, F. (2010). *La construction contemporaine des paysages fluviaux urbains. Le cas de deux villes nord méditerranéennes : Perpignan et Montpellier.* PhD thesis, AgroParisTech, Paris.

Sheller, M. and Urry, J. (2006). The new mobilities paradigm. *Environment and Planning A*, 38, 207–226.

Steinberg, P. and Peters, K. (2015). Wet ontologies, fluid spaces: Giving depth to volume through oceanic thinking. *Environment and Planning D: Society and Space*, 33, 247–264.

Urbain, J.-D. (2003). *Secrets de voyage. Menteurs, imposteurs et autres voyageurs impossibles.* Payot, Paris.

Vallerani, F. and Visentin, F. (eds) (2018). *Waterways and the Cultural Landscape.* Routledge, London/New York.

VNF (2013). Étude sur les retombées économiques. La location de bateaux habitables sans permis en France. Report, Voies Navigables de France, Béthune.

VNF (2019a). *Colloque. Le transport fluvial à l'heure de la transition énergétique. Synthèse des débats.* Voies navigables de France, Béthune.

VNF (2019b). Les chiffres du tourisme fluvial en 2018. Report, Voies Navigables de France, Béthune.

Wateau, F. (1989). Gens de l'eau. Structure familiale de la batellerie du Nord de la France. *Ethnologie française*, 19(4), 350–361.

Wiegmans, B. and Konings, R. (eds) (2017). *Inland Waterway Transport. Challenges and Prospects.* Routledge, London/New York.

Willemin, V. (2008). *Maisons sur l'eau.* Alternatives, Paris.

11

Temporary Mobilities and Neo-Nomadism

Arnaud LE MARCHAND

Laboratoire IDEES, CNRS, Université du Havre, Le Havre, France

11.1. Introduction

The furtive but significant reappearance of people who are constantly or at least often on the move, for professional reasons or according to a neo-nomadic lifestyle, has raised questions about the reasons for this phenomenon: is it only a matter of obeying injunctions or is it the result of chosen divisions?

We will begin by presenting the results of research on these flows, from the perspective of changes in work and from that of cultural movements. These results make it possible to understand the issues, for the law and urban planning, but also with regard to politics, in these practices. The measures that could be taken, in order to be calibrated, require the use of methodologies specific to these phenomena, which are not very standardized, for which data are lacking, and which therefore require multiple, faceted approaches. Nevertheless, there are major research works that integrate these questions into a general sociology, in an admittedly paradoxical but significant way. As in any emerging field, there are still ongoing debates, because the phenomenon is complex, notably on the question of the origins of its practices.

11.2. State of current knowledge and major references

Temporary migration is movement without relocation, when people stay away from their home for a substantial period of time, on average less than 2 years, in OECD countries. The reason for this may be professional or private. In these cases, people use temporary housing: lodgings, hotels, rental or mobile housing, squats.

11.2.1. *Socioeconomics of temporary labor migration*

This phenomenon was first studied in relation to the seasonality of certain activities. As early as 1912, a pioneering work, *Seasonal Trade* (Webb and Freeman 1912), which studied seasonal occupations in the British area, addressed this theme in relation to itinerant hotel staff, one of the first European labor markets. The debate then focused on financial compensation for regular intermittence. It is, of course, present in Anderson's (1923) *Hobo*, although the latter primarily traces the lives of the homeless in Chicago. A seminal article in industrial relations theory also focuses on itinerant harvesters in the United States in the 1950s (Kerr 1953). This research is more in line with the sociological approach to wages than with mobility studies. Mobility remains, as it were, in the background of the studies, as a necessary, and implicit, condition that is not investigated.

These temporary movements have been studied for 19th century Europe by historians and geographers. Brunet (1951) and Béteille (1981) highlight the regularities and regional habits of seasonal migration. Brunet links them to local factors in the host regions: development of intensive farming and disappearance of day laborers. Béteille shows the structuring of space and the importance of regional communities among these travelers. For the end of the 19th century, however, Bompard et al. (1990) note the importance of intersectoral mobilities (industry and agriculture), the decline of regional regulations, and the extension of areas of movement.

While economic sociology's approach to mobility differs and is less normative than that of institutional economics, it is primarily interested in the networks of relations that facilitate, support, or force these temporary mobilities (Granovetter 2000), their spatial dimensions remaining secondary. It is through a book written by journalists, *Nomadland* (Bruder 2017), that the physical mobility of employees who do not experience upward social mobility, and in particular of retired employees working for Amazon, was recently reintroduced into the public debate. This reintroduction was the occasion for the invention of a neologism: workamper. This term was already used in Amazon's communications concerning employees who came to work during peak periods and parked their campers near the warehouses.

In this book, these practices are seen as forms of adaptation to the social crisis in the United States, aggravated by the subprime crisis: the emphasis is on the presence of the elderly to point out the failings of the retirement system. The same observation can be made about studies in the French-speaking world. For a long time, this phenomenon has been absent from reflections on labor mobility. The notion of labor mobility covers two aspects: social mobility, i.e., changes in qualification, sector of activity, and careers, and so-called residential or geographic mobility, which covers movements, especially on an inter-regional or international scale, and therefore migrations. In the Marxist tradition, the problem surrounding the reproduction of labor power can lead to a study of the role played by temporary mobility. In Noon's analysis of labor problems in Africa in the 1950s, translated and discussed by Naville (Naville and Noon 1952), temporary migration is seen as one of the causes of the maintenance of low wages. It is thus less an object in itself than a means of understanding another phenomenon.

Twenty-five years later, in Gaudemar's (1976) work on labor mobility, there is no mention of workers with variable workplaces. Similarly, in the survey of the Fos and Vitrolles area conducted by labor sociologists in 1977 (Bleitbrach et al. 1977, p. 208), a caravan is mentioned but not commented on. However, from the end of the 1980s (Enjolras 1988), when the theme of precariousness made its appearance, mobile populations and travelers made a discreet but real comeback in the works that were part of this paradigm. First of all, through the appearance of problems linked to the place of mobile populations in social services, and then, in works on regional economics (Marchand 1988), through the observation of what was seen at the time as a failure of mobility: employees moving around, without managing to settle down, and periodically returning to unemployment.

Health concerns also motivate certain studies. In the 1990s, Pison and his team studied the consequences of seasonal migration to cities for the spread of AIDS in Africa, emphasizing the protective role of family networks, where they exist, for these temporary migrants (Pison et al. 1993).

Since then, these temporary migrations have continued to grow. In France, in 2015, inter-regional mobility along with moving house seemed less likely to help people find or keep a job than it did during the Trente Glorieuses (period of 30 years following the end of World War Two), according to Sigaud (2015a), and tended to decrease. Behind this observation lies another form of mobility: one that does not involve moving in the administrative sense; people go to work temporarily in another region, without changing their address, or do not have a fixed address at all. These temporary migrations can also be international, especially since the OECD countries are looking to discourage the settlement of economic migrants from outside the EC. There is an injunction to return and to maintain the temporary nature of labor migration. If, at the European level, the substitute worker is a substitute for the migrant, at the national level, the worker in a mobile habitat or in a household replaces the employee/householder.

Early work focused first on the most skilled segment of the workforce, such as managers (Crague 2004), and then on blue-collar workers or more low-skilled workers (Le Marchand 2011; Lefebvre 2012). Long-distance transport workers, living in their vehicles, can be included in this work. In this perspective, temporary migration is a response to the injunctions of flexibility, which have their place in the description of capitalism in the 21st century. However, they also result from negative expectations about job stability on the part of employees who are already in a precarious situation. Some will refuse to move, if they own their homes for example, because they are not sure of how long the companies and the jobs might last.

Under these conditions, they prefer to make temporary migrations rather than seeking to settle down. These temporary migrations can explain the growth of non-ordinary housing, and in particular mobile or transient housing. This would be a return to the Parisian "zone" which has become a moving space in 21st century France. This evolution could be compared to those in other European countries, and in Asia, in China, and even in Japan, since the departure of day laborers from their reserved neighborhoods: the *yosebas* (Aoki 2003; Le Marchand 2010). The importance of tourism and logistics has created a new demand for these mobile workers, but other sectors are also concerned.

11.2.2. *Neo-nomadism and countercultures*

Another approach has considered temporary migrations, in parallel, as arising from a neo-nomadism understood as a counterculture. This other body of work (Frediani 2009; Pourtau 2012; Reitz 2017) focuses on segments of populations considered to be marginal: such as travelers, old and new, seasonal young workers, and even rootless youngsters. This work initially questions the adoption of mobile or packable housing as a choice, in opposition to the injunctions to a more normal lifestyle, in the conventional sense. It is often justified by the actors themselves with an anti-urban or anti-system discourse or one critical of modes of consumption. The history of this movement is very interesting for a sociology of mobility, as it provides an example of how political and religious factors, combined with cultural contestation, can contribute to alternative forms of mobility.

Neo-nomadism has emerged as a form of habitat whose revival is linked to criticisms of the dominant way of life, or to the hippy movement, then to the development of a public going from music festivals to festivals, to sports practices, such as surfing, or even influenced by beatnik literature, with a pre-eminent importance given to the book by

Jack Kerouac. But in her introduction to Frediani's (2009) pioneering work, Judith Okely suggests another origin, referring to antinuclear protests as one of the laboratories of the New Age Traveller movement. The neo-nomadic movement in England would find its origin in the first protest marches against atomic weapons, which took place in England between 1958 and 1965 (Aldermaston Marches), and in West Germany, from 1961, during which some participants perceived themselves to be pilgrims, traveling in a world of misfortune.

The experience of the protesters during these marches, which took place on Easter weekends, had a spiritual dimension, reinforced by the departure from ordinary material life (Nehring 2013). Some who had lived in trucks, which can be seen in photographs from the time, during the event, would have decided not to return to sedentary life. This experience of protest mobility would have been prolonged in a nomadic life, initially carried out by some individuals, joined with the passing of years, and by the disruptions of new arrivals, in particular again in England, around the protest camp at Stonehenge, at the beginning of the 1980s. This type of habitat was also present in the hippy movement, whose creation is linked to pacifism as much as to a style of music. Like other currents of the counterculture (MacKay 2004), the traveler phenomenon stems from this social movement, endowed with a spiritual dimension as well as a dystopian fantasy, with war and nuclear winter, and a utopian dream world, of building a world different from the one leading to nuclear apocalypse. A similar story, with a strong feminist implication, would explain the *wagenplatz* (urban mobile housing camps) in Germany (Marsault 2018).

These first neo-nomads were joined, from the 1980s onward, by others coming from the punk movement, bearers of another dystopian fantasy. An intuition of the climatic problems at the very origin of the punk movement in England can be suggested. The summer of 1976, now considered as a marker of global warming, was one of the circumstances of its birth. Savage (2002, p. 263) writes that there was an apocalyptic climate in England that summer due to the extreme drought and unbearable temperatures (over 35°C in London) for the time. In this context, the slogan *No future* marked an awareness of the finiteness of industrial societies, which, combined with the eviction of urban squats, led to secession nomadism. This hybridization between punk and hippie also gave rise to the free parties (Pourtau 2012).

Later, Frediani noted that the traveler world did not organize itself around a shared ideology: its dynamics being essentially individual and its actors claiming above all a cultural autonomy, or the right to organize events outside the market economy. The social, or even political, dimension has reappeared more recently and is the result of a repression of mobile housing, perceived as an injustice. While this injustice is not always denounced in the same terms by all the participants, it is not surprising to find a critical dimension because it was present at the very origin of the movement.

In fact, it is also the increasing poverty and precariousness of young people that will grow this movement in the UK (Frediani 2009) and France (Bernardot et al. 2014). Neo-nomadism and the movements linked to precariousness then fall under the sociology of marginality and of this social space called in France the "zone". The sociology of the zone describes an inhabited space, in a paradoxical rejection or adaptation to neoliberal norms and modern comfort, and movable from one interstice to another (Beauchez et al. 2017, p. 5). The sociology of mobile housing falls into this field. This sociology does not really question the issues related to the mutations of work. Yet, as we have seen, some of the people living in mobile housing have made these choices, constrained by the logics of labor segmentation. That is to say, both approaches, through the injunctions to professional mobility and through the adoption of counterculture values, come together, as there is an intersectionality of these fields. Of course, the neo-nomadism linked to the reorganization of work, for example, in industry, does not necessarily share the alternative values of travelers. But the latter are also workers, whose way of life is not completely detached materially from the rest of society.

11.3. Challenges for contemporary societies

Temporary migration involving transient or mobile housing, as well as neo-nomadism, constitutes several challenges for contemporary societies.

Strictly from a transportation perspective, these mobilities are an alternative to commuting. People temporarily lodge close to their place of work (although this is not always possible), rather than commuting back and forth. But legal systems are ill-equipped to guarantee rights for these practices because they are constructed by positing fixed employment and normal housing as norms and mobilities that conform to them. These temporary migrations therefore circumvent urban planning and legislation, as they are partly unplanned.

From a housing perspective, they question the norms of ordinary housing, especially because housing made up of caravans or converted trucks, for example, is, from the point of view of sedentary people, unworthy housing. As the Belgian jurist Bernard (2012) wrote, these practices threaten the dominant, accepted norms because these transient inhabitants do not consider their dwellings unworthy. Mobile, rental, and transient dwellings challenge a common conception of comfort. The fact that housing is also caught in the net of mobility can be denounced as an abuse, a harmful acceleration or impoverishment, or a detachment from ordinary social ties.

The temptation is then great to authorize them only as ethnicized cultural practices, for the Western European Romany in particular, with consideration of their human rights (Donders 2016), but still subject to strong constraints. The economic reasons make them acceptable when they concern large construction sites that resemble special economic zones in which tax, labor, and urban planning laws are applied with much greater flexibility than in the rest of the national territory. But these tolerances do not imply that these local arrangements can be spread further. Certain exceptions, whether economic or cultural, are then all the more accepted as the general rule is confirmed.

These practices concern workers, whether they care or not, from the construction and public works sectors, from the energy sector (the nomads of the nuclear and wind power industries), and from industrial maintenance, as well as multiskilled workers, such as the seasonal workers who alternate between agricultural, tourist, and cultural activities. Many of these workers belong to both worlds. But they extend beyond these reserved areas. On the one hand, because the employees who use them can be found in places other than large relatively isolated sites: moreover, this type of housing is spreading to other sectors, such as temporary hospital work, social work, or abattoirs. The mobile or transient housing of neo-nomads is becoming a mode of housing, adapted to new urban mobilities, sometimes adopted by people who are neither poor nor excluded. In fact, they are forms of paradoxical integration, in societies that tend to consider them as residual, outside the tourist sphere. Consequently, these temporary mobilities give rise more to bargaining – that is, ad hoc solutions that do not give rights – than to negotiated rules.

These new forms of mobility therefore raise questions about the practice of social dialogue, and territorial social dialogue when it exists. Although the issue of mobility is now considered to be one of the themes calling for normative negotiation (Gazier and Bruggeman 2016), between social partners and with the actors in the territories concerned (territorial social dialogue), it must be noted that this is, once again, a classic conception of mobility. Representative actors and public authorities can initiate exchanges of information, consultations, look for rules for professional transitions, such as job changes, or for (relatively) definitive changes of workplace. But temporary mobility has not yet entered this field of social dialogue and collective bargaining.

However, if we accept a broad conception of regulation, including remote interactions, we will note that the adaptation of offers and prices in the so-called budget hotels for employees on the move, the creation of service areas for seasonal workers in certain ski resorts, the interventions of the public authorities to solve parking problems, as well as the press articles sometimes devoted to the housing of certain employees outline the emergence of a codependence recognition process that could benefit from being more negotiated. For the time being, some associations of residents in rental or mobile housing are beginning to be recognized as representatives (Halem in France, Halé in Belgium). But there is little trade union or employer involvement in these negotiations.

On the part of local authorities, these mobilities should encourage them to rethink the facilities offered or sold to people in temporary mobility. Not only sites such as service areas for travelers and their eventual opening to other groups, but also other collective facilities, such as public showers or baths, laundries, or places to shelter mobile residents from extreme climatic events (heat waves, floods, etc.). Urban planning could take into account these types of habitats for new mobilities. However, the tendency to consider them only under the condition of cultural identity, for the Romany alone for example (Donders 2016), or for the conditions of exercise of certain recognized professions (circus performers, people working on the rivers) results in not recognizing the extent of the phenomenon, as well as its plasticity. It should be possible to think of it independently of its two modes of conditional acceptance, as a recomposition of the way of living and moving. It is an innovation, both culturally and economically, which calls into question many inherited distinctions.

Thus, some of the existing public shower facilities are not located in bathhouses, but in municipal swimming pools or in facilities managed by associations dedicated to specific groups, such as the homeless or drug users, like the Caarud in France. In 2015, according to the survey carried out by the Addiction Federation, 84.5% of these associations' drug user assistance centers provided one or more showers, also used by homeless people not suffering from addiction problems. For these associations, the drug user is a nomadic figure, an archetype of the vulnerable neo-nomad (Rivoirard 2016), almost a ghost of the zone. These particular offers are justified by health concerns (AIDS, hepatitis) and a desire to reduce harm. The care function in these cases pre-dated those related to hygiene. However, this addition may have served as an experiment, a warning to encourage the reopening of municipal bathhouses. These developments give a new meaning to the question of public collective facilities, such as municipal swimming pools, or private facilities, such as laundries or campsites.

The decentralization of social policies has been the subject of debate as to its effects. In several configurations, it has seemed to lead to its disappearance behind policies of renewal and attractiveness, oriented more toward buildings and constructions than toward people (Donzelot et al. 2003).

If these ways of getting around and living were to continue to spread, other questions would be asked, which are already potential. Environmentally, is this an alternative model to commuting that could be sustainable on a larger scale?

How can we rethink the political participation of actors moving in the territories they visit and in which they work? How can we rethink the rights associated with domiciliation, when this can become mobile, intermittent, and networked? The integration of the people concerned, and possibly the social improvement of the processes underway through consultation, is therefore an objective to be achieved, but for the time being, it seems that it is the refusal to negotiate that predominates, both among powerful actors (employers and public authorities) and among actors with little negotiating power (seconded employees and the marginalized).

It is without a doubt just as foreseeable that fears that were mobilized to justify the repression of travelers, and particularly the Romany in Europe, will be revived. For how can we think of security and sanitary control if a portion of the population is no longer fixed, while the Covid-19 crisis showed in 2020 the importance of seasonal workers in Europe or in India? Here, again, it should be remembered that the migration of Chinese workers has led to the decline of the *hukou*, the Chinese system of administrative control through residence permits (Tao et al. 2015); these mobilities, however vulnerable they may be, call into question administrative practices.

Finally, this perspective leads us to rethink, from an economic point of view, the distinction between generic factors of production, because they are mobile, and specific factors of production, because they are localized, which has structured the regional economy to a great extent. This distinction goes back to the work of Philippe Aydalot (Matteaciolli 2004) and the attempts to renew the paradigm of the regional economy, to move from natural factors of production to a more endogenous vision. If we accept that some local production requires highly specialized seasonal workers who adopt a neo-nomadic lifestyle, this distinction between specific localized factors and mobile, and therefore generic, factors becomes blurred.

The emergence of these practices appears retrospectively predictable, because they are consequences of the reorganizations of production and the relative withdrawal of the welfare state, but they were unforeseen. This unwelcomed occurrence justified their rejection and their consideration by successive improvisations. It is possible to think that after a still undefinable threshold, this attitude can no longer be maintained. It will then be necessary to negotiate, and not only to bargain, the temporary migrations and the place of the neo-nomads in the public space.

11.4. Survey methodologies, analysis with missing data

First of all, it is necessary to admit that this phenomenon is intrinsically volatile, with practices that are often furtive, which makes its measurement necessarily unclear. Because of the nonstandard nature of these practices, conventional statistical methods are not well suited to studying them. In general, the statistical apparatus is always a little behind certain social developments, and the interviewers' grids have a certain inertia, all the more so because changing them too often limits the capacity for comparison. From the moment when questions about workers' housing, for example, ceased to be seen as of primary importance in relation to the measurement of unemployment (Le Marchand 2011), mobile housing and temporary geographical movements ceased to be included in the census boxes. These remarks also apply, and have for a long time, to home-based work (Lallement 1990, p. 199), whose legal representation is not that of statistics nor of the actors themselves.

These differences also reflect the porosity of the boundaries between this type of work and employment and other domestic, manufacturing, or artisanal devices, of which remote coworking is only a new form. Almost by design, the worker in mobile housing is decoupled (White 2011, p. 123) from ordinary integration, and his "entry into the territory" (Sigaud 2015, p. 4), or rather his passage through it, is not always accompanied by statistical recording. Nevertheless, there are sectoral surveys, conducted by occupational physicians, on nuclear workers (Barbat et al. 2013) and on steeplejacks (Vignal et al. 2017), for whom this moving around, and for some the use of mobile housing, is an attested reality.

On this issue, research must deal with missing data and unreliable figures and exploit all possible traces. Nevertheless, there is an upward trend in temporary international migration, which for the OECD as a whole was more than 6% in 2017. For some European countries, this increase has been continuous throughout the 2010s: from 2010 to 2015 in Belgium and Germany, the increase in the number of incoming seconded workers was 72.9% and 67.5%, respectively (source: Eurostat 2010–2015).

The data are unreliable because respondents hide their status as nomads or temporary migrants to avoid harassment or are outside the scope of administrative investigations. This leads to a preference for surveys (Ravalet et al. 2014), field surveys, and indirect statistical approaches, as in problems of unobservable economics.

Another approach using the mobile habitat faces similar difficulties, those related to the definition of the phenomenon. This type of habitat is designated by multiple qualifiers. Delpech and Veyrac Ben Ahmed (2014) have thus identified, according to texts, more than a dozen expressions that allow us to understand it (ephemeral, temporary, etc.). The uncertain limits of the phenomenon also generate difficulties in producing statistics or quantitative reasoning on mobile or temporary habitats, which is still necessary. Censuses are problematic because some of the people concerned will try to avoid a survey, which may involve eviction or even demolition of the dwelling. American sociologists have developed a method of identifying *colonias* in Texas, i.e., small blocks of mobile or dismountable dwellings, through the use of Google Earth or other satellite images. But they recognize that estimating the number of inhabitants requires a direct survey of the identified sites, with the usual problems of authoritarian censuses (Ward and Peters 2007).

It is remarkable, moreover, that the first satellite surveys of the *colonias* did not make any links with the shale gas boom. Another classic solution is to look for proxies, i.e., variables that evolve like those that remain difficult to measure. This indirect approach, however, implies proposing relationships between the observable variable and temporal migrations that are considered acceptable by both the actors concerned and the research community, as has been emphasized by ethnomethodological investigations of survey practice (Maynard and Schaeffer 2001). This can be met with conservative caution on the part of researchers or a lack of global vision on the part of actors: for example, indirect observation of the growth in the consumption of laundry services is easily accepted as an indirect measure of temporary mobility, while recourse to statistics on the number of members of groups dedicated to Facebook, such as the virtual community of "seasonal workers in mobile housing," is not received as a reliable measure, even if indirect and partial, of the dynamics of these practices.

Under these conditions, the qualitative approach is essential. But it faces several pitfalls. The tried and tested approach, which consists of getting to know a site in depth, for example, a camp, possibly through the installation of the researcher who is part of the site, undoubtedly allows for a better understanding of the realities faced by the inhabitants of converted trucks. But it risks, in a somewhat paradoxical way, preventing seeing certain mobilities, because of the focus on a single site, about which the researcher would try to know everything.

In addition, life-course approaches, which aim to reconstruct the trajectories of certain actors, make it possible to avoid this limitation (Reitz 2017; Loiseau 2019). They have the disadvantage, which is also their value, of requiring a lot of time to gain the trust of the actors. This often limits the size of the samples taken and induces bias. However, this research, using various and sometimes unstable methods, converges on one result: that of the growth of these practices, a growth that is partly cyclical, but also structural. The triangulation of these methods makes it possible to validate these results, which are admittedly partial, but which reflect significant changes.

In order to pursue this systematization of different methods, it would be necessary to network researchers involved in different fields, including industrial sites and special economic zones, or engaged in long-term studies. But to explain without going into too much detail, this observatory of temporary migration and neo-nomadism should work with some of these temporary migrants. It is therefore necessary to find a mechanism to bring an observatory to life, involving researchers and actors, associations, or unions representing them, to coproduce knowledge and data on these issues.

11.5. Place in general sociology

The major research works focus on cultural or social aspects of the phenomenon. Following the work of Kenrick and Clark (1999) and Marcel Frediani on *travellers* in the United Kingdom, Pourtau (2012) developed an approach to neo-nomadism through the prism of the sociology of deviance and youth. He analyzes it as a very marginal practice, including those within the technoid sound system movement, and always temporary, constituting a stage in a deviant path, before a return to normal and sedentary life. According to this author, it fulfills the function of an airlock in a journey, before a return to a life more compatible with the dominant norms. But he notes that *travellers* are rare. He understands *travellers* in the sense of young people living almost exclusively in trucks, invested with sound systems, and following or organizing free parties and teknivals. This can be translated in return by the hypothesis, verified in certain places where young people live in trucks, that the "ravers" are only one of the components of this group whose dynamic is not reduced to that of the techno movement.

Other work also focuses on the converted vehicles of *new travellers* (Reitz 2017) and the meaning of this way of living, or on the objects carried by traveling executives. Finally, there is a whole current of anthropology that describes professional groups such as sailors, or ethnic groups such as the Roma or the Tuareg. The international journal *Nomadic People* provides a good overview of these works. They are all the more useful for understanding these mobilities, since in many cases, ethnic borders become porous and the camps multicultural. As a result, some concepts and results can be transferred from one field to another, especially for the analysis of situated action in a shifting network (Loiseau 2019).

Zygmunt Bauman's theorizations, via the opposing metaphors of tourists and vagabonds, provide a critical framework, which allows us to reinscribe these phenomena in a general framework and sociology.

The famous chapter "Touristes and vagrants" in *Globalization: The Human Consequences* implicitly refers to temporary migration and neo-nomadism without naming them. It opens with the sentence: "Nowadays we are all on the move" (Bauman 1998, p. 119, our translation).

This seems contradictory to this statement further on:

As capital has emancipated itself from space, it no longer needs traveling workers (and its most technologically advanced vanguard almost no longer needs any work, mobile or immobile) (Bauman 1998, p. 143, authors' translation).

Apart from the interpretation according to which Zygmunt Bauman thinks that travelers do not work (as wage earners?) or are potentially unemployed, this statement seems to be contradicted by the *mingongs* in China, the seconded workers in Europe, the *workampers* in the United States. In the same way, we have identified meeting points, modern fountains, notably laundries, which he considered to have disappeared, whereas their activity is on the rise again (as is that of the bathhouse). One possible explanation is that Bauman studied the ideology of capital and power. In this perspective, he suggests that capital no longer sees workers, while modular production, infrastructure, and agricultural work, but also the tertiary sector, need travelers, mobile as well as immobile workers.

But in the sphere of pure ideology, there is no longer any need for it, hence the end of public services and the policies of eradicating vagrants, etc. Remembering that Zygmunt Bauman thinks in terms of duality and the excluded third party (Davis 2008) can help to remove this contradiction. According to this author, societies are organized around a fundamental dichotomy, which implies an injunction to be classified in one group or the other, while those who are unclassifiable are excluded in the sociological sense. Mobility and immobility are essential criteria in the contemporary world.

But the recognized mobility is that of the upper classes (the supertourists); those who are mobile without being among the dominant are the vagabonds. This explains the assertion at the end of the same page: there are no tourists (the superconsumer) without vagabonds because they are produced by the changes generated by the activity of the highly mobile, and it is not possible to let the tourists go free if one does not lock up the vagabonds, as they are elements of disorder. For if the excluded third party exists, then its members must be repressed or locked up. Rosa's (2014) version of this reasoning distinguishes between those capable of accelerating (production, ships, technology, the pace of work) and those still capable of imposing a deceleration (institutional actors of the welfare state, civil servants, doctors, ecologists); the neo-nomads are then excluded because either they travel without acceleration or they park, and then slow down flows (of goods, for example), without being authorized to do so.

Beyond the limits of academic research, documentary makers have also produced films. In France, one thinks of Gabrielle Culand's films, such as *Vagant, une génération sur la route*, which notably succeeded in filming recruitment discussions in which having a converted truck was an advantage, and Alexandra Tilman's

Cadences (2014), which follows an ex-worker turned DJ. On industrial sites, the film *Flamanville brûle-t-il?* by Stany Cambot, which traces life on the campsites occupied by employees of the Flamanville EPR work site, gives an understanding of the changes within the labor market leading to temporary migrations, explained by the workers concerned themselves. In December 2020, Chloé Zhao's film *Nomadland* was released, putting into fiction the observations of Bruder's book. There are photographic works such as that of Ferjeux Van der Stigghel, which integrates an anthropological reflection on the inhabitation and intimacy of *travellers*. These works are valuable because the use of images is a way not only to document situations (and to constitute an archive) but also to make people understand and see interactions situated in special spaces.

11.6. Status of scientific debates and controversies in the field

The quantitative evaluation of the phenomenon is not the only problem under debate. The division between adaptation to injunctions and the autonomous choices of actors is just as difficult. Behind the discourses claiming professional choices, or invoking anti-urban ideologies, we can analyze divisions. These previous courses of action can explain the choice of seasonal or irregular mobility, justified or irregular mobilities, which are then justified because they suit the people concerned. Adaptation to injunctions and eccentric choices are more intertwined than really distinguishable. For while these practices may retain a utopian dimension, they are also part of reorganizations of production and consumption, which make them functional, despite their official invisibility.

The focus on the constraints that led people to make these choices ignores the requisite dispositions that enable them, and the learning and socialization that result from them. Some observations are consistent with research on the determinants of motility (Kaufmann 2005). The family is one of the frameworks for acquiring the know-how to move, and beyond an initial formation of a motility capital (Kaufmann and Widmer 2005). Beyond the family circle, the neighborhood can constitute a learning network; it has already been noted that there is a strong presence among young people traveling from festival to festival, of people coming from suburban housing estates (Chobeaux 2011). The distance from cultural life felt by adolescents whose families do not live in the city may be a motivation to acquire this motility, with the help of other young residents of the housing estate, to compensate for the spatial disconnection. Motivation related to cultural ties would in this case be no different from the mechanisms related to the search for seasonal jobs, for example. In this case, the anticipation of the precariousness of jobs, even those with permanent contracts, pushes one to develop these skills so as not to have to move. From this point of view, travel is not incompatible with a territorial anchorage that one seeks to preserve.

But if anticipations play an essential role, family memories or memories carried by other collectives are also possible explanations. One of the difficulties is to approach this question of resources drawn from a past of homelessness without falling into an outdated essentialism. That is to say, without freezing collective identities that would act as hidden motivations for these mobilities. For all that, working-class memories of nomadism exist; the intertwining of the fairground and travelers with the populace is a reality that is being rediscovered, which can explain why certain groups can accept living as travelers more easily than others. These memories that become resources can be found in objects, such as the motorhome or the converted truck, which have fairground genealogies, and in the history of American hobos. Social networks also have long histories, as the study of the determinants of international migration has shown, which can also shape the motility of those who are part of them. Hence the interest of historical research linking mobility and habitat in the long term, a theme that is being revived (Canepari et al. 2016). For it is a minority habitus, but its distribution may not follow that of other social capitals.

As the history of antinuclear marches in Great Britain reminds us, these practices may have been acquired during protests, during political experiences of contestation. Some of these actions in temporary migrations, such as the pallet camp, can be found in the registers of action of new social movements. This result can be extended: it is sometimes on the occasion of events generating a shift and a questioning of daily routines that the learning of mobility can take place.

The imaginary world, from the hobo route to the hippies via the beat generation and pilgrimages, is one of the factors leading to the adoption of neo-nomadism. It is similar to tourist mobilities, for which the imaginary world of the elsewhere is a prerequisite. This could make neo-nomads, like temporary labor migrants, spatial intermittents, tourists "living the journey," as much for professional reasons as for a refusal of norms.

11.7. References

Anderson, N. (1923). *The Hobo: The Sociology of the Homeless Man.* University of Chicago Press, Chicago.

Aoki, H. (2003). Homelessness in Osaka: Globalisation, Yoseba and disemployment. *Urban studies*, 40(2).

Barbat, D., Bejeau, D., Bergaut, F., Boulay, M.H., Devaux, M.J., Diem-Lam, L., Hemery, J.M., Meyer, A., Rousselet, A., Sauvagere, J. (2013). Vie, travail, santé des salariés de la sous-traitance du nucléaire. *Références en santé au travail*, 136.

Bauman, Z. (1998). *Le coût humain de la mondialisation*. Hachette, Paris.

Beauchez, J., Bouillon, F., Zeneidi, D. (2017). Zone: l'espace d'une vie en marge. *Espaces et sociétés*, 171(4), 7–18.

Belorgey, J.M. (1988). *La gauche et les pauvres*. Syros, Paris.

Bernard, N. (ed.) (2012). *La norme à l'épreuve de l'habitat alternatif?* Die Keure/La Charte, Brugge.

Bernardot, M., Le Marchand, A., Santana Bucio, C. (2011). *Habitats non-ordinaires et espace-temps de la mobilité*. Le Croquant, Bellecombes en Bauge.

Béteille, R. (1981). Une nouvelle approche géographique des faits migratoires: champs, relations, espaces relationnels. *Espace géographique*, 10(3), 187–197.

Bleitbrach, D., Chenu, A., Bouffartigue, P., Broda, J., Ronchi, Y. (1977). Production et consommation dans la structuration des pratiques de déplacement CRET. Report, Université Aix Marseille, Marseille.

Bompard, J.-P., Magnac, T., Postel-Vinay, G. (1990). Emploi, mobilité et chômage en France: migrations saisonnières entre industrie et agriculture. *Annales. Economies, sociétés, civilisations*, 1, 55–76.

Bruder, J. (2017). *Nomadland. Surviving America in the Twenty-First Century*. Norton, London.

Canepari, E., Mésini, B., Mourlane, S. (2016). *Mobil Hom(m)es. Formes d'habitats et modes d'habiter la mobilité (XVIe–XXIe siècles)*. Éditions de l'Aube, La Tour d'Aigues.

Chobeaux, F. (2011). *Les nomades du vide: des jeunes en errance, de squats en festivals, de gares en lieux d'accueil*. La Découverte, Paris.

Crague, G. (2004). Des lieux de travail de plus en plus variables et temporaires. *Économie et statistique*, 369–370.

Davis, M. (2008). Bauman on globalisation. The human consequences of liquid world. In *The Sociology of Zygmunt Bauman*, Hviid, M.J., Poul, P. (eds). Ashgate, Farnham.

Delpech, V. and Veyrac-Ben Ahmed, B. (2014). Habiter l'atypique. Quelles réalités présentes pour quel avenir. In *Colloque de l'ASRDLF*, July.

Donders, Y. (2016). Protecting the home and adequate housing. Living in a caravan or trailer as a human right. *International Human Rights Law Review*, 5, 1–25.

Donzelot, J., Mével, C.,Wyvekens, A. (2003). *Faire société : la politique de la ville aux États-Unis et en France*. Le Seuil, Paris.

Enjolras, B. (1988). Mobilité, précarité : vers un nouveau rapport salarial. *Espace, populations, sociétés. La population face à l'emploi – Population and Work Opportunities*, 561–566.

Frediani, M. (2009). *Sur les routes : le phénomène des New Travellers*. Imago, Paris.

Gaudemar, J.-P. (1976). *Mobilité du travail et accumulation du capital*. Maspéro, Paris.

Gazier, B. and Bruggeman, F. (2016). Dialogue social et dialogue social territorial au début du XXIe siècle. Un essai de théorisation. *Négociations*, 26(2).

Granovetter, M. (1990). *Le marché autrement. Les réseaux dans l'économie*. Desclée de Brouwer, Paris.

Kaufmann, V. (2005). Mobilités et réversibilités : vers des sociétés plus fluides ? *Cahiers internationaux de sociologie*, 118(1), 119–135.

Kaufmann, V. and Widmer, E. (2005). L'acquisition de la motilité au sein des familles. État de la question et hypothèses de recherche. *Espaces et sociétés*, 1(120/121), 199–217.

Kenrick, D. and Colin, C. (1999). *Moving On: The Gypsies and Travellers of Britain*. University of Hertfordshire Press, Hatfield.

Kerr Clark, J. (1953). *The Harvest Labor Market in California*. Lloyd H. Fisher, Cambridge/Massachusetts.

Lallement, M. (1990). Une forme d'emploi le travail à domicile. In *L'emploi, l'entreprise et la société. Débats Economie-Sociologie*, Michon, F., Segrestin, D. (eds). Economica, London.

Le Marchand, A. (1987). *Entre identité et itinérance, le Languedoc dans tous ses états*. CRES Université P. Valéry, Montpellier.

Le Marchand, A. (2010). Voyage parmi les précaires de Séoul et d'Osaka. *Multitudes*, 4, 43.

Le Marchand, A. (2011). *Enclaves nomades. Habitat et travail mobile*. Le Croquant, Bellecombes en bauge.

Lefebvre, B. (2012). *Ethnographie des travailleurs en déplacement. Voyages en Europe sociale*. L'Harmattan, Paris.

Loiseau, G. (2019). Odologie et présence des gens du voyage en France. Blocages, passages et noeuds des espaces de vie voyageurs. PhD thesis, Université Le Havre, Le Havre.

Marsault, R. (2018). Éléments d'anthropologie punk sur l'espace des Wagenburgen berlinoises. *Journal des anthropologues*, 1(152/153), 265–281.

Matteaciolli, A. (2004). *Philippe Aydalot, pionnier de l'économie territoriale*. L'Harmattan, Paris.

Maynard, D. and Schaeffer, N.C. (2001). La pratique des sondages vue par l'ethnométhodologie. In *L'ethnométhodologie. Une sociologie radicale*, de Fornel, M. (ed.). La Découverte, Paris.

McKay, G. (2004). Subcultural Innovations in the campaign for nuclear disarmament. *Peace Review*, 16(4), 429–438.

Nehring, H. (2013). *Politics of Security: British and West German Protest Movements and the Early Cold War, 1945–1970*. Oxford Press, Oxford.

Noon, J. and Naville, P. (1952). La mécanique des bas salaires en Afrique Noire. *Présence Africaine*, 13, 202–218.

Pison, G., Le Guenno, B., Lagarde, E., Enel, C., Seck, C. (1993). Seasonal migration: A risk factor for HIV infection in rural Senegal. *Journal of Acquired Immune Deficiency Syndromes*, 6(2), 196–200.

Pourtau, L. (2012). *Techno : une subculture en marge*. CNRS, Paris.

Ravalet, E., Dubois, Y., Kaufmann, V. (2014). Grandes mobilités et accès à l'emploi. *Reflets et perspectives de la vie économique*, liii(3), 57–76.

Reitz, M. (2017). Assembler son quotidien sur la route : une ethnographie de l'habiter mobile contemporain. PhD thesis, EPFL, Lausanne.

Rivoirard, A. (2016). Le toxicomane : une figure de l'errant ? *Le sociographe*, 53(1), I–XIII.

Rosa, H. (2014). *Aliénation et Accélération. Vers une théorie critique de la modernité tardive*. La Découverte, Paris.

Savage, J. (2002). *England's Dreaming. Les Sex Pistols et le punk*. Allia, Paris.

Sigaud, T. (2015a). Mobilité géographique ressource ou fragilité pour l'emploi. *Cahier du CEE*, 125.

Sigaud, T. (2015b). Accompagner les mobilités résidentielles des salariés : l'épreuve de l'entrée en territoire. *Espaces et sociétés*, 162(3), 129–145.

Tao, L., Hui, E.C.M., Wong, F.K.W., Tingting, C. (2015). Housing choices of migrant workers in China: Beyond the Hukou perspective. *Habitat International*, 49(2), 474–483.

Vignal, B., Soulé, B., Rogowski, I (2017). Étude épidémiologique des blessures chez les cordistes français. Report, Université Lyon 1, Lyon.

Ward, P. (2007). Self-help housing and informal homesteading in peri-urban America: Settlement identification using digital imagery and GIS. *Habitat International*, 31, 205–218.

Webb, S. and Freeman, A. (1912). *Seasonal Trades. London School of Economics and Political Science*. Constable, London.

White, H. (2011). *Identité et contrôle. Une théorie de l'émergence des formations sociales*. Grossetti, M., Godart, F. (trans.). EHESS, Paris.

Filmography

Cambot, S. (2019). *Flamanville brûle-t-il ?* Echelle Inconnue.

Culand, G. (2012). *Vagant. Une génération sur la route.* Program33.

Tilman, A. (2014). *Cadences*. Vimeo.

12

Towards a Rhythmology of Mobile Societies

Guillaume DREVON[1,2] and Vincent KAUFMANN[2]

[1] *Urban Development and Mobility Department, Luxembourg Institute of Socio-Economic Research, Esch-sur-Alzette, Luxembourg*
[2] *Laboratoire de sociologie urbaine (LaSUR), École polytechnique fédérale de Lausanne, Switzerland*

12.1. Limitations of the concept of mobility

The general objective of this book is to think collectively about different forms of mobility, their social, spatial, and temporal diversity through contributions that focus on both a detailed description of the literature and the perspective of empirical studies on a European scale. All of the chapters show the intricacies of different forms of mobility as well as the diversity of the intentions that underlie them and push people to move, on a neighborhood scale or to the other side of the world, being either very spatially anchored or on the contrary a traveler or nomadic at heart. The contributions highlight the major political issues associated with mobility. Among them: the dependence on mobility, the acceleration of the pace of of life or the mechanisms of exclusion, and precarity linked to migration and reversible mobilities. The chapters in this book also show that mobility is part of a closed circle of concepts that comprehensively circulate through a wide variety of disciplinary fields and domains. Mobility is thus a concept that transcends disciplinary divisions and allows, depending on the object, to think on different temporal and spatial scales.

However, we noted in Chapter 1 that an approach to mobility organized by object (everyday local mobility, residential mobility, migration, and even atypical mobility)

Mobility and Geographical Scales,
coordinated by Guillaume DREVON and Vincent KAUFMANN. © ISTE Ltd 2023.

runs the risk of segmenting analyses and contributing to the development of compartmentalized research that refers, on the one hand, to specific disciplines and, on the other hand, to specific objects and fields. The mobility turn as proposed by John Urry aims to go beyond this state of affairs by considering, in the tradition of Michel Bassand, that all forms of mobility form a system by mixing various objects and by including the different spatial and temporal mobility scales mentioned above.

However, more than 20 years after the publication of Urry's (2000) manifesto, it is clear that research on mobility is still profoundly associated with disciplines and struggles to transcend the traditional fields of everyday mobility, residential mobility, tourism, and migration. This is evidenced by the titles of conferences, scientific journals, and international networks or, more anecdotally, by the profiles of positions advertised in international research. This persistence is certainly linked to the shaping of research on specific subjects. Whoever wants to make a career in the social sciences must specialize in a specific subject and mobility as a system is certainly not one available to them. In our book, the references cited by the various authors often attest to this state of affairs, particularly with regard to empirical research.

It is obvious that research on mobility is not reaching its full potential and is very often confined to certain fields, struggling to integrate the spatial, temporal, and social dimensions of the phenomenon in a broad and generous approach. This situation needs to be overcome and three major challenges need to be addressed through research:

– Firstly, the concept of mobility allows for a holistic approach to the analysis of contemporary societies. It is important that this vision is translated into a conceptualization work specific to this broad approach. Reversibility and motility clearly go in this direction, but approaches to mobility are often not very transversal.

– Secondly, the study of mobilities focuses interest on movement, whether social or spatial, thus implicitly putting aside the instituted, the fixed, and what remains and more generally what does not move. The challenge is to avoid making invisible what is immobile and to avoid producing new analytical blind spots.

– Thirdly, the research that has been carried out on mobility issues has not made it possible to highlight the levers for action that would make it possible to meet the major challenges facing contemporary societies in the areas of climate change, globalization of trade, and growing inequalities. As a result, the impact of this work is often limited.

In relation to these three challenges, this book demonstrates that in order to think about mobility, but also immobility and its different spatial and temporal scales, in a comprehensive way, it is important to adopt an approach that allows us to think about the intertwining of the different forms of mobility. Such a grid must allow us to move between the different fields of the social sciences, and between their different terrains and issues.

With this in mind, we hypothesize that the notion of rhythm has the necessary conceptual qualities to respond to the identified issues.

12.2. Thinking about the entanglement of mobilities using forms of rhythm

One of the essential points raised in this book concerns, in our opinion, the possibility of thinking collectively about the different forms of mobility. In this respect, the various contributions show that the forms of mobility coexist in a constantly changing world. This constant change suggests a complex entanglement of the different forms of mobility. Thus, within the same space–time, different regimes of mobility cohabit, motivated by a multitude of goals, obligations, projects, but also hopes. This configuration implies a differentiation of the regimes of commitment in the practice of mobility. These regimes may be driven by the promise of an upwardly mobile professional career, the possibility of a moment of relaxation, a simple stroll around the neighborhood, or the prospect of a better life in another part of the world.

In this perspective, forms of mobility are composed according to an aesthetic order, but above all they depend on the rhythm of movement. Rhythm is understood here as a speed of crossing, but more generally as a rhythm that testifies to different regimes of mobility. Thus, through rhythmic forms, it is easy to distinguish the hurried worker, the tourist, the newcomer, or the stroller moving through public space. Rhythm thus gives meaning to movement, an unprecedented density that collectively illuminates different forms of mobility. This exercise can be carried out on the forecourt of a train station, in the heart of a public space, or even in large tourist resorts. This approach gives pride of place to anthropology and more broadly to ethnographic methods. However, the rhythmology of mobility that we propose is also likely to draw on methods of Big Data analysis and, more broadly, quantitative analysis of behavior.

Our rhythmanalytic proposal of mobility is based on a vast legacy of the study of rhythms, which we propose to outline here. Already present in Plato's work, the concept of rhythm is marked by a long evolution in use and in conceptualization. In order to avoid a long digression that would take us away from a reflection on forms of mobility and the way of thinking about them together, we will limit the presentation of the conceptualization of rhythm to the major authors in the social sciences. Since the beginning of the 20th century, the concept of rhythm has been present in various fields that have fueled a long genealogy of rhythmanalytic hypotheses (Sauvanet 2018). In philosophy, rhythmanalysis first appeared with Gaston Bachelard in 1936 (Bachelard 1936), then with Maldiney (1973) and attained new relevance at the beginning of the

1990s (Wunenburger 1992) then at the end of the 2000s with the publication of the *Rhuthmos* journal.

In parallel with philosophical approaches, the concept of rhythm has been present in sociology since the beginning of the 20th century. Simmel (1900) highlights the progressive separation between the cyclical rhythms of nature (seasons, fluctuations in quantity of food) and the rhythms of human activity by putting its role in this separation of city life, of the commodification of time, and of the individualization of lifestyles through the division of labor into perspective. Simmel observes that the rhythm of life, which refers to the "sum of actions," is more sustained among the inhabitants of large cities, describing in particular an "intensification of nervous life." The sum of actions as an analytical prism of rhythm is also taken up by Rosa (2010), for whom rhythm corresponds to the number of episodes of actions and experiences per unit of time, thus putting the experiential dimension already described by Simmel into perspective. Lefebvre (1981, 1992) put forward the notion of rhythmanalysis by introducing it in 1981 in the third volume of *Critique de la vie quotidienne*, then by developing it in his work published posthumously in 1992. The notion of rhythm is also present in *Production de l'espace* (Lefebvre 1973), then in 1974 in a synthesis article (Lefebvre 1974). In his conception, Henri Lefebvre puts into perspective two types of rhythm.

His proposal is to build a sociology of everyday life by considering jointly time and space in a project of rhythmology, which tends to analyze the arrangement of social times and the modalities of their deployment. These arrangements can thus be defined as rhythms likely to show forms of life in their spatial and temporal dimensions (Drevon 2019). In this perspective, the proposal of rhythmology developed in this Chapter 12 corresponds well to the study of the entanglement of forms of mobilities. Thus, putting into perspective different rhythms of mobility is likely to show different forms of life that cohabit within the same spaces and the same temporalities.

12.3. Responding to the challenges of mobility research with a rhythmology of mobile societies

To respond to the three identified challenges facing research on mobility, the rhythmological analysis of contemporary societies offers very stimulating avenues for reflection.

First of all, in the face of climate change, the rhythmology of mobility allows us to see the impact of mobility on the environment and fragile spaces. This impact is materialized through the intensity, extent, and frequency of practices as well as their consequences in terms of energy consumption. This approach paves the way to broader reflections on the regulation of mobility. Surprisingly, the regulation of mobility remains a hot and controversial topic. Based on the argument of the hindrance to individual liberties, the regulation of mobility is nevertheless a major theme of sustainability policies. It also refers to reflections on the saturation of spaces by traffic and the congestion of public space during rush hours.

Considering this, the rhythmology of mobile societies is likely, on the one hand, to provide tools for observing the paces and forms of mobility that overload traffic, oppress natural environments, and congest public spaces. Rhythmology is also capable of providing political alternatives for regulation by proposing a new choreography of the rhythms of mobility that would limit pressures on space–time by spreading out, recomposing, and reorienting flows. This political perspective of regulating mobility through rhythms makes it possible to avoid the pitfall of a brutal and homogeneous slowdown, which, as the economic crisis following the Covid-19 health crisis shows, involves considerable damage at both the economic and social levels.

Work on mobility logically tends to focus on movement, whether social or spatial. Thus, contemporary societies are marked by all kinds of movements generated by daily mobility, long-distance or local tourism, and, on the social level, the multiple changes in roles, jobs, and lifestyles. This way of interpreting the world gives pride of place to what is moving and can be considered dynamic on the individual, collective, and territorial levels. On the other hand, it does not emphasize the immobile, the fleeting, and the captive, and thus risks making vulnerable social phenomena and groups invisible. Urry (2000) denounced the fact that the social sciences insist above all on the analysis of the solid, institutionalized world, leaving aside what comes under the heading of flows in the broad sense; with the mobility turn that he proposed, the perspective is reversed, and with it the opposite observation is made. Rhythmology allows us to respond to this limitation of the concept of mobility. By including the diversity of appearances, it reduces the dichotomy between intense movement on the one hand and immobility on the other.

Rhythmology suggests integrating the analysis of the different nuances of movement. For example, it proposes including the nonmobile, the captive, and people with limited mobility in its analytical focus. The rhythmology of contemporary societies makes the bet of temporal and spatial inclusion by orienting the focus on the more ordinary, even banal rhythms.

As mentioned in Chapter 1 of the book, research on mobility over the last 20 years has largely focused on the transformation of the relationship with time and, in particular, on the temporal pressures imposed by the injunction to activity. This perspective of the analysis of mobile societies has considerably fed the currents of critical analysis of neoliberalism. It has also accompanied reflections on well-being and the search for slowing down as an aspiration in contemporary lifestyles. As Rosa (2010) suggests, alienation is a particularly salient symptom of the effects of time pressure and saturation on mobile individuals. In our proposal, rhythmology is perfectly adapted to the fight against the different forms of alienation associated with time pressure. It allows, indeed, for putting in perspective the forms of life that imply rhythmic pathologies related to various forms of saturation. It also allows us to contribute to the search for the right rhythm that favors emancipation and the reappropriation of time. In short, rhythmology proposes to understand the diversity of relationships to time in the different types of mobility and thus to identify the pathological forms and, on the contrary, the happy forms.

By focusing on time, the notion of rhythm allows us to go beyond the identified limits of research on mobility and to give a broader theoretical framework to the systemic conception of mobility dear to Michel Bassand.

Thus, permanence can be considered in rhythmic terms in the same way as flexibility, and the analysis of mobilities in the broader paradigm of rhythmology allows us to avoid focusing the researcher's attention on what translates into movements in geographical space at different scales. Moreover, the rhythmology of mobile societies allows for the introduction of an important political dimension to the analysis of mobilities (Antonioli et al. 2021). It proposes the design of new choreographies of mobility to limit the pressure on living environments and support the transition of lifestyles. Rhythmology also proposes to fully welcome the plurality of rhythmic forms by transcending the categorization of mobilities according to their spatial and temporal scales and by thinking about the entanglement of diversity. Finally, the rhythmology of mobile societies aims to contribute to the debate about the search for the right rhythm that reconciles, on the one hand, the good life and the preservation of the nonhuman, and on the other hand, personal emancipation and the culture of connection with others.

12.4. References

Antonioli, M., Drevon, G., Kaufmann, V., Gwiazdzinski, L., Pattaroni, L. (2021). *Manifeste pour une politique des rythmes*. Presses polytechniques et universitaires romandes, Lausanne.

Bachelard, G. (1936). *La dialectique de la durée*. Boivin, Paris.

Drevon, G. (2019). *Proposition pour une rythmologie de la mobilité et des sociétés contemporaines*. Alphil/Presses universitaires suisses, Neuchâtel.

Lefebvre, H. (1974). La production de l'espace. *L'Homme et la société*, 31(1), 15–32.

Lefebvre, H. (1981). *Critique de la vie quotidienne. De la modernité au modernisme.* L'Arche, London.

Lefebvre, H. (1992). *Éléments de rythmanalyse : introduction à la connaissance des rythmes.* Syllepse, Paris.

Maldiney, H. (ed.) (1973). L'esthétique des rythmes. In *Regard Parole Espace.* L'Âge d'homme, Lausanne.

Rosa, H. (2010). *Accélération : une critique sociale du temps.* La Découverte, Paris.

Sauvanet, P. (2018). Actualité de la recherche en rythmanalyse(s) : quelques éléments pour un état des lieux, suivis d'un retour sur quelques malentendus. In *Rythmanalyse(s) : théories et pratiques du rythme : ontologie, définitions, variations*, André, J. (ed.). Lyon, France.

Simmel, G. (1900). *Psychologie de l'argent.* Allia, Paris.

Urry, J. (2000). *Sociology beyond Societies: Mobilities for the Twentyfirst Century.* Routledge, London.

Wunenburger, J.-J. (1992). *Les rythmes : lectures et théories.* L'Harmattan, Paris.

List of Authors

Samuel CARPENTIER-POSTEL
Laboratoire ThéMA
CNRS
Université Bourgogne Franche-Comté
Besançon
France

Garance CLÉMENT
Laboratoire de sociologie urbaine
(LaSUR)
École polytechnique fédérale
de Lausanne
Switzerland

Laurie DAFFE
Laboratoire de sociologie urbaine
(LaSUR)
École polytechnique fédérale
de Lausanne
Switzerland

Guillaume DREVON
Urban Development and Mobility
Department
Luxembourg Institute of Socio-Economic
Research
Esch-sur-Alzette
Luxembourg
and
Laboratoire de sociologie urbaine
(LaSUR)
École polytechnique fédérale
de Lausanne
Switzerland

Caroline GALLEZ
Laboratoire Ville Mobilité Transport
(LVMT)
Université Gustave Eiffel
Champs-sur-Marne
France

Camille GARDESSE
Lab'Urba
École d'urbanisme de Paris
Champs-sur-Marne
France

Juliana GONZÁLEZ
Laboratoire de sociologie urbaine
(LaSUR)
École polytechnique fédérale
de Lausanne
Switzerland

Vincent KAUFMANN
Laboratoire de sociologie urbaine
(LaSUR)
École polytechnique fédérale
de Lausanne
Switzerland

Arnaud LE MARCHAND
Laboratoire IDEES
CNRS
Université du Havre
Le Havre
France

Mathilde LOISELLE
Faculty of Planning
Université de Montréal
Canada

Sébastien LORD
École d'urbanisme et d'architecture
de paysage
Université de Montréal
Canada

Christophe MINCKE
Institut national de criminalistique
et de criminologie
Brussels
Belgium

Emmanuel RAVALET
Mobil'homme
Laboratoire de sociologie urbaine
(LaSUR)
École polytechnique fédérale
de Lausanne
Switzerland

Pascal VIOT
Laboratoire de sociologie urbaine
(LaSUR)
École polytechnique fédérale
de Lausanne
Switzerland

Index

A, B

acceleration, 16, 20, 24–26, 33
access to mobility, 39, 40, 51
accessibility, 39, 44–47, 52
atmosphere, 95
biographical, 121, 125

C

capital, social, 48
capitalism, 16–18, 20–22, 27, 34
commuting
　cross-border interregional, 165
　fluctuating, 162, 166
　intensive, 163, 165, 168–170, 175
　intensive daily, 162, 163, 165
　long, 122
　long-term, 164
　weekly, 165, 166, 172

D

demonstration
　political, 197, 198
　street, 195
dependence on mobility, 51
domination, 16, 18, 21, 23, 35

E

equity, 40–46, 54
event
　leisure, 195
　traditional, 192
　urban, 196
　with a global reach, 196
experience
　social, 96
　travel time, 64

F, I, J

flexibility, 38
fragmentation, 79
immigration, 133, 137–147
individiual, 16, 17, 22, 23, 26, 31
injunction, 162, 170
　to be mobile, 162, 170
justice, 37, 38, 40–44, 46–48, 52, 53

L

law, 38, 39, 42, 49–51, 53, 54
life
　nomadic, 225
　pace of, 241
lifestyle
　neo-nomadic, 221
limit-form, 30, 31
liquidity, 20

M

major
  event, 186–190, 192, 196
  mobility, 162, 163, 168, 172, 173
    work-related, 161–163, 168, 169, 172, 175
migrants
  economic, 223
  temporary, 223, 230, 231
    labor, 235
migration flows, 38, 39, 48, 51
mobile methods, 99
mobility/mobilities (*see also* major *and* rhythms), 161–164, 167, 169, 171–173, 175, 185–198, 241–246
  access to, 39, 40, 51
  alternative forms of, 224
  at major events, 194
  atypical, 241
  daily, 186
  dependence on, 51
  hybrid, 163
  intensive, 162, 163, 169, 173
  interdepartmental, 223
  labor, 223
  professional, 226
  residential, 242
  reversible, 241
  seasonal, 234
  soft, 190, 191
  spatial, 161, 171
    hybrid, 161
  temporary, 221, 223, 227, 228
  tourist, 235
  turn, 6
  upward social, 222
  urban, 227
motility, 17, 27
multitasking, 73, 77

N

navigation
  inland, 201–203, 208, 210, 216
neo-nomadic movement, 225
neo-nomadism, 221, 224, 226, 231, 232, 235
neo-nomads, 225, 229, 233

P, R

pathways
  inland waterway transport 203, 205
  navigable, 202–204
  waterborne, 201, 208
project-based city, 16, 18, 19, 33
representations
  of time, 71
  social, 15–17, 29, 34, 35
rhythmanalysis, 243, 244
rhythmic forms, 243, 246
rhythmology, 241, 243–246
rhythms, 241, 243–245
  cyclical, 244
  of mobility, 244

S, T

seasonality, 222
sedentariness, 87, 93
social
  representations, 15–17, 29, 34, 35
  specialization, 110
spatial scales, 1, 2, 4–6, 9
stranger, 133
subjectivity, 93–102
survey
  ad hoc, 149
  quantitative, 149
time
  free, 72
  travel, 63–79
  waiting, 64, 66, 70, 78
totalitarianism, 25

U, V, W

urban
  event, 196
  quality, 91
  space, 87, 88, 93, 94, 97, 108, 110, 145

value, 7
walkability, 87, 89–98, 101–103
waterways, 201
  inland, 203, 204
  large gauge, 203, 204
  urban, 209
weak links, 28

Printed in the USA
CPSIA information can be obtained
at www.ICGtesting.com
BVHW051909080823
668357BV00002B/15